MOUNTAIN

DATE DUE

MAR 8 2004	
MAR 2 9 2004	
MAY 0 5 2004	
NOV 7 2014	
JUL 1 – 2015	

BRODART, CO.   Cat. No. 23-221-003

MEADOWS

MASSACRE

By Juanita Brooks

*Foreword and Afterword
by Jan Shipps*

UNIVERSITY OF OKLAHOMA PRESS   :   NORMAN

By Juanita Brooks

(ed.) *On the Mormon Frontier: The Diary of Hosea Stout* (Salt Lake City, Utah, 1964)

Dudley Leavitt, Pioneer to Southern Utah (St. George, Utah, 1942)
(ed.) *A Mormon Chronicle: The Diaries of John D. Lee, 1848–1876.*
With Robert Glass Cleland (San Marino, 1955)

John Doyle Lee: Zealot-Pioneer Builder-Scapegoat (Glendale, 1962)
The Mountain Meadows Massacre (Stanford, 1950; new edition,
Norman, University of Oklahoma Press, 1962, 1970)

(ed.) *Journal of the Southern Indian Mission: Diary of Thomas D. Brown*
Logan, Utah, 1972)

(ed.) *Not by Bread Alone: The Journal of Martha Spence Heywood, 1850–56*
(Salt Lake City, Utah, 1978)

LIBRARY OF CONGRESS CATALOG CARD NUMBER: 62–18053
ISBN: 0–8061–0549–6 (cloth)
ISBN: 0–8061–2318–4 (pbk.)

16   17   18   19   20   21   22   23   24   25   26   27

Contents

Illustrations

Foreword
by Jan Shipps

Rarely in the writing of the history of any controversial or tragic event has a single historical work had such a far-reaching impact as has *Mountain Meadows Massacre*. Rarely, too, has any historical monograph stood the test of time so well. First published in 1950 and published in a new edition in 1962, the book went through nine printings in hardback before the editors of the University of Oklahoma Press decided to issue a paperback edition.

While the publication of notable historical works "in paper" is nearly always appreciated, the appearance of this celebrated monograph in a new format merits more than an ordinary welcome. Although this is not a new edition, as such, new material has been added to bring the work up to date. Readers are provided with a revised, detailed map of the site where the tragedy occurred. Included also is a recent photograph of the area showing the new memorial that was installed there in the summer of 1990 and on which the names of all the victims are inscribed.

Juanita Brooks, sometime college English teacher, fulltime Mormon wife and mother, and lifelong resident of Saint George in Utah's southernmost region, its Dixie, began more than fifty years ago to work on the project that led to the writing of *Mountain Meadows Massacre*. Although she went on to complete other major scholarly ventures, this book, described on the dust jacket of the second edition as a "near-classic treatment" of the terrible tragedy, became the author's masterpiece. Despite enormous advances in the fields of western and Mormon history during the

v

past half century, this book has never been bettered from the standpoint of the information it provides about what transpired when a party of emigrants from Arkansas attempted to take the southern route from Great Salt Lake City to California in September, 1857, and—except for eighteen young children—were murdered by members of a Mormon militia unit and their Indian allies. Nor does any subsequent historical account contain better answers to the inevitable and pressing questions about where the blame for the massacre must be placed, what roles Mormon church President Brigham Young and Latter-day Saint officials in southern Utah played in precipitating the tragedy, and what possible reasons might explain the mass murder of this particular "Gentile" emigrant party. Brooks's work also contains the authoritative explanation of how the entire blame for the massacre was shifted onto the shoulders of John D. Lee and how, with the connivance of the Mormon church, he was made the scapegoat. Excommunicated for his part in the butchery, he was allowed— following conviction by a jury of Latter-day Saint peers and subsequent execution—to carry to his grave Mormondom's guilt for this horrible and barbaric act.

Brooks was a natural storyteller and gifted writer whose Mormonness was as much a part of her identity as her gender or family of origin. That she would choose the remote, virtually isolated region of the Great Basin where she grew up as locale and her own people, the staunch Latter-day Saint pioneers in southern Utah, as her subjects could have been anticipated. But since literature was her chosen field of study, it is somewhat surprising that she made her mark as a historian. For this, accidents of time and place were primarily responsible.

Born and bred in Utah's Dixie, Juanita grew up knowing about what happened at nearby Mountain Meadows in the days when her grandfather was young. What she knew, however, was what most Mormons of her generation "knew," that is, that in 1857 an Indian attack on a wagon train had resulted in an appalling loss of life and that non-Mormons usually blamed the Saints for the massacre of the innocent travelers. She was not aware that most of the older Latter-day Saints in Dixie knew an altogether different version of the story. Not until she was twenty, when she was approached by an elderly Mormon settler who wanted her to record things he said his eyes had witnessed, but his tongue had never uttered, did she begin to suspect the awful truth.

Although she arrived at Nephi Johnson's deathbed too late to hear his story, she was not too late to hear him yell "BLOOD! BLOOD! BLOOD!" and to have the reason for that frightened exclamation explained by others at his bedside.[1] Learning that the aged Saint had been at Mountain Meadows led Brooks to believe that the story of the tragedy that she had been told was just that—a story. Only gradually did she come to realize that the reality of Mountain Meadows and, of equal consequence, the secrecy that kept the perpetrators and their descendants from acknowledging and dealing with their guilt, presided like a gruesome specter over Mormon memories in southern Utah. While not always perceptible, the massacre and the secrecy that surrounded it were always there.

Establishing herself as a free-lance writer in the 1920s, Brooks built a reputation with articles based on pioneer diaries. This led to a position with the Historical Records Survey during the Great Depression and, later, to a position as a collector of pioneer diaries for the Huntington Library. Both positions gave her access to a great body of primary source material that would prove invaluable when she began systematic research on the lamentable affair at Mountain Meadows.

Recognizing that Mormons as well as Indians were involved, Brooks worked during the years of the Second World War to create a clear chronology of the massacre, an incident she came to understand in terms of the bloodshed and carnage attending the Utah War that the United States had mounted against the Saints in 1857. She used diaries and other documentary evidence

---

[1]A full account of this incident is found in Levi Peterson, *Juanita Brooks: Mormon Woman Historian* (Salt Lake City: University of Utah Press, 1988), 40–41; chapter 6 of this prize-winning biography, "The Story She Was Born To Tell," tells the story of the writing of *Mountain Meadows Massacre*.

to delineate a picture of the wartime ambience in which the killing occurred, as well as to verify the names and ascertain the actions of the Saints who participated—the list included her own grandfather—and to discover when the decision to commit the deed was made and how that decision was turned into action. In the process of writing up her findings, Brooks also demonstrated that with the decision to sacrifice John D. Lee, the LDS church committed itself to suppressing the truth about what had happened. As the current dean of American church historians, Robert T. Handy, noted in 1951 when he reviewed *Mountain Meadows Massacre* for the *Journal of Religion*, this allowed the church "to protect itself against an unpleasant incident in its own history."

The book's main text is surrounded by a multiplicity of separate parts: two statements by the author, a preface, acknowledgments (first printed in the second edition) come before; an addendum, thirteen appendices, and a bibliography follow. Taken together, these various notes, additions, and direct presentations of evidence are an indication that this is not an ordinary monograph. Its history is hardly as significant as the story it tells, yet this has been a pivotal work. As is reported in the "Addendum" to the second edition, Juanita Brooks's research made enough facts available to the First Presidency and the Council of the Twelve Apostles of the LDS church for them to act on April 20, 1961, to authorize John D. Lee's "reinstatement to membership and former blessings," a consummation that had been devoutly wished by his family and descendants since his disgrace nearly a century before.

Of more general importance, this work set a precedent for future Mormon historians willing to follow the documentary evidence wherever it leads. In her original "Preface," Brooks started out by making clear that she was and had ever been a loyal and active member of the LDS church. She realized that "*we* have tried to blot out the affair from *our* history [emphasis mine]," but argued that, "with the old antagonisms gone," she could do her church a service by telling the true story. Although substantial church callings (assignments) were withheld from "Sister Juanita" after her account of the massacre was published, she was not cut off. She continued to bespeak her LDS loyalty from the platform that monthly testimony meetings provide to all faithful Saints, and if the recognition she coveted never came from the LDS church officials in her lifetime, the fact that her work was not officially condemned proved to be an auspicious portent for the future study of the Mormon past.

When the Mormon History Association met on the campus of Dixie College in Saint George in 1978, Juanita Brooks was presented with a special award for her lifetime of research and writing about the Latter-day Saint past. Although this award encompassed all that she had done, the decision to honor the author at home in Dixie emphasized the immense importance of her study to the Saints in her region. Without any question, this award was also a direct reflection of the collective appreciation of a new generation of Mormon historians just then beginning to understand what implications follow for themselves and their church when all the evidence found in the documentary record of the LDS experience is faced head on.

In addition to its importance as a historical work and above and beyond its significance as precedent to the Mormon historical enterprise, *Mountain Meadows Massacre* stands as a monument to the power of history in human life. Knowing the truth will never set the Saints free from what happened in 1857 in any ultimate sense. Yet the courage Juanita Brooks showed in insisting on revealing the facts has had real consequences. For all time, the Saints have been set free from the necessity of denying their responsibility for what happened in that lonesome meadow.

Author's Statement—I

Twelve years have passed since this book appeared. It found a very sympathetic audience among the people of Utah, especially among the historians and teachers of the institutions of higher learning. If no recognition came from the authorities of the Church of Jesus Christ of Latter-day Saints, neither did any official condemnation.

While the publication was a welcome consummation of years of work, the republication provides its own special brand of gratification. It indicates that public interest has created a demand for the book; that hundreds of people who were not able to get a first edition copy will want a second. It also provides an opportunity to correct and amplify the text and to enrich it with illustrations.

In the meantime, two other books have appeared which have stimulated interest in this subject. The first, *A Mormon Chronicle: The Diaries of John D. Lee*, edited by Dr. Robert G. Cleland and Juanita Brooks (1955), was published by the Henry E. Huntington Library. Although the diaries do not begin until February, 1848, and there are long lapses between some of them, they do give a clear and intimate picture of this man through his mature years and later life. The second, *John Doyle Lee, Zealot—Pioneer Builder—Scapegoat* (Glendale, Arthur H. Clark Company, 1962), is my own attempt to assemble and crystallize the life of this man from unpublished diaries and contemporary sources as well as from the published ones.

Equally important in developing my understanding of the life

xi

and times of this man has been the two-year labor of editing the diaries of his contemporary and associate, Hosea Stout. This new research has strengthened the conclusions of the first edition and made more puissant the argument that this tragedy could only have happened in the emotional climate of war.

Author's Statement—II

I AM PLEASED that with this fourth printing of the new edition of *Mountain Meadows Massacre* the University of Oklahoma Press has given me permission to add material which might amplify or alter my earlier conclusions. Strangely enough, several important items have been made available to me within the past two years. Some of these clarify earlier conclusions; others raise questions as yet unanswered. I shall discuss these items briefly under three headings. Citations by page number only refer to this volume.

I. INDIANS

Recently I was given access to an electrostatic copy of the daily journal of Brigham Young. Under date of September 1, 1857, the entry reads:

> Kanosh the Pavaunt chief with several of his band visited me gave them some council and presents. A spirit seems to be takeing possession of the Indians to assist Israel. I can hardly restrain them from *exterminating* the Americans.

This seems very significant. The "Journal History of the Church" under this same date tells of the visit of Jacob Hamblin and twelve Indian chiefs from the south [p. 41]. President Young talked with them all, but it seems that Kanosh was given private audience. He was the chief who had killed Captain John W. Gunnison and several of his men as they were camped on the Sevier River on October 28, 1853. Whether or not Kanosh and his band were at the Mountain Meadows we do not know, but we can now be more certain that the Mormon war strategy was to use the natives as "the battle-ax of the Lord," as some of the early missionaries had stated [p. 33].

An entry in the Journal of Abraham Cannon for Tuesday, June 13, 1895, gives Samuel Knight's account of the massacre. By this time the Church leaders were encouraging participants to tell their stories to trusted agents. Knight said that he had told this account to only one other person—Daniel H. Wells—evidently just before the second trial of John D. Lee. The account agrees closely with other stories: the boastful attitude of the emigrants, the poison springs, etc.

> . . . a messenger came from the authorities in Cedar City, but whether they were military or ecclesiastical authorities that gave this command Brother Knight does not now remember. This message, which he accepted as an order that could not be disobeyed without imperiling his own life, commanded him to go South, in the neighborhood of St. George and Santa Clara, and instruct the Indians to arm themselves and prepare to attack the emigrant train. This attack it was proposed to make at the junction of the Santa Clara and the Mogotsu. . . . Brother Knight did not return with the Indians, but remained to do some necessary work on the ranch which he and another brother owned near where Santa Clara now stands, but after laboring there for two days, he and his companion, feeling anxious to know what had occurred at the Meadows, mounted their horses and started for the place. . . .

Samuel Knight did not name his companion, nor did he give the real reason for their remaining two days: to let the horses recuperate. These express trips were to be taken without regard for horseflesh, and the ride down at full speed would tax their animals to the limit. The point to be made here is that the orders came from Cedar City, and were both military and ecclesiastical.

> . . . As Brother Knight passed on the way to his ranch at the north end of the valley he saw the militia camped at a place where Joseph Burgess's house now stands, and on reaching his home he heard considerable shooting, which made his wife very nervous, she

having but recently given birth to his first child. He . . . remained at his home until a message came requiring him to hitch his team to his wagon, there being only one other team in the valley, and proceed with it to the south end of the valley. . . .

Knight gave the story as it has been told here, with the wagons going on ahead, the women and older children following, and the men in the rear. He named no living man as participating.

That same night Haight, Dame and others took supper at Knight's house, and he learned from their conversation that none of the general authorities of the Church had sanctioned or encouraged in any way the dastardly deed of which these fanatics were guilty.

Here, as always, there was definite clearance of all the general authorities of the Church, letting the local men divide the responsibility as they could.

Of Kanosh and his band from the vicinity of Nephi we cannot be sure, but Chief Ammon, brother of Chief Walker who had died earlier, was there with a large band of Piedes from Beaver area [p. 252], as well as the Tonaquint Indians from Santa Clara. It seems that the Indians from the Lower Virgin and Muddy tribes were also present, for Perry Liston and Jehiel McConnell were sent to that area. [pp. 132, 136]. Lieutenant George W. Wheeler, surveying in Nevada wrote: "An old Fellow by the name of Toshob was chief of these bands on the Muddy; a wily, treacherous, cold-blooded old scamp, who was well known to have been the leader of the Indians that were engaged in the 'Mountain Meadows Massacre,' that horrible murder of helpless emigrants, both male and female, old and young . . . ." [U.S. Army, Engineer Department, Preliminary Report upon a Reconnaissance through Southern and Southeastern Nevada, made in 1869, by First Lieut. G. M. Wheeler . . . Assisted by First Lieut. D. W. Lockwood . . . Washington, Government Printing Office. 1875. 72 pp. B.L. call no. fF841.U51, page 23.]

As has been noted, every letter and order had at least one sentence regarding the Indians. Dame's message to the men in the field was most definite: ". . . but on no Conditions you are not to precipitate a war with the Indians while there is an army marching against our people."

In line with the early plan, the Indians had been gathered from far and near, so many that the Mormons found "they had started a fire they couldn't put out," as one expressed it.

II. The Spirit of the Times

During the fall of 1962, as I worked at editing the Hosea Stout *Diaries*, I had occasion to go into the Military Records in the State Archives, at that time housed on the third floor of the Historical Society Building. Here I found a booklet made by James H. Martineau, the cover carefully lettered and embellished. On the front page was the caption:

ORGANIZATION
OF THE
IRON MILITARY DISTRICT
JUNE 1857
COL WM H. DAME
Organizer
JAMES H. MARTINEAU
Assistant

The following pages contain a list of the names of all persons enrolled in the Iron Military District, and their organization into tens and fifties, by Wm H. Dame agreeably to "General Orders No. 2," published in the Deseret News, No. 6 vol. 7.

The pages following contain a list of the men in each company, beginning with Company 1 at Beaver and continuing through Company 9 at Washington, Washington County.

A letter dated August 5, 1857, indicates that during the summer some changes had been made in the personnel of the Officers' Staff. Now the companies were designated by the letters A through I, and combined into four battalions. A note at the end added:

Please send us some Battallion and Regimental returns. We are now organized as a Regiment, and await further orders. Please send us the No. of the Regiment, Brigade, and Division, with any other information you may please to communicate.

Yours truly

Wm H. Dame

Col Comg Iron Mil. Dist.

Aug 23 1857 P.S. This was prepared at date but there being no mail, it has been delayed until the present time

J. H. M. *Adj.*

Three days after the body of this letter was written, George A. Smith arrived at Parowan, with Josiah Rogerson, Sr., accompanying him as clerk. During his stay in the south, Jesse N. Smith was his teamster. Beginning on the fifteenth of August, accompanied by William H. Dame, James H. Martineau, and perhaps others, he made a tour of every settlement in the area. In each place the troops were mustered and drilled, following which a general meeting was held. George A. Smith himself acted as mail carrier back to Salt Lake City on August 23. A second letter was part of the mail:

HEADQUARTERS IRON MILITARY DISTRICT
PAROWAN AUGUST 23 1857

Lt. Genl. D. H. Wells

SIR

I have the honor to report that I have just returned from a tour through this District, have mustered and drilled the troops upon their own parade grounds and inspected their arms and ammunition; and following is a report of the same:

[The armament is set forth in a diagram showing reports of Companies A through I, with totals as follows:

Muskets	99
Rifles	190
Colt's Revolvers	17
Pounds of Powder	192 ¾
Pounds of Lead	335 ½
Swords	24]

The Field and Staff officers not enumerated in this return, but are well armed.

The command feel calm, quiet, and willing to act upon any command that may be given and any orders from head Quarters will be cheerfully obeyed. We can place 200 effective men in the field if necessary. Every effort is being made to secure the grain in every settlement, and your previous orders are being strictly carried out. Every inlet of the District south of Beaver is now guarded. If a hostile force is found to be approaching us, we shall immediately express to you, and await your further orders; Unless attacked, in which case we shall act on the defensive, and communicate immediately with you.

WM H DAME

Col. Comg Iron Military District

J H MARTINEAU *Adjutant*

As subsequent events show, they "acted on the defensive," before orders arrived from headquarters. The participants as named by John D. Lee show that no man from Beaver, Parowan, or Paragoonah was present. Participants were largely from Cedar City, with not more than two or three from each of the other southern settlements: Hamilton's Fort, Pinto, Kanarraville, Harmony, Washington, and Santa Clara. Lee names only forty-two of the fifty-four said to have been present.

Of those who made depositions, Philip Klingonsmith was a private, as was also Samuel Knight. Daniel S. Macfarlane was a sergeant; Nephi Johnson, second lieutenant. John M. Higbee was a major, as was also John D. Lee.

These records make it doubly clear that the massacre at Mountain Meadows was committed by a military group under military orders by men fired by what was later called "The Spirit of the Times." Spurred on by the inflammatory speeches of their Church leaders, their own determination not to be driven again, their private vows to avenge the blood of the Prophets, the promises in their Patriarchal Blessings that they would be permitted to do so—all these carried some weight. But military orders brought them to the scene; military orders placed each man where he was to do his duty.

After it was over, not a man of them would ever be the same again, either in his own heart or in the eyes of his neighbors.

III. How Many People Were Killed?

I am embarrassed that I did not earlier give closer scrutiny to this question. The monument and plaque had been in place for twelve years before I began this work; the number slain had been accepted. Only in the past year have I been forced to agree with Major J. H. Carleton that the number 123 people killed is greatly exaggerated. [57 Cong. 1 sess., *House Doc. 605*].

The item which really set me to work on the problem was handed to me at Logan in September, 1968, by Dr. Don D. Fowler, Director of Desert Research Institute, Reno, Nevada. It was an anonymous account of the Mountain Meadows Massacre secured from the Library of Congress. [BAE Ms #3141—Historical Notes—Rept. on Mountain Meadows Massacre, Anonymous]. The account was wrong on almost every point: first in the story itself, and second, in the failure of the typist to decipher the handwriting. Such small errors as *Darins* for *Darius*, *Bay* Wash for *Big* Wash, *Dane* or *Dand* for *Dame*, and several blanks where the word could not be interpreted, gave evidence of the poor handwriting.

The correct spelling of *Schurtz*—so often written *Shirts*—and the notation near the end that, "My son was employed by this second party to go with them through the Muddy as Interpreter. When he got to the Clara he was ordered back [by] Mormon Authority," made me conclude that the writer was Peter Schurtz.

Whoever he was, he had everything wrong about the massacre itself: that Isaac Haight led the men on the ground; that the order of march was "the men leading, followed by the women, the children coming last. Those children who could not walk were carried ahead by Lee in a wagon." Later he tells that "Among the emigrants were two sisters, twins, so much alike the Indians from superstition would not kill them. Lee took his pistol and shot them both. . . . Haight was the originator and cause of all the Whites going out. I cannot say about Dane. I have heard that Daned was there, and also that he had proved his absence. . . ."

Clearly the last part of his story had been gathered from folk-lore and general whisperings. But the first paragraphs held me:

About 12 o'clock on Sunday I saw John D. Lee in the town of Harmony with about 45 Indians mustered in, in military style. The following Sunday he returned with the same Indians. In the after-noon he got up before the congregation, among which were Billy Young, Henry Barney, Darins [*sic*] Schurtz, Jim Davis, and others I do not recollect. (Ingram and wife was also there) and told the history of the "*Mountain Meadow Massacre*" as it is called, which had just taken place. He represented it as a vision which had oc-curred to him some time, probably six months before, told the number killed, which was *96*. . . .

Wrong as he was on so much of the story elsewhere, he might also have been wrong in recording the number slain, and yet this was important. A difference of twenty-seven people means much! I counted again the personnel of the Arkansas Company [pp. 45, 46] and found twenty-three men, ten women, and thirty-four children—a total of sixty-seven, of whom eighteen children were saved. Now the total slain would depend upon how many other families were along, and how many independent packers. From several references I found these last referred to as "about 12 men."

I turned to the report of the Indian agent at Provo, George W. Armstrong. Writing on September 30, 1857, he gave a magnified account the offenses of the emigrants and pictured the massacre as a purely Indian affair: ". . . The Indians followed them to a place known as Mountain Meadows where they attacked the camp and after a desperate fight they killed fifty-seven men and nine women." [p. 143] No mention was made of any children in-volved!

An item in Lee's *Confessions*, written years later, states: "I thought then that there were some fifteen women, about ten chil-dren and about forty men killed, but the statement of others that I have since talked with about the massacre on the Mountain Meadows, and the ten who died in the corral, and young Aiden killed by Stewart at Richards' Springs, would make the number up to one hundred and twenty-one." [*Mormonism Unveiled: ...* (St. Louis: Sun Publishing Company, 1882) p. 244]. In this item, Lee is certainly confused, for his first total of 65 people is not built up to 121 or even to the 96 he admitted at church. Armstrong's total of 67 and Lee's first total of 65 approximate rather nearly the 67 given by Mitchell of the Arkansas train.

To turn now to another confused source, a letter signed by Mrs. Frances Haynes, Riverside, California, July 17, 1932, and addressed to the Bancroft Library:

> Do you have any information in your Library that gives the names of the eleven miners or plainsmen who rode into Los Angeles in the fall of 1857 and reported the murder of the Emigrants at Mountain Meadows in Utah? ...
> My father Zebulon P. Fawcett said he was one of the band ...
> My father said he crossed the Plains with that Emigrant train and because he and a few others did not want to camp at the Meadows, they went on, but the ones left behind agreed to overtake them in a few days. ...

Confused as this letter is, there might well be some truth in the statement that the eleven miners, plainsmen, "Missouri Wildcats" or whatever else the group might have been called, did not stop longer than a day or two. They would have no reason to do so, for they had no families nor any cattle herd to care for. They would naturally push on, glad to be out of Mormon country and ignorant of the storm that was brewing. At any rate, this challenges further research.

More complete and reliable than any of these sources is a photographic copy of "Information derived from Claim No. 8479 U.S. Court of Claims, National Archives, submitted in 1911 by Malinda Cameron Thruston, Administratix for the estate of William Cameron (Camron?) deceased. (Indian Depredations)." This was mailed to me by Mr. L. T. Gremaux, 953 Colusa Avenue, Berkeley, California. It will bear study from many angles. Malinda Cameron Thruston was a daughter of William Cameron and his wife, listed third from the last in the Mitchell report, both of whom, with five of their children, were killed. According to her account:

> She married one Henry Dalton Scott and resided in the vicinity of Clarksville. On March 29, 1857, she along with her husband and three children . . . , as well as her husband's brother Richard Thomas Scott, set out for Stockton, California by wagon. (According to Malinda her husband's sister [unnamed] was residing in Stockton, having arrived there in 1854.)
>
> She met her father and the rest of the family named above somewhere in the Cherokee nation . . . her father's party consisted of about four wagons . . . arriving in Salt Lake City on about Aug. 3, 1857, where upon the advice of the Mormons, the wagon train divided in order that the stock have sufficient feed. Malinda and her family . . . in three other wagons continued traveling a day's journey on Aug. 3. . . . The two were to rejoin on the other side of Salt Lake City and continue on to California via the Northern or Humboldt Route.
>
> On Aug. 5, 1857 Malinda's father came to their wagon and informed them that the Mormons had recommended that, because of the amount of livestock in the train, they take the Southern Route to California to take advantage of the better graze along the route. . . . her father took the Southern route along with the largest part of the wagon train. . . .
>
> In her first affidavit dated 15 Oct. 1877, Malinda stated that her parents, all her brothers, her sisters, and Joseph Miller [her brother-in-law] as well as his child William Miller, were killed . . . The other three children [two boys and a girl] were captured and later returned to Malinda's sister, Nancy Littleton. She further stated that her cousin, Nancy Cameron, was also captured, and as of the date of the affidavit, was still with the Mormons and aged about 32 years.

Here is the first hint that I have found of the identity of the missing child, though varying stories abound as to who brought her up and who married her. Some of her descendants may find this interesting.

This account explains that not all who crossed the plains together went on via Mountain Meadows, and there is also evidence that several other wagons remained in Salt Lake City to follow in later companies. Among this group was Mr. Frank E. King, who remained in Salt Lake City three months before proceeding south. He spent the winter in Manti, and remained in that area until 1863, when he joined the first company to Marysvale. Here he lived until 1905.

Mr. Josiah F. Gibbs, who had been a neighbor for twenty-five years, never heard Mr. King mention the Mountain Meadows Massacre; thus he was surprised when Charles King, a son, told him in 1910 that his father had traveled across the plains in the Fancher company. Mr. Gibbs immediately wrote, asking specific questions, which are given herewith, with their answers:

Q.—Kindly give me the names of as many members of the company as you can remember.
A.—Fancher, Dunlap, Morton, Haydon, Hudson, Aden, Stevenson, Hamilton, a family by the name of Smith and a Methodist minister.
Q.—Give the Christian names of the two Dunlap girls and their ages.
A.—Rachel and Ruth, aged sixteen and eighteen years respectively.
Q.—How many wagons and carriages in the train?
A.—Forty.
Q.—How many men capable of carrying arms, and about how many women—married and single, large girls included?
A.—About sixty men, forty women and nearly fifty children.
Q.—About how many horsemen in the train?
A.—About twelve, as near as I can remember.
                    [Josiah F. Gibbs, "The Mountain Meadows
                    Massacre," Salt Lake *Tribune*, 1910, p. 13.]

Here again is the number of twelve horsemen, and the total of 110 persons. But this is *before* the train left Salt Lake City. Of the people he knew, only three families were on the list of Arkansas emigrants sent in by William C. Mitchell: Fancher, Dunlap, and Aden, which makes a total of thirty family heads named, certainly not all that were in the original group.

The testimonies of Mormon participants that they had man for man in the last fatal march sets the number at about forty. If there was an equal number of women plus sixteen older children, the number would fit Lee's report, but both these "if's" may well be wrong. The total number remains uncertain. We can be sure only that, however many there were, it was too many.

In 1932 the local people erected the monument [p. 221] which still stands on the edge of the bank worn down by erosion. In April, 1966, representatives of the Mormon Church purchased from Mr. Ezra Lytle the two and one-half acres upon which the monument stands. At once the leaders adopted a policy of "discouraging" visitors. On June 2, 1966, the Forest Service sign and also the Old Spanish Trail sign on the opposite side of the road disappeared. Although forest rangers at both Enterprise and Cedar City were notified, the place was still unmarked as late as December 2, which meant that for one full season, tourists searched in vain for the monument.

Nor was any work at all done on the access road to the place, so that by January, 1967, it was totally impossible for any car to reach the site. Sometime after August 4, 1966, the picnic table in the valley was lifted out by heavy equipment and hauled away, with a report to the forest ranger at Cedar City that it had been washed down by a flood. That this report was false was amply evident to every one of the several persons who went to investigate.

By early summer of 1967 the furor of tourist groups and traveling clubs forced the County Commission to repair the road and to keep it open and passable. This they continue to do.

Interested persons might be able to bring pressure enough to have a new sign built near the main highway, pointing out the location and correcting the inscription on the first plaque, at least by striking the two words AS LEADER and changing the figures of the number killed.

JUANITA BROOKS

Preface

AT THE OUTSET, let me make myself clear. I am a member of the Church of Jesus Christ of Latter-day Saints, commonly called Mormon; I was born into the church and have been raised in it. Anyone who is interested enough to look up my history will find that I am, and have always been, a loyal and active member.

I am interested in the reputation of my church. When one has served in and sacrificed for a cause over a long period of years, that cause becomes dear, more dear, perhaps, than it is to those who draw their livelihood from it. Hence, in trying to present this subject with a desire only to tell the truth, I believe that I am doing my church a service.

Since the Mountain Meadows Massacre occurred, and especially since the execution of John D. Lee for his part in it, we have tried to blot out the affair from our history. It must not be referred to, much less discussed openly. Years ago, that might have been the best stand to take in the interest of the church, but now, with the perspective of time, with the old antagonisms gone, we should be able to view this tragedy objectively and dispassionately, and to see it in its proper setting as a study of social psychology as well as of history.

There is no satisfaction in rehearsing the horrible details. The few known facts have been enlarged upon and colored by many different writers with many different purposes. My excuse for adding my name to the long list of those who have given time and thought to this subject is the fact that I have some new material to present which should add to the general understanding of what went on, and why.

To the descendants of the men who were involved, I say that my own grandfather was there. What part he took I do not know, except that in his late life he always insisted, as many others did, that he had nothing to do with it. There is evidence that he was in the vicinity at the time and that he knew what was going on. If he did not help with the massacre, he still did nothing to prevent it.

This study is not designed either to smear or to clear any individual; its purpose is to present the truth. I feel sure that nothing but the truth can be good enough for the church to which I belong.

I wish to thank all who have encouraged me in this undertaking—the many, many loyal members of the church in high places and low who share my feeling that our history is our history, and that, with all its dark spots, we will accept it as it is. We will let the accomplishments of the Mormon pioneers weigh against their mistakes without apology.

Especially am I indebted to Robert G. Cleland and Leslie E. Bliss, both of the Henry E. Huntington Library, for making this study possible by giving me a fellowship under the grant made by the Rockefeller Foundation for the study of the history of the Southwest. Without this aid, I might never have been able to complete this work. Their help and guidance have been invaluable to me.

JUANITA BROOKS

ST. GEORGE, UTAH

Acknowledgments

Bεcausε I felt that I must bear full responsibility for the first edition of this book, I named no one specifically as giving me assistance. Now I wish to make grateful acknowledgment to the following people:

Dale L. Morgan, who supplied material from the National Archives which I could never have secured otherwise; who questioned and argued with me through the mail; who gave me much bibliographical material and directed me in its arrangement; and who was never too busy to pay attention to my problems;

Stanley S. Ivins, who gave me the benefit of his years of research, especially in the newspaper files and in the biographies of some of the men involved;

Miss Ettie Lee, whose loyalty is beyond price;

A. R. Mortensen, formerly of the Utah State Historical Society, for his repeated attempts to find a publisher for this second edition, and for his enthusiastic defense of the first;

John Wesley Williamson, whose pictures add much to the present volume and whose support through a painful crisis will never be forgotten;

My husband, William Brooks, whose unbounded faith in me is a constant source of strength;

And all the many unnamed friends who have spoken out in my defense through the intervening years.

All of the illustrations, with the exception of those of John D. Lee arriving at Mountain Meadows on the day of his execution and John D. Lee seated on his coffin, for the use of which I am indebted to the Utah State Historical Society, are from the collection of John Wesley Williamson.

JUANITA BROOKS

1

Into the Wilderness

To UNDERSTAND properly the Mountain Meadows Massacre, one must know something of the stormy history of the Mormon church. This church had its beginnings in western New York during the revivalist period of the early 1800's, when preachers stirred whole counties into frenzy with their lurid eloquence, and sporadic sects sprang up over the countryside like mushrooms. During this time of revival and exhortation and hell-fire preaching, the fourteen-year-old youth, Joseph Smith, claimed to have had his first vision. In it he was told that the true church of Christ was no longer upon the earth and was promised that, if he proved worthy, the time would come when he, himself, would help to establish it. He believed that fulfillment of this promise had begun when, on April 6, 1830, at Fayette, New York, a group of six young men organized the church which was to become known as "The Church of Jesus Christ of Latter-day Saints." Later the members of the church became known as "Mormons," and the church itself as the Mormon church, because of a book published by Joseph Smith, *The Book of Mormon*. This purports to be a history of the ancestors of the American Indians translated from gold plates, the location of which Joseph Smith said was revealed to him by an angel.

So zealous were the proselytes of this new faith that the church membership increased with amazing rapidity, in some cases whole congregations being converted at once. Caught up in the westward movement of the time, the church transferred its headquar-

3

ters to Kirtland, Ohio, near the shore of Lake Erie, a little east of Cleveland.

From here they branched out, in 1831, to Independence, Jackson County, Missouri, then on the extreme western frontier. This place, they believed, God had designated as their center stake and had set apart as their inheritance. Frictions developed with the early settlers—frictions aggravated by both sides and inherent in their fundamental differences. In less than two years some twelve hundred Mormons had moved into Jackson County, had set about clearing land and building homes and towns, had talked too freely of God's promises to them, and had voted as a unit on civic matters. Tensions grew. Skirmishes became minor battles, and both sides made appeals to state officers to defend them.

Many things contributed to the difficulties; political, social, and religious differences were agitated until, in the excitement, mass meetings sometimes became unrestrained mobs who rode through the countryside, pillaging and burning. Some Mormon leaders were tarred and feathered; others were whipped to unconsciousness. In one night ten cabins at Big Blue River were demolished, and families were driven to shelter in the woods. Mormons organized for defense, thereby stirring their enemies to greater atrocities.

Following a clash on November 4, 1833, in which one Mormon and two non-Mormons were killed, the lieutenant governor, Lilburn Boggs, called out the militia to restore order. The commander, Colonel Thomas Pitcher, demanded that the Mormons surrender their arms and give up some of their leaders to be tried in the courts. No sooner had the Mormons complied than the mob gathered and began sacking the Mormon villages, in one night driving twelve hundred people from their homes and forcing them to take shelter in the undergrowth along the river bottoms, exposed to a biting November wind.

Word of this outrage aroused the sympathy of the citizens of adjoining Clay County, so that they offered the Mormons shelter and temporary homes. From here they moved north a little later to the sparsely settled areas of Caldwell County. Again they set about clearing land and building homes; again, when they began to be too numerous, their troubles were repeated. Differences could not be reconciled, and radicalism and extremes on either side led again to violence.

A tragic culmination came in October of 1838, when a band of ruffians fell upon a little settlement at Haun's Mill. Some of the Mormons fled to the woods and took shelter in the brush, but a group hid in an old blacksmith shop, among them a number of children. Of this group, eighteen were killed and a number seriously wounded. When one small boy begged for his life, a mobocrat answered, "Nits make lice," and blew out his brains. That expression was echoed twenty years later on the hillside at Mountain Meadows.[1]

Feeling in Missouri became so intense that whole areas were in a state of civil war. Governor Boggs, petitioned by both sides for support and protection, took his stand firmly against the Mormons. In October, 1838, he issued the order: "The Mormons must be treated as enemies and must be exterminated or driven from the State if necessary for the public peace." Following the surrender of Joseph Smith and other Mormon leaders, General Lucas tried them by court-martial and sentenced them to be shot for treason in the public square at Far West. The man commissioned to carry out the order was Alexander Doniphan, a man who dared to defy a military superior.

"It is cold-blooded murder," he wrote to the General. "I will not obey your order. My brigade shall march for Liberty tomorrow morning at 8 o'clock, and if you execute these men I will hold you responsible before an earthly tribunal, so help me God." The order was not executed.

Forced to find another home, the Mormons were described by John D. Lee as a people "stripped and peeled," but, unlike the

---

[1] David Lewis, a survivor of the Haun's Mill massacre, wrote a vivid account of that outrage, giving the events which led up to the attack and naming both victims and their assailants. At the time of the massacre, Lewis was thirty-three years old; his story was written six years later, after he had come to Utah.

A photostat is in the Henry E. Huntington Library.

5

sapling that dies under such conditions, they sent down roots again. This time, their central city, Nauvoo, was to grow out of a mosquito-infested bog on the bank of the Mississippi River in Illinois. In five years they transformed it into a busy town, the center of a rich farming district—a town where business prospered, a printing press was set up, a temple begun, and a municipal university projected. With a population of fifteen thousand, it was the largest city in the state. Through bitter experience Joseph Smith had learned to protect his people under the law, so he secured for his city a charter which made it almost independent of the state and which gave it an army for its protection.

The very prosperity of Nauvoo carried with it the seeds of trouble. The Mormons were already too numerous, and daily their numbers were increasing. They still voted as a unit, playing the Whigs and Democrats against each other for favors and eventually arousing the ill will of both. Proud of their accomplishments and secure in the protection of their charter, they perhaps became overconfident. Joseph Smith even aspired to the presidency of the United States, sending his missionaries out to campaign for him along with their preaching. All this had encouraged more vehement opposition from without, and now there was division within as well. Some members who were out of harmony with the leaders had been excommunicated, and they defiantly set up a paper, *The Nauvoo Expositor*, which attacked Joseph Smith so vigorously that he, as mayor of the city, pronounced it a nuisance and ordered it destroyed. Public reaction was instant and violent. Mormon leaders were arrested and housed in the jail at Carthage, Illinois, under promise of protection, to await trial. Unwilling to delay for the action of a court, a mob gathered about the jail, their fury mounting until they attacked the prison cell and killed Joseph Smith and his brother Hyrum. Thus, on June 27, 1844, was climaxed more than eleven years of strife between the Mormons and their neighbors of the western frontier.

Contrary to the hopes of their enemies, the Mormons did not scatter at the death of their prophet. Instead, they enshrined him in their hearts as a martyr who had sealed the truth of his testi-

6

mony with his blood. They would work all the harder to carry out his plans and to maintain his "Kingdom." Seeing this, their enemies determined that they must be driven from Illinois.

Some wit sardonically labeled as "wolf hunts" the series of organized raids upon Mormon homes which followed. Bands of armed bandits scoured the country, driving off stock, breaking windows and furniture, driving out women and children, and then shooting to frighten them further as they ran for shelter into the fields. Then began the burnings. A mob would ride up to a farmhouse, order the family out, give them a generous few minutes in which to salvage such necessities as they could, and allow them to watch the glow of their burning home against the sky, or to compare its blaze with that of the granary and haystack. If the owners resented it or had too much to say, it was sometimes fun to enliven the party by giving the father a taste of the blacksnake in full view of his terrified children or by stripping him and smearing his body with hot tar.

Again both sides appealed to higher tribunals: the natives to have their state rid of the menace of the Mormons, the Mormons for their rights as American citizens. Finally, in October, 1845, a truce was arrived at in which Brigham Young, successor to the martyred Joseph Smith, promised to move his people en masse in the spring, as soon as there should be grass for the cattle. The anti-Mormons agreed not to molest the people until that time.

During the winter, the Mormons worked desperately to prepare for the move—repairing their wagons, building new ones, and securing supplies. By January, the mob had become restless. Would the Mormons really leave, they wondered, or would further encouragement be necessary? A nail spike has goaded many a plodding ox into a gallop; perhaps some pointed reminders would speed up the move. Why not have some fun with them before they got away? Perhaps, also, they could be persuaded to sell their property at a cheaper figure.

Posses led by pseudo-officers began to ride the city in search of arms or apostles, and burnings began again among the farms. Hysteria gripped the Mormons. Sarah Sturdevant Leavitt wrote

7

bitterly of how she and her husband were forced to sell their fine forty-acre farm for a pair of unbroken steers, and forty thousand burned bricks, out of which they had planned to build a new home, for an old bed quilt. For her fancy high-post beds she got some weaving done, while the light cherry stand and the commode and all the pretty dishes were left for the mob—facts which she never forgot to her dying day, nor lost an opportunity to tell. She was only one of the many who were so filled with fear that they left before they were prepared to go. Abandoning their home, she and her husband took temporary shelter, along with other families, in a schoolhouse. One night a heavy foreboding of evil awakened her, and she convinced her husband that they must flee at once if they would save their lives. Hitching up his team in the darkness, he pulled to the banks of the Mississippi River, where other wagons were gathering, all impelled by the certainty that to remain longer would mean death.

On the morning of February 4, 1846, blocks of ice choked the Father of Waters. With the break of day the ferries began running. All day long and until dark at night they ran, carrying first a vanguard of young men organized under competent leaders to prepare the camping place. The families followed, moving as fast as ferriage was available, all preferring the uncertainties of winter to the threats of their enemies. Before night a road had been marked out, a camping place cleared, and some wood assembled on Sugar Creek, nine miles from the landing place. Here rude temporary shelters were erected against a bitter wind.

Day after day the ferries ran; people landed on the west bank and moved on to the camp at Sugar Creek, where within a few weeks nine babies were born—nine new lives ushered in amidst misery everywhere, hunger and cold and fear. On February 14, a heavy snow fell. "There were many families that night in our camp in waggons without covers, who were receiving the driving snow amid their women and children & also their goods which rendered their condition truly uncomfortable," Hosea Stout wrote the next day from the shelter of his tent.

On the twentieth of February the temperature fell to twenty

degrees below zero, freezing the mighty river all the way across. As ancient Israel crossed the Red Sea on dry land, so this modern Israel now crossed the Mississippi River on a bridge of ice, a special providence of God, they told each other. At the end of ten days, three hundred wagons made up the settlement along Sugar Creek; on March 28, Brigham Young, writing to the governor of Iowa to ask for clemency for his people as they traveled west, reported that the company now consisted of "400 wagons, very heavily loaded."

With most of the Mormon leaders out of Nauvoo, tensions were eased so that other members could live in their homes "until the water runs and the grass grows," according to the agreement made the fall before. April and May saw a constant stream of wagons across the prairie. The poorest of the Saints were last to get away—families without wagons or teams, orphaned children, people old and infirm. During July, eight men caught harvesting crops near Nauvoo were mercilessly whipped with long switches as a warning to all. By September, guns and cannon were brought into play in an exchange "battle," and the remaining Mormons were driven to the riverbank on foot, taking along only such things as they could carry. Ferried across, they must wait for wagons to come back for them. Brigham Young had declared that all who wished to stay with the Saints should do so, which meant that those more fortunate must assume responsibility for those who had nothing. Only a great co-operative effort could have carried out this promise.

The first wagons inched along through the mud and slush of a wet spring, taking five months to cover the four hundred miles across Iowa to Council Bluffs on the Missouri River, a distance which the later emigrants traveled in less than half the time. En route the first groups established two temporary settlements, Garden Grove and Mount Pisgah, where some families remained to build cabins, clear land, and plant crops for the use of those who should come later. The headquarters and general gathering place was at Winter Quarters on the west bank of the Missouri River, where a community of small cabins and dug-outs was built.

At all these places exposure and malnutrition took a heavy toll. The Jonathan H. Hale family lost both parents and two daughters within a week; George A. Smith's third wife and four children all died of scurvy; Hosea Stout lost one wife and four children between the departure from Nauvoo and the departure from Winter Quarters—to cite only a few instances. The total Mormon deaths for this year are estimated at well over six hundred.

While the Mormon church was scattered in temporary camps the width of Iowa, events were shaping in the nation's capital which were to affect its members vitally. The Mormon representative there, Jesse C. Little, had been alert to try to secure contracts for building mail posts or forts, or performing any service by which the Saints could earn money to help with their enforced migration. With the declaration of war upon Mexico, it was decided to call five hundred young men from the Mormon ranks to march with the troops to California. While this would weaken the Mormons somewhat, it would transport this number at government expense, and their advance pay would help purchase necessities for needy families.

So strongly had the Mormons felt regarding the treatment they had received and the failure of the government to protect them in their rights, that when Captain James Allen arrived to enlist them, none wished to volunteer. Only after Brigham Young had preached and exhorted and commanded was the required number raised.

For years the eyes of the church leaders had been turned to the West. Brigham Young had taken pains to seek out all the information he could from trappers and explorers, so that he might select a place where his people could live unmolested. In the spring of 1847, he led a band of pioneers toward the mountains to mark out a route, to take measurements and make calculations, and to select the location for the permanent home of his people. In July, 1847, when he looked over the valley of the Great Salt Lake, he knew that he had found the place.

After exploring the country round about, tentatively marking out the city, planting crops, and making some provision for the safety and comfort of those who were to remain, the Mormon leader took a few scouts and started, late in August, back to the body of the Saints on the Missouri.

In the meantime, one detachment of the Mormon Battalion had arrived in the Salt Lake Valley, and several companies from Winter Quarters had followed on the heels of the pioneer group, so that some eighteen hundred people wintered in the embryo city. The next year four thousand more arrived. In 1849 the Mormon emigrants were caught up in the great rush of gold-seekers on the plains, but they were not materially affected by the hysteria that drove others to seek their fortunes. They wanted only to gather with their people in the new Zion.

As new companies arrived each year, Brigham Young began to establish towns and villages wherever there was water. Timber was an advantage but not a necessity; crops would grow wherever water could be obtained. It was good strategy, too, for the Saints to have possession of every spring and stream, thus closing the land to colonization by the Gentiles, who might later become numerous enough to begin again the troubles so lately experienced. Thus, within a few years, little settlements began to dot the valleys to the north and to march in a thin line south along the Old Spanish Trail to the sea.

In 1850 a territorial government was set up for Utah, with Brigham Young appointed as governor and with three other Mormons and six Gentiles completing the official personnel. From the beginning, most of the federally appointed officers from the outside met with difficulties in Utah. They resented the unquestioning allegiance of the members of the church to Brigham Young, which made him in fact the ruler, no matter what position anyone else held in name. On the other hand, the people viewed the government appointees with suspicion. Life in the territory was so difficult for them that one after another of the officials returned to the states bearing reports that pictured the Mormons as insubordinate and traitorous.

In the fall of 1856, the Mormon leader initiated a movement known as the Reformation, which was a vigorous call to repentance among the people. In every town and hamlet, even in the distant forts where only a few families lived, appointed missionaries catechized each person individually. Although the questions asked referred to loyalty to the church, to the Christian principles of honesty and integrity, and even to matters of personal cleanliness,[2] the whole process was a soul-searching affair, often attended by high emotion. Once having either answered the questions satisfactorily or confessed his sins and irregularities, the

[2] This version of the "Catechism" is found in the diary of John Pulsipher, who at the time was living at Fort Supply. Beginning on page 101, he says:

"On Sunday, May 10, [1857] Pres. Bullock said the time had come to catechize this people—& asked Bros. Robinson, Crandall, & Thompson to assist so the four sides of our Fort were all waited on at the same time.

"CATECHISM

"Have you committed murder, by shedding innocent blood—or consenting thereto?

"Have you betrayed your brethren or sisters in anything?

"Have you committed adultery by having connection with a woman that was not your wife or a man that was not your husband?

"Do you pay your tithing promptly?

"Have you spoken against any principle contained in the Bible, Book of Mormon, Doctrine & Covenants, or any principle revealed through Joseph the Prophet or the authorities of the Church?

"Do you teach your families the Gospel of Salvation?

"Do you wash your bodies & have your family do so as often as cleanliness requires or circumstances permit?

"Do you preside over your family, as a servant of God—and is your family subject to you?

"Do you fulfill your promises, do you pay your debts or do you run into debt without prospect of paying?

"Have you taken anything that did not belong to you without the owners knowledge or consent?

"Have you borrowed anything that you have not returned or paid for?

"Have you found lost property & not returned it to the owner or used all diligence to do so?

"Have you lied about or maliciously misrepresented any person or thing?

"Have you branded any animal that you did not know to be your own?

"Have you taken up strays & converted to your own use without accounting to the proper Authorities?

"Do you work 6 days & go to the house of worship on the 7th?

"Have you taken the name of Deity in vain?

"Have you been intoxicated by strong drink?"

Copies of the Pulsipher diaries are at Brigham Young University and the Utah State Historical Society; the Henry E. Huntington Library has a photostat.

person was rebaptized in renewal of his covenants. In general, the effect of this movement was to arouse the people to new religious consciousness, but for some who had lived through the persecutions of Missouri and Nauvoo and whose covenants included a hope that God would avenge the death of the Prophet and the sufferings of His Saints, the Reformation served to encourage fanaticism. It also helped to cement their group solidarity and to make them feel that Zion must stand against the sins of the world.

In awakening the Saints to their duties, the Reformation also seemed to set them more directly against the government officials who, they felt, were ruling without consent of the governed. Thus frictions were aggravated and tensions became more strained.

It will not be possible here to follow the details of the growing troubles or to measure the guilt of the two sides. Bitter, accusing letters were exchanged; long reports were filed. One difference led to another, until Justice Stiles reported that he was intimidated in his own court, and his official records were stolen and burned. Justice Drummond also returned to Washington, D. C., and in a long letter accompanying his resignation listed his grievances, among them the charge that the court records had been destroyed with the knowledge and approval of Brigham Young, and that the officers of the government were constantly insulted and harassed. He insisted that affairs in Utah were in a treasonable and disgraceful state.

Mormon protestations that affairs had been misrepresented were ignored; proof that the records were safe did not change the fact that they had been taken without sanction from the office of the judge. Finally President Buchanan decided to send an army to Utah to quiet the "rebellion." This decision was made in the late spring of 1857; unofficial word of the oncoming army reached Utah on July 24, 1857; the Mountain Meadows Massacre occurred on the following September 11.

Whether or not the policies of Brigham Young were such as to justify the sending of an army to Utah, and whether or not the President of the United States was wise in his approach to the problem, will not seriously concern us here. We are concerned primarily with the approaching army as a factor in the attitude of the people of Utah, the first fatal development in a situation which culminated in the murder of some 120 men, women, and children in an isolated area in southern Utah.

2

Defense of Zion

Had brigham young planned and timed it, had he set the stage deliberately, he could not have had a more dramatic occasion for announcing that an army was moving upon Utah. Every year since the first group of pioneers had entered the valley of the Great Salt Lake, the Mormons had set aside the twenty-fourth of July as a holiday, but this tenth anniversary was made a very special celebration. Weeks before, invitations had been sent throughout the territory, bidding the people gather at Silver Lake, at the head of Big Cottonwood Canyon in the mountains east of the city, for a three-day outing.

On the morning of July 22, the trek up the canyon began, the individual outfits ranging from smart carriages, fringed and tasseled, to heavy, ox-drawn wagons, behind which the family cow plodded. Three open-air pavilions had been erected at the appointed place, and six bands kept up continuous music.

With characteristic Mormon attention to detail, the record shows that 2,587 persons were present, that they had come in 464 carriages and wagons, with 1,028 horses and mules and 332 oxen and cows. The record lists also the songs and speeches, the music and prayers; but the loveliness of the setting, the couples romancing, cronies observing and gossiping, and children playing are left to the imagination.

People visited with friends from other settlements, comparing experiences and reminding each other of the changes which the last ten years had brought. In what had been a barren desert now lived some thirty-six thousand people in a hundred towns and villages. Great Salt Lake City, the center of their Zion, fairly exuded an atmosphere of vigor, of growth, of expectancy of great things. New businesses were springing up almost overnight, and public buildings were constantly under construction. The public square had been enclosed in a high rock wall, within which an adobe tabernacle large enough to accommodate two thousand people had been finished; ground had been broken for a temple. On the block to the east, the Lion House and the Beehive House stood, also behind protecting rock walls, while the Council House and the Social Hall looked as if they might have been transplanted bodily from New England. Their city was, in fact, becoming large and great.

In every hamlet and village, homes were being built and trees planted. Best of all, every citizen could become an independent landowner, a fact appreciated especially by converts from the factories and mines of Europe. As they visited and celebrated, the people talked over the many advantages of being in Zion. Though they had known privation and hunger here, they enjoyed security; no mobs rode at night. Truly this was the Kingdom of God spoken of in the Scripture, the Zion which should be established in the tops of the mountains and exalted above the hills.

About noon on the day of the twenty-fourth, when the festivities were at their height, four travel-weary men rode into camp: Mayor A. O. Smoot, Judson L. Stoddard, Nicholas Grosbeck, and Porter Rockwell, already a distinctive figure with his long braid of hair looped up and tied like an Indian's. These men sought out Brigham Young, who in turn called his council into a private session to hear their report.

The afternoon festivities went on undisturbed. The dance at night grew hilarious as the different groups of musicians vied with each other in lively tunes. When the time came for dismissal, Daniel H. Wells called the people to order to give instructions for the breaking of camp the next day and then announced that they had just received important news from the East. The mail contracts had been canceled, the service suspended, and special

*Modern Utah, showing the relationship
of Mountain Meadows to present-day cities.*

riders had brought word that an army was on its way to put down the rebellion in Utah.

At first the audience received the news quietly; then whisperings ran through the crowd like a sudden breeze across a field of grain. To put down a rebellion! Was not the flag of the United States even now floating above the pavilion? Had they not made a special ceremony of planting it on a tall pole fastened in the top of the tallest pine? An army? An armed mob! Converts new from Europe might not know what that meant, but those who had lived through the persecutions of Missouri and Illinois could not be deceived; they had had experience with armies and troops too many times before!

As the crowd broke up, groups collected to talk about this unexpected development. "Remember what Brother Brigham said just ten years ago?" they reminded each other. He had predicted that "if our enemies would give us just ten years unmolested, we would ask no odds of them; we would never be driven again." Well, the ten years were up, ten years to the day.

The leaders, more conscious of the storm that had been gathering in the East, were perhaps not so surprised at this move on the part of the government as were the ordinary Saints, who had been busy at building homes and getting established. True, many remembered the stinging public denunciation that Brigham Young had given Judge Brocchus when that worthy questioned the morals of Mormon women, but only the authorities sensed the full extent of the irritations and provocations which had sent so many government officials back to Washington, D. C., in protest. Those who knew smiled at the deception of Judges Stiles and Drummond with regard to the court records, but did not know how heavily that deception weighed in the balance against the Mormons. They sensed the unfriendly attitude of the Indian agent, Garland Hurt, but could not know of the long reports he sent questioning the motives behind their Indian missions, wherein he called the missionaries "rude and lawless young men, such as might be regarded as a curse to any civilized community."[1]

[1] Garland Hurt, writing to George Manypenny, May 2, 1855. The tension

18

In the tabernacle two weeks earlier, both Brigham Young and Heber C. Kimball had suggested, without knowing just what action might be taken against them, that trouble might be brewing. Now they both proceeded to denounce the government in good, round terms. On Sunday, July 26, Heber C. Kimball gave one of his characteristic fiery speeches:

> Send 2,500 troops here, our brethren, to make a desolation of this people! God Almighty helping me, I will fight until there is not a drop of blood in my veins. Good God! I have wives enough to whip out the United States, for they will whip themselves. . . .
>
> Will we have manna? Yes, the United States have 700 wagons loaded with about two tons to each wagon with all kinds of things and then some 7,000 head of cattle, and there is said to be 2,500 troops with this and that and the other, that is all right. Suppose the troops don't get here, but all these goods and cattle come; well, they would be a mighty help to us. That would clothe up the boys and girls and make them comfortable, and then remember there is 15 months provisions besides. . . .[2]

Already, on January 14, 1857, the legislature had passed an act to reorganize the militia of Utah Territory, or, rather, to reactivate the Nauvoo Legion. Daniel H. Wells was named commander-in-chief, and his General Orders No. 2, issued on March 27, 1857, indicate that he knew there might be trouble: "As the

between Hurt and his Mormon neighbors grew to be such that he fled the territory in the fall of 1857. In a letter to A. S. Johnson, dated October 24, 1857, he gives the reasons for his action: "Believing that I have maintained my position among them for the last three or four months under circumstances of the most extreme hazard to my life, I determined on the 27th day of September last to try to make my escape, and seek protection with the army then enroute to Utah."

[2] *Deseret News*, August 12, 1857. Kimball went on: "Poor rotten curses! and the President of the United States, inasmuch as he has turned against us and will take a course to persist in pleasing the ungodly curses that are howling around him for the destruction of this people, he shall be cursed in the name of Israel's God, and he shall not rule over this Nation, because they are my brethren, but they have cast me out and will cast you out, and I curse him and all his coadjuters in his cursed deeds in the name of Jesus Christ and by the authority of the Holy Priesthood, and all Israel shall say amen."

good never wish for war, and the wise are always ready for it, let us continually seek that our weapons may be made bright and ready by our industry, and preserved so by a continued peace." Now, with war an immediate possibility, he issued to the Nauvoo Legion, numbering some two thousand men, an order declaring that Utah was about to be invaded by a hostile force, so that every member must be prepared to defend his homeland.[3]

On August 6, Franklin D. Richards, brigadier general commanding, in his orders to the officers serving under him in the 2d Brigade, 1st Division, declaimed:

We have experienced the repeated desolation of our homes. Our women have been ravished. Our prophets and brethren have been imprisoned and murdered, & the people *en masse* have been exterminated from their midst.

We have appealed to Judges [?] and Governors of those States for redress of our wrongs in vain, and when we applied to the Presidents of the United States for our rights we were told *"your cause is just, but I can do nothing for you."*

We now appeal to the God of our Fathers & Prophets for protection against the hostilities of any Mob that shall invade our Territory, and invoke the aid of the heavens to strengthen us in defending ourselves against further aggressions.

You are required to hold your Regiments in readiness to march at the shortest possible notice to any portion of the Territory. See that the law is strictly enforced in regard to arms and ammunition and cause that each Ten be provided with a good wagon four horses or mules, or Oxen (where horses or mules cannot be had) as well as the necessary clothing rations Tents &c. for a winter campaign and make immediate returns to this office of the men in each Ten who have charge of the Wagon animals Tent &c. Let your influence be diligently employed for the preservation of the grain and report without delay any person in your District that disposes of a Kernel of grain to any Gentile merchant or temporary sojourner, or suffers it to go to waste. . . .

[3] Brigham H. Roberts, *Comprehensive History of the Church of Jesus Christ of Latter-day Saints,* IV, 239.

The opportunities that occur of obtaining arms & ammunition from the passing emigrants should not escape your carefull attention.

Finally avoid all excitement and be Ready![4]

The tone of this document leaves no question about the Mormon determination to fight or as to the reason which prompted them. The order to "report without delay any person in your District that disposes of a Kernel of grain to any Gentile merchant or temporary sojourner" was a recognition of the military emergency. As the war psychology developed, any trading with passing emigrants might be considered equivalent to giving aid and comfort to the enemy.

From these orders, carried to every southern village in August, grew many of the tensions and frictions which finally culminated in the Mountain Meadows Massacre. The people of the southern settlements had already shown themselves reluctant to sell food to travelers, for they were far from supplies themselves and had seen near famine. Previously the plain law of self-preservation had made them loath to part with their grain, but now military orders made it mandatory that they store it. As early as January 15, 1856, Erastus Snow had written of conditions in the south:

> The southern settlements of Iron County raised a surplus of provisions last year, but the Northern settlements raised little or none. But the old grain on hand and the surplus in their neighboring settlements will be ample for the people until another harvest, if rigid economy is observed. But they are determined that no supplies shall be furnished emigrants or others bound for California;

---

[4] The military records of the 2d Brigade, 1st Division, of the Nauvoo Legion were carefully kept in a single volume, the original of which has now been sold to a private collector in the East. Typewritten copies are at the Brigham Young University, Provo, Utah, and the Henry E. Huntington Library, San Marino, California.

From the various orders issued to this brigade, it is easy to follow the course of the "Mormon War," as far as Mormon resistance is concerned.

and all such persons who fail to supply themselves before reaching those settlements may expect to grub their living across the desert.[5]

During the weeks following the announcement of the coming army, the feeling of resentment and harassment grew in intensity. Brigham Young expressed himself with characteristic forthrightness in a letter of September 4, 1857, to his nephew, John R. Young:

The government have called 2 two regiments of Infantry, and one of Dragoons with two batteries of artillery; and placed the army under command of that blood-thirsty old villain, General Harney, with orders to come to *Utah* and regulate the "Mormons." This has been done without investigation or even taking into consideration our own reports, or looking at any circumstance which would withdraw the pretext, which they have for years been seeking, to make a final or fatal blow at the kingdom. We had determined years ago, if a mob again attack us, whether led by their own passions, or constitutionally legalized by the General Government or Government of any of the States or territories, that we will resist their aggressions; by making an appeal to God, and our own right arms, for that protection which has ever been denied us by Christianized and civilized nations. . . .[6]

Speeches became more and more inflammatory, such speeches as have been used by patriots and zealots in many causes to stir the heart to anger and strengthen the arm for battle. From one end of the territory to the other, the people of Utah retold and relived their past sufferings, the mobbings and burnings and final expulsion from Nauvoo. They would never be driven again; they would fight first.

The spirit was widespread and contagious. Even John Taylor, ordinarily mild and peace-loving, became a vigorous proponent of war. Speaking in the tabernacle to a large assembly, he said:

[5] The full text of this letter is published in the *Deseret News*, January 23, 1856.
[6] This letter was copied into the private journal of John Stillman Woodbury, the original of which is at the Brigham Young University. The Henry E. Huntington Library has a photostatic copy of the journal.

We have had to stoop to our enemies heretofore and bear many things from them worse than death; but if there is anything that gives us joy and consolation, at least I can speak for myself, It was when I heard the Brethren say, "You are free, brethren, you are free; and you may prove yourselves before God and man that you are willing to defend yourselves against tyrants and oppressors." When I heard this, I was full of joy, and who would not be? Who would not rather die than bow down to the yoke of the enemy? It would sweeten death to a man to know that he should lay down his life in defense of freedom and the kingdom of God, rather than to longer bow to the cruelty of mobs, even when the mob have the name of being legalized by the nation. I thank God, and I rejoice that this people are determined to be free of mobocracy and oppression, and that they are determined to have peace, if they have to fight for it.[7]

To this stirring appeal, the whole congregation responded with a loud and hearty Amen!

Since this sounds suspiciously like treason, as do many of the preachments of Mormon leaders during this time of stress and excitment, it might be well to examine here the Mormon attitude

[7] This speech was delivered in the tabernacle at Great Salt Lake City, Sunday, September 13, 1857, and published in the *Deseret News* for September 23, 1857. John Taylor said also:

"What was your object in coming here? Was it to rebel against the general government? (President Brigham Young: To get away from Christians.) Pres Young said it was to get away from Christians, from that unbounded charity which you had experienced amongst them. In consequence of their treatment you had come away to seek a home in the desert wilds, and to obtain that protection among savages which Christian philanthropy denied you. We came here because we could not help it, and now we have got an idea to stay here because we can help it. . . .

"What have you heard taught here? Nothing but the law of God and obedience to the laws of the land. Nobody but the most blackhearted villians that ever lived would have gone among our enemies and represented things otherwise. You comprehended liberty, and you will have this boon. Many of your fathers have fought for this, and you are resolved to enjoy it. . . ."

In the same speech he asked the questions: "Would you, if necessary, brethren, put the torch to your buildings and lay them in ashes, and wander homeless into the mountains, rather than submit to their military rule and oppression?" The congregation manifested a unanimous affirmative.

toward the government. From the first, the leaders had often expressed great love for the Constitution of the United States. Joseph Smith often spoke of America as a land of promise, a land "choice above all other lands," where the people "shall be free from bondage and captivity, and from all other nations under heaven." The Constitution, he maintained, was an inspired document, formed by wise men under the direction of God. Brigham Young had often said that he had no complaint against the government, but did have one against the damned rascals who administered the government.

Within the bounds of this political organization, they believed their business was to establish the Kingdom of God upon the earth, a material kingdom as well as a spiritual one. This would prepare them for the millennium, which was close at hand, "even at the door." Through their persecutions they had developed a high state of group solidarity and loyalty; they had survived hardships and were beginning to prosper. Other nations and kingdoms would diminish, but the Kingdom of God would eventually overspread the whole earth. Now, under the tensions of this crisis, Brigham Young spoke of cutting the thread which held them to the United States, so that the business of establishing the Kingdom might go on without interference. Soon after word of the approaching army arrived, he spoke of this:

> The time must come when there will be a separation between this kingdom and the kingdoms of this world. Even in every point of view, the time must come when this kingdom must be free and independent of all other kingdoms.
>
> Are you prepared to have the thread cut today? , , , I shall take it as a witness that God desires to cut the thread between us and the world when an army undertakes to make their appearance in this Territory to chastise me or to destroy my life from the earth. . . . We will wait a little while to see; but I shall take a hostile move by our enemies as an evidence that it is time for the thread to be cut.[8]

[8] Brigham Young, in a speech delivered on August 2, 1857, as reported in the *Deseret News* for August 12, 1857.

In the weeks that followed, he referred often to the possibility of separation from the United States, and many of the faithful who listened to him went home and recorded his sayings in their diaries. Hosea Stout, whose daily entries are full of current happenings, wrote on September 6, 1857: "President B. Young in his Sermon declared that the thred was cut between us and the U. S. and that the Almighty recognized us as a free and independent people and that no officer apointed by government should come and rule over us from the time forth."[9]

The next week Jesse B. Martin, newly arrived with a company of emigrants, wrote in his pocket diary: "Sunday, Sept. 13, This morning I went to the tabernacle & there heard Brother Brigham speak, he told us that if we would assert our independence we should be a free people but if not in the name of Israel's God the kingdom should be rent from us."[10]

The theme was evidently repeated the next week, for John Pulsipher, who had moved his family in from Fort Bridger ahead of the approaching army, attended conference in early October, and recorded his version of the sermons: "Bro. Brigham felt sorry that our enemies were so anxious to make war on an innocent people—but he was firm that if government does sustain this approaching hostile forse & will not let us have peace then the thread is cut that bound us to them & we will be free. Many predictions in regard to the Triumph of Israel."[11]

Whether for defense of their rights or for ultimate independence, the fervor of war spread, until by mid-August a military organization had been set up in every town and village; every able-bodied man in the territory was mustered into service. Military drills and inspection of arms were systematic and regular.

As a part of the general policy that Mormon economy should be independent of the outside and should consume only what it

[9] Photostatic copies of the Hosea Stout diaries are at the Henry E. Huntington Library. Typewritten copies are at the Utah State Historical Society and the Brigham Young University.

[10] Photostatic copy at the Henry E. Huntington Library.

[11] Copies as in note 9 above.

could produce, there had been early efforts by the Saints to manufacture their own ammunition, powder, and lead. They had had trouble before and might have again, but, in any event, bullets were needed to get game and to insure safety from wild animals and Indians. As early as 1855, when some of the Indian missionaries to Las Vegas discovered a stratum of lead-bearing ore, President Young had made immediate plans to develop the mine and smelt lead. The story of this venture is an epic in hardship, for the rough, hot country, the starvation diet, the lack of fuel, and the distance from any settlement had doomed the project from the beginning.[12] Now, with the approach of the army and the resolution to resist it, ammunition was an urgent necessity, and for a short time the project was reactivated. But the difficulties were so great that it was soon clear that, if Zion were to defend herself, she must have another source of ammunition.

On August 15, 1857, Brigham Young wrote to the Saints in the Carson Valley, instructing them to dispose of their property and come home to Utah, giving as the reason for this order a detailed description of the army and its purpose. "Bring all the arms and ammunition you can," he told them. "Buy all the powder, lead, and caps you possible can, but do not tarry to go over into California, or at least to detain you any length of time."[13]

The Carson Saints raised $1,260, and with this sum purchased

[12] *Nevada State Historical Society Publications*, Vol. V (1925). This account is printed from original sources in the archives of the Latter-day Saints church historian, Salt Lake City. The account covers pages 119–284 of the publication.

[13] The full text of Brigham Young's letter to the Carson Saints, taken from the "Church Letterbook No. 3," follows:

PRESIDENT'S OFFICE
S.L. CITY
AUG'T 15, 1857

ELDER CHESTER LOVELAND, AND THE BRETHREN IN CARSON CO:
DEAR BRETHREN:

We have concluded that it is wisdom that you should dispose of your property as well as you can and come home. If you cannot sell to advantage lease your places, and get your pay in advance.

We send this counsel to you by Express that you may avail yourselves of the present emigration to dispose of your property. We want you to secure as much ammunition as you can. Be wise, 'and not let the right hand know what the left

ammunition which they brought back with them to the valley, arriving there early in November.[14]

Not only the Carson Saints were summoned back to Zion to join in a decisive stand against the United States Army. Elders en route to Hawaii were turned back; those already there were charged to close up their business, pay the church debts, and come home. The printing press, with which the *Western Standard* had been put out in San Francisco, was offered for sale, and the brethren were counseled to be ready to leave at a moment's notice. Five trusted men were stationed in the East to manage affairs of the church there and to direct the European immigration.

That the Mormon leaders expected the war to be serious and possibly of long duration is shown by their orders to store and cache grain against a possible siege and their plans to divert their immigration to Utah north through Canada or south through Panama, as well as their immediate action to mobilize manpower.

hand doeth.' 'A hint to the wise is sufficient.' Make no noise about your business, but let all things be done quietly and in order. You are aware that you sell at better advantage if you can keep your own counsel.

The express party will remain and assist you in fitting up and return with you on the Northern route. Brother W. R. Smith, who went to California with Capt'n Hooper's stock, will it is presumed be ready to come with you.

Come in one company, and keep together so that you can protect yourselves against all foes, both white and red.

We learn there is an army of from twenty five to thirty five hundred men now enroute for this Territory, besides some ten or twelve hundred teamsters &c. seven hundred wagons with ox teams loaded with supplies; and about four hundred more mules and horse teams loaded with personal effects, camp equipage, &c, seven thousand beef cattle. The supplies are designed to last them fifteen months after they arrive in this Territory. We do not expect them to come *here*, although the last we heard of them, 100 of the wagons were 180 miles on the way, and a train of 30 wagons were starting out every other day, and the troops were to start off the 15th of the last month; they are to march on foot.

My counsel is for you to leave your farms with as good gentiles as you can, if you cannot sell to advantage, for we would just as soon own the property as not. Buy all the powder, Lead, and Caps you possibly can, but do not tarry to go over into California, or at least to detain you any length of time.

BRIGHAM YOUNG

[14] See the narratives of Peter Wilson Conover and Oliver B. Huntington, copies of which are in the files of the Utah State Historical Society.

An eloquent summary of the situation and the Mormon attitude toward it is given in a letter written from New York by Samuel Richards to his brother, Henry, in Hawaii:

In view of the invasion of our territory [Utah] by the United States Troops, our mission is to call all the Elders home from the States and Europe that they may take care of their families, and from hence forth Israel take care of themselves, while the world goes to the Devil. A great exertion will be made to get every family possible out of the States, as should they remain, and difficulties exist between us and the government it would be very unsafe for Saints to remain in the States. This week is the last number of the "Mormon" that will be issued, and everything will be made to bend as far as possible towards clearing the country. We go to Liverpool to stop emigration from coming into the States, and assist in turning it up towards the head of the Lakes, Upper Canada, and after next Season, they have to meet the Saints in the mountains by a *new* northern Route, through the British possessions. The States evidently have commenced a war with us, and are determined to put an end to us or our religion, neither of which they can do, as they have commenced a job they never can accomplish, we may expect a mighty howling from the regions below (the States). The Gentiles can never again put their yoke on Israel, and some funny times will be seen before they will acknowledge our Independence. One thing is certain, they cannot exterminate the Saints, neither can they make them forsake their religion. About 700 Freighted wagons, carrying 5000 each, are on the way to the mountains for the Troops, besides the wagons etc. necessary to accompany the Troops and carry the camp equipage, arms, etc., of 2500 Troops. Won't we have lots of good things in the valley if the Troops couldn't get in, and all the trains arrive safe.

We met the trains and most of the Troops as we came down. Our emigration were getting along well, and will be in at an early date. Since Government has refused to carry the Mail, the express company have abandoned their stations on the route. There are none now between Bridger and the Bever [*sic*] River, called Genoa 100 miles from Florence.

Our movements outside will be governed by the state of things in the mountains. God Bless you, Henry, and we'll go it for the Kingdom. The Lord preserve us and ours and his saints.[15]

Not enough attention has been given to the songs which the Mormons composed and sang during this period as an expression of the emotional climate. In addition to many short doggerel verses and "DuDah" jingles, at least two serious battle songs emerged, both still included, one with minor changes, in the present Latter-day Saints hymnbooks. The first, "O Ye Mountains High," was used to impress upon Captain Van Vliet, of the United States Army, the fact that the Mormons meant to fight. Legend says that Brigham Young had the Scotch singer, Brother Dunbar, sing it twice so that the visitor could get its full significance. An excerpt will show its general tenor:

> *In thy mountain retreat, God will strengthen thy feet*
> *On the necks of thy foes thou shalt tread*
> *And their silver and gold, as the Prophets foretold*
> *Shall be brought to adorn thy fair head.*
> *O Zion, dear Zion, Land of the free!*
> *Though thou wer't forced to fly to thy chambers on high*
> *Yet our hearts shall be ever with thee.*

These were not just empty words; these were a call to battle, though not so eloquent or direct as "Up, Awake Ye Defenders of Zion," which begins:

> *Up, awake, ye defenders of Zion,*
> *The foe's at the door of your homes*
> *Let each heart be the heart of a lion*
> *Unyielding and proud as he roams.*
> *Remember the wrongs of Missouri*
> *Forget not the fate of Nauvoo*
> *When the God-hating foe is before you*
> *Stand firm and be faithful and true.*

[15] This letter was copied into the diary of John Stillman Woodbury, a companion of Henry Richards in the letter, or inserted later by the copyist. See note 6 above.

Written by Charles W. Penrose, this song asks the faithful: "Shall we bear with oppression forever? Shall we tamely submit to the foe, while the ties of our kindred they sever, and the blood of the Prophets shall flow." The melody, "Red, White, and Blue," was well known and stirring enough to quicken the pulse of every Mormon and to justify violence in defending their church.

Among the soldiers of Johnston's army there was also the thought of approaching battles, for they learned early that the Mormons meant to resist their entrance into the territory. Captain Jesse A. Gove wrote, on September 18: "If the Mormons will only fight, their days are numbered. We shall sweep them from the face of the earth and Mormonism in Utah shall cease. Our campaign will then be at an end. I sincerely hope that they will, at least, go far enough to compel us to take quarters instead of hiring."[16]

Thus the groundwork was laid for war, and the wonder is that more blood was not shed, as there certainly would have been had the clash come in September or October instead of the spring following. The massacre at Mountain Meadows, though far from the center of the war activities, was a definite outgrowth of the war-mongering of the preceding month—a fire, kindled, that got out of control.

[16] Captain Jesse A. Gove, *The Utah Expedition*, 58.

3

The Zealous South

THE EXCITEMENT that was sweeping the whole territory at the approach of the army was perhaps most intense in the isolated southern settlements. Most of the people who had been called to the south had been with the church through the persecutions of Missouri and Illinois; Tarleton Lewis, the bishop of Parowan, had been wounded at the Haun's Mill massacre and survived only because the mob thought he was dead. Others had lost relatives and friends in that tragedy and longed for an opportunity to avenge them. Their current reading was limited almost entirely to the *Deseret News*, which was printing in serial form the life of Joseph Smith, their prophet, and retelling the suffering many of them knew firsthand. Always the crimes of their enemies were a favorite theme for testimony, sermon, and even recreation.[1]

When the first colonists arrived in the south, in late 1851, they had formed a military organization,[2] and, as other settlements

[1] James H. Martineau, writing to George A. Smith from Parowan on March 13, 1856, said, "The play, called 'The Missouri Persecutions,' was performed a few nights since, and every one seems highly pleased with it, which of course, pleases me, and encourages me to try my hand again. The time it occupied in its performance is just three hours." "Journal History of the Church," under date listed.

[2] The first settlers to southern Utah were en route in December, 1850, and from Fort Peteetneet (now Payson) George A. Smith wrote back to Brigham Young on December 20:

"Yesterday I organized the Iron County militia into 4 companies, one of horse 35 in number, rank and file, and two of infantry, ranking near the same in number; also one artillery company, 12 in number, forming the whole into a Battalion, which is known by the name of the Iron Battalion.

were established, this was extended to them. Although there had been little activity other than an occasional muster, the machinery was in existence, and in January 1856, a company of minutemen on horseback had been organized for emergencies. Now, with word of an approaching army, even by rumor, what had been an empty form became reality, and purpose was injected into drills and inspections.

On August 4, George A. Smith left Provo for the southern towns, delivering the military orders to the commander of each. They were to be in readiness to march at the shortest possible notice to any part of the territory; they were to be equipped for a winter campaign and prepared for a long siege. Every able-bodied man was called into service.

Because of these developments, the Indians assumed a new importance. Though the Indian missions had been established with the professed purpose of raising the natives from their low and degraded condition and teaching them the arts of civilized life, beneath this aim was the fact that it was good strategic policy to court their friendship—small, isolated settlements would have been in constant jeopardy but for the good will of the natives. Apart from this, some of the early missionaries had seen the Indians as a possible ally in case of trouble with the Gentiles; one had even referred to them as "the battle-ax of the Lord," which they

---

"Our military organization may appear strange to some of the officers of the Nauvoo Legion, and in fact some of the Iron County officers thought it rather odd. But it was organized to suit the wants of the camp under the present conditions."

About a year later, when a settlement was made at Cedar City, John D. Lee, the recorder, wrote on November 5, 1851: ". . . the militia of Cole Creek were organized into a Battalion which caused the Iron Battalion together to grow into a regiment over which Geo. A. Smith was elected Colonel, James A. Little Lieut. Col., and Matthew Carrathers, Major."

As a footnote to his letter quoted in note 1 above, Martineau added:

"P.S. We have just had a muster and Col. Dame organized a company of minute men—horsemen out of the other companies. Jas. Lewis, Capt., C. Y. Webb 1st Lieut., and J. H. Martineau 2nd Lieut."

Notations are all from the "Journal History," under the dates cited.

might learn to use with skill.[3] Now, with actual war impending, Brigham Young took steps to secure their active support. To withstand the United States Army successfully, he must not overlook any possibility of help.

In addition to the orders which he carried to the local military officers, George A. Smith had also an important letter to Jacob

[3] Thomas D. Brown, who kept the records of the first Indian mission to the south, "Journal of the Southern Indian Mission, April 15, 1854–April 1856," gives careful minutes of the meetings. Because the aims and ideals of the group are more truly shown by the record of the whole meeting rather than by single isolated remarks, I quote more fully from the entry made Sunday, May 14, 1854, entered on pages 35–38 of the original record:

"At 10 o'C A.M. we met under Patriach E. H. Groves presiding. Song Come all Ye sons of Zion. Bro. Groves prayed in faith. The Recorder, by request, and the subject he chose was 'lengthening the cords and strengthening the Stakes of Zion,' and upon union in this Stake. A good spirit prevailed. Father Groves speaking of order in receiving, keeping, feeding, and working the Indians said, 'Take not their wild habits and liberty from them at once, but by degrees, and help them to farm, but let them labor for their food. . . .'

"Bro. Jno Lott, glad to stand in this mission and be one of us. I have been reared in the church and know nothing but Mormonism. Spoke of Joseph Smith, the Prophet, of the rise of this Church, of his suffering, tarring and feathering, and other persecutions, because his Father in Heaven required it at his hands. I lived with Jos. in Missouri. The Saints of God endure not for a good name among men, but because it is required of us by the good Father in heaven. We suffered from damned Sectarians in Mo., driven, robbed, and murdered. I hope to see the day when the blood of martyrs will be avenged, and these damnable rebels make restitution, or the children suffer for the wickedness of their fathers. We will do good God being our helper.

"Brother Lewis reviewed the principles of the previous speakers, all good and for good. All the scenes Bro. Lott has recounted I shared in, my Brother Benjamin was killed Missouri, and I am alive to avenge his blood when the Lord will. The second time I heard a Mormon preach, he declared holding up a Book of Mormon that this was a record of the red men, and of God's dealings with their fathers, and we should one day carry this work to the Indians, and we are now living among them, and to teach them of this work. We must treat them like children, by degrees, to quit their savage customs. Shall we have no opportunities? We shall. No conquest without a struggle, no victory without a fight. Be diligent, faithful and patient, and the Lord will reward you when you have been proved. Ephriam is the battle axe of the Lord. May we not have been sent to learn how to *use* this axe, with skill? . . ."

The original of this journal is in the archives of the Latter-day Saints church historian.

Hamblin, outlining the part which the Indians might play in the coming crisis. This letter has been often quoted, but in an edited form which omitted the significant message it bore. It read:

PRESIDENT'S OFFICE

GREAT SALT LAKE CITY

AUGUST 4, 1857

ELDER JACOB HAMBLIN,

You are hereby appointed to succeed Elder R. C. Allen (whom I have released as President of the Santa Clara Indian Mission.) I wish you to enter upon the duties of your calling immediately.

Continue the conciliatory policy towards the Indians, which I have ever recommended, and seek by works of righteousness to obtain their love and confidence, for they must learn that they have either got to help us or the United States will kill us both. Omit promises where you are not sure you can fill them; and seek to unite the hearts of the brethren on that mission, and let all under your direction be knit together in the holy bonds of love and unity.

We have an abundance of "news." The Government have at last appointed an entire set of officials for the Territory. These Gentry are to have a body guard of 2500 of Uncle's Regulars. They were to start from Fort Leavenworth July 15th 400 mule teams brings their personal dunnage, & 700 ox teams 15 months provisions, 7000 head of beef cattle are to arrive here to supply them. General Harney it is supposed will command the expedition. There errand is entirely peaceful. The current report is that they somewhat query whether they will hang me with or without trial. There are about 30 others whom they intend to deal with. They will then proclaim a general jubilee [and] afford means and protection to those who wish to go back to the States. We feel first rate about all this and think every circumstance but proves the hastening of Zion's redemption.

All is peace here and the Lord is eminently blessing our labors; Grain is abundant, and our cities are alive with the busy hum of industry.

Do not permit the brethren to part with their Guns or ammunition, but save *them* against the hour of need.

34

Seek the Spirit of God to direct you, and that he may qualify you for every duty is the prayer of your

> Fellow Laborer in the Gospel
> of Salvation
> BRIGHAM YOUNG[4]

In the version of this letter written in the manuscript record, "Annals of the Southern Utah Mission, Book A," by James G. Bleak, and also printed in *Jacob Hamblin, Personal Narrative*, by James A. Little, the phrase "for they must learn that they have either got to help us or the United States will kill us both" is not included. Neither is the entire paragraph which gives the "abundance of news." The reason for this deletion seems clear.

Not only did George A. Smith carry significant orders to both the military and the Indians, but his preaching to the people in general was of such an inflammatory nature that it roused them to a high emotional pitch. Because of this, the fatal relationship between his visit and the massacre which followed scarcely a month later can hardly be overemphasized.

Legends regarding his sermons persist in southern Utah. One is from Parowan to the effect that there had been trouble with some boys in the village stealing fruit. The public whipping which the local authorities ordered as punishment was resented by some of the parents. When Apostle Smith arrived, he listened to both sides of the controversy, and in his public speech gave as a solution the counsel that they plant their public square to fruit, so that their children might have what fruit they wanted without having to steal. He went on to suggest what trees to plant and how to prepare the ground. He reminded them that bones make good fertilizer; a few bones at the roots of a tree would nourish it a long time. Then, speaking of the approaching army, he said, "As for the cursed mobocrats, I can think of nothing better that they could do than to feed a fruit tree in Zion."

[4] This letter is found in the "Church Letter Book, No. 3," pp. 737–38. The original is owned in the family of Jacob Hamblin, Mrs. Mary H. Beeler of Mesa, Arizona, having it in 1945.

That the people as a whole were deeply affected by his visit is shown by many entries in private diaries. He stayed with his family in Parowan until Saturday, August 15, when he started, in company with William H. Dame, colonel commanding, Captains C. C. Pendleton, Jesse N. Smith, Elias Silas Smith, C. Dalton, D. Cluff, Jr., and others to visit the settlements south and complete the military organization in each. James H. Martineau, who made the official report of this trip, not only told of the activities in each village, but described the roads—"Peter's Leap," "Haight's Jump Up," and "Jacob's Twist"—gave the summer temperatures in the various places, commented upon the lack of water and the condition of the crops, and noted the Indian farms of the area.

Jesse N. Smith, who kept a journal religiously over many years, also made entries regarding this trip. One of these would seem to show an additional cause for excitement among the people of the south:

> Tues. August 19, We were overtaken by an express rider with advice from Salt Lake City to the effect that it was desirable to watch the approaches to the Territory from the Western border, lest we be surprised by a detachment of the U. S. Troops from that quarter, as it was known an Army was marching on the Territory. Reached Washington; bathed in the Rio Virgin; partook of some melons; started in the evening for Fort Clara. . . .[5]

This warning was undoubtedly responsible for the conversation, later referred to by George A. Smith, in which Isaac C. Haight said that, should such a detachment appear, there would be no time to wait for instructions as to what he should do.

Among the local people who commented upon this visit was Perry Liston of Cedar City, who wrote:

> 1857. This fall I cradled 82½ acres of grain in 22½ days, this

[5] The original Jesse N. Smith journals are in the archives of the Latter-day Saints church historian, but a typed copy was made for the family. This has been reproduced in serial form in "The Kinsman," a monthly sheet being issued by George A. Smith, Route 2, Box 261, Mesa, Arizona.

being the year the government sent troops to destroy the Mormons. We got word just before harvest, so we were constrained to hurry up our harvest and hide up the grain in obedience to council.[6]

William Adams, who lived in Parowan, wrote later in his "Autobiography":

The year 1857 was a trying time for the saints, extermination from our homes, fleeing to the mountains, destruction of our property all were calculated upon. We were preparing for the worst, caching our flour in the mountains. The saints in the north were moving south ready to put the torch to their homes. . . .[7]

At Harmony, Rachel Lee, a wife of John D. Lee, made the following entries in her diary:

16th [August, 1857] there was no meeting held this day but preparing to receive G. A. Smith.

17th George A. Smith and company having arrived last evening and this morning the brethren paraded in order to show the officers of this place how to discipline their men aright.

Martineau of Parowan commanded the movements. At seven o'clock met in the meeting house. After singing and prayer by E. H. Groves *President G. A. Smith delivered a discourse on the spirit that actuated the United States towards this people*—full of hostility and virulence, and all felt to rejoice in the Lord God of our fathers. After singing, prayer by Prest. I. C. Haight. The company left for the Rio Virgin.[8]

But from none of these accounts, suggestive as they are, comes so direct or so eloquent a story of the activities of George A. Smith in the south and their effect upon the people as he himself

[6] A photostatic copy of this journal is in the Henry E. Huntington Library; typescripts in the Brigham Young University library, the state historical society files, and the Washington County library, St. George, Utah.

[7] Copies are in the depositories listed above.

[8] This original journal is owned by the Henry E. Huntington Library.

gives in a report made immediately upon his return to Great Salt Lake City. Speaking freely and frankly, and before he knew of the tragedy which followed so closely after him, he declared:

I visited the different settlements hurriedly until I reached Parowan in the county of Iron, the place of the first settlement in the southern part of the territory. When I arrived there it appeared that some rumor or spirit of surprise had reached them, for there were active operations going on, seemingly preparing for something that was near at hand. As I drove in at the gate I beheld the military on the square exercising and was immediately surrounded by the "Iron Battalion" which seemed to have held its own very well, since it was organized in that place. They had assembled together, under the impression that their country was about to be invaded by an army from the United States and that it was necessary to make preparation by examining each other's arms, and to make everything ready by preparing to strike in any direction, and march to such places as might be necessary in the defense of their homes.

As it will be well recollected, I was the president of the company that first made the settlement there. I was received with every feeling of enthusiasm, and I never found them in better spirits. They were willing any moment to touch fire to their homes and hide themselves in the mountains and to defend their country to the very last extremity. Now, there had not been such preaching as that when I went away; but the spirit seemed to burn in my bones to visit all these settlements in that southern region. Col. Dame was about organization of the military of that district under the law of last winter. As the colonel was going along to organize the military, I got into the carriage and went on a mission of peace to preach to the people. When I got to Cedar, I found the battalion on parade; and the colonel talked to them and completed the new organization.

On the following day I addressed the saints at their meeting house. I never had greater liberty of speech to proclaim to the people my feelings and views; and in spite of all I could do, I found myself preaching a military discourse, and I told them in case of invasion it might be necessary to set fire to our property and hide in the mountains, and leave our enemies to do the best they could.

It seemed to be hailed with the same enthusiasm that it was at Parowan. That was the same sabbath that Bro. Young was preaching the same kind of doctrine and I am perfectly satisfied that all the districts in the southern country would have given their unanimous vote.

I went to Penter [Pinto] and there addressed a house full of people in the evening, and then proceeded to Cedar the next day. They had heard they were going to have an army of 600 dragoons come down from the east into the town. The major [Isaac C. Haight] seemed very sanguine about the matter. I asked him, if these rumors should prove true, if he was not going to wait for instructions. He replied there was no time to wait for instruction, and he was going to take his battalion and use them up before they could get down through the canyons; for, said he, if they are coming here, they are coming for no good. I admired his grit; but I thought he would not have the privilege of using them up, for want of opportunity.

I don't know whether the inhabitants of Parowan intended to whip a regiment of dragoons or not; but it is certain they are wide awake and are not going to be taken by surprise. There was only one thing that I dreaded and that was a spirit in the breasts of some to wish that vengeance for the cruelties that had been inflicted upon us in the States. They did feel that they hated to owe a debt and not be able to pay it; and they felt like an old man that lives at Provo, Bro. Jameson, who has carried a few ounces of lead in his body ever since the Haun's Mill Massacre in Missouri and he wants to pay it back with usury; and he undertook to preach at Provo and prayed God would send them along, for he wanted a chance at them.

Now I never felt so, if the Lord brings us in collision with them, and it is His will, let us take hold, not in the spirit of revenge or anger, but simply to avenge God of his enemies, and to protect our homes and firesides; but I am perfectly aware that in all the settlements I visited in the south, Fillmore included, one single sentence is enough to put every man in motion; in fact, a word is enough to set in motion every man, or to set a torch to every building, where safety of this people is jeopardized.[9]

---

[9] This was published in the *Deseret News*, September 23, 1857. See also the "History of Brigham Young," October 31, 1857.

This report is of especial interest because it is such a frank picture of his own activity in giving "military speeches," and of the intensity of feeling general in the south. Made as it was in Great Salt Lake City on September 13, and reported in the *Deseret News* for September 23, before John D. Lee arrived with his "awful tale of blood," it makes admissions that all were reluctant to make later; it indicates too direct a relation between his activities and the following tragedy. The conversation wherein Haight declares that there will be no time to wait for counsel in the event of an invasion is followed by the apostle's admission that he "admired his grit." It would seem that he approved of the ardor of the southern leader and said nothing to dampen his spirits.

His moral responsibility is increased by the fact that a basic teaching of the church was obedience to authority. As Heber C. Kimball said earlier and repeated in effect many times, "If you do things according to counsel and they are wrong, the consequences will fall on the heads of those who counseled you, so don't be troubled."[10] This teaching was general from all those in authority —from Brigham Young down through to the bishops. In this case, while George A. Smith did not counsel his subordinates to use violence, he let them feel that he admired their spirit and would not condemn them if they found it necessary to take matters into their own hands.

Jacob Hamblin, faced with his new responsibility for the Indians and concerned about making them understand their part in the approaching war, decided to take a group of the chiefs to Great Salt Lake City for an interview with the great Mormon chief, Brigham Young. His handwritten diary, as yet unpublished, says:

I started for Great Salt Lake City in company with Thales Haskell and Tutsegabit [the Yannawant Chief]. He had felt anxious for a long time to visit Brigham Young. We fell in company with

10 Heber C. Kimball, on August 1, 1847, as reported in William Clayton's "Journal," 334.

George A. Smith. Conosh [the Puavant Chief] joined us. Other Indian chiefs also joined our company. When we arrived in the City there were ten of them went up to see Brigham Young, the Great Mormon Chief.

We encamped on Corn Creek on our way up; near a company of Emigrants from Arkansas, on the——[11]

Here the account stops abruptly, for the next leaf is torn out. The doings of the chiefs are indicated, however, by this entry in the "Journal History of the Church," under date of September 1, 1857:

> Bro Jacob Hamblin arrived in G. S. L. City from the Santa Clara Mission with 12 Indian chiefs who had come to see Pres. Young. One of them was the head chief; his name was Tutsigabot. There was also a chief of the Piedes and of the Deserts and Santa Clara and Rio Virgen and of Harmony; Also Kanosh chief of the Pavants and Ammon, Walker's brother were in the company. Pres. Young had an interview for about one hour with the Indians.

What Brigham Young told the chiefs in that hour was not recorded, but we might hazard an opinion that it was not out of harmony with his written instructions that "they must learn that they have either got to help us or the United States will kill us both." Even with the help of his best interpreters, they could understand each other imperfectly; their conversation probably was made up of signs and grunts and monosyllables, or short, broken sentences at best. Yet there must have been some common understanding, if one is to judge from the immediate attitude of the Indians toward the "Mericat" emigrants. At that time Brigham Young had to be sure of his allies, for he was conducting a war against tremendous odds. The previous Mormon policy had been to keep the natives from stealing and plundering and to teach them the peaceful pursuits of farming and cattle raising, but now

[11] The original Jacob Hamblin diary is in the archives of the Latter-day Saints church historian.

Brigham Young seemed determined that he would no longer "hold them by the wrist," as he told Captain Van Vliet a few days later.

The Indians must have started back home immediately, for in seven days they were harassing the emigrants at Mountain Meadows, and in ten days they participated in the massacre of the company. Jacob Hamblin, on the other hand, went out to the town of Tooele, some forty miles west of the city, to visit with his family there. Incidentally, he courted a neighbor girl, Priscilla Leavitt, won her consent and that of her mother, and brought her back to Great Salt Lake City to marry her. The records of the Endowment House show that the ceremony was performed on September 11, 1857.

In the meantime, Thales Haskell had visited his sister who lived at Little Cottonwood. Here he met Margaret Edwards, a newly arrived emigrant girl from Wales, courted her, and married her. The two couples started south in the same wagon, but, one day out of the city, they were overtaken by a horseman who ordered Jacob to go in all haste to manage the Indians of the South. His diary says that he arrived at his ranch on the upper end of Mountain Meadows on September 18; from subsequent happenings this would seem to be accurate, for the Duke company had passed by just a day or two before and he sent horsemen to overtake them.

Family legend says that he returned on the road as far as Fillmore to meet his bride and escort her home, and some stories persist concerning her experience when she reached the place of the slaughter.[12] The fact that Hamblin testified in court later that

[12] Children of Priscilla Leavitt Hamblin say that their mother often told how, as they left Great Salt Lake City to return to Santa Clara, they were overtaken by a horseman who ordered Jacob to ride ahead in haste to manage the Indians of the south. This he did, leaving his bride to follow in the wagon with Thales Haskell and his young wife, an emigrant girl who could not yet speak English.

Jacob arrived at Mountain Meadows after the massacre, to find the Indians following the Duke train of emigrants, expecting to attack them at the first opportunity. He sent Dudley Leavitt and others to follow and prevent another massacre by helping the Indians to stampede the cattle of the emigrants. Hamblin then returned on the road as far as Fillmore, where he met his wife and friends.

he had met Lee at Fillmore, and that the original copy of Special Orders No. 5 bears on the back the notation, "Received fr. Jacob Hamblin Sept. 26, 1857," might give weight to this legend.

Through all this excitement, the seasonal tide of emigrants to California had gone on without interruption. Throughout the summer, companies arrived in Great Salt Lake City, where they expected to rest and get fresh supplies for the last desperate lap of the journey. Most of these proceeded by the more direct northern route, but later arrivals, fearful of the snows in the Sierra and knowing of the Donner disaster, chose the longer southern road by way of the Old Spanish Trail.

The "Journal History of the Church" mentions briefly the arrival of many emigrant trains in Great Salt Lake City. After mid-July it records:

July 20, 1857. About noon a company of emigrants, mostly from Illinois, enroute for California, arrived in Great Salt Lake City.

July 25, 1857. A Company of California emigrants arrived in the city. Richard Pettit and Joseph Thompson, overhearing C. J. Landon, an apostate, telling the emigrants what damned rascals the Mormons were, gave him a tremendous beating.

July 27, 1857. Another company of emigrants arrived in G. S. L. City.

August 3, 1857. A company of emigrants arrived in Great Salt Lake City with a large herd of cattle.

August 4, 1857. Another emigrant train with a large drove of cattle arrived in G. S. L. City. . . . George A. Smith left Provo at noon and delivered general orders to Gen. Aaron Johnson at

When they reached Mountain Meadows, the two men told the girls to stay in the wagon under the cover, which was tightly drawn and securely fastened all around, while they went out to look over the country. Unable to restrain their curiosity and impatient with waiting, the girls did not obey, but climbed out to do some exploring themselves. What they discovered sent them back to the wagon in terror, and the husbands returned to find them trembling and crying. To the end of her days, Priscilla was haunted by that sight of putrefying, dismembered women's bodies.

Springville. Near Santaquin, he broke his wagon and remained until the next day.

August 5, 1857. Another very large company of emigrants enroute to California arrived in G. S. L. City. . . . George A. Smith and company continued to Nephi, where they delivered Gen. Wells' orders to Major Bradley and camped for the evening four miles south of the Sevier River.

So the record goes on, following the daily travels of George A. Smith on his journey south (which we have already discussed) and listing other emigrant arrivals on August 10, 11, and 28. Which of these is the company that met disaster at Mountain Meadows? That cannot be decided definitely; some of the groups undoubtedly took the northern route. Since Jacob Hamblin met the company at Corn Creek, near Fillmore, on August 25, it would seem that the group was the one listed on August 3 or 4.

Why, of all those listed, should this particular train alone have been wiped out, except for a few small children? What unhappy combination of circumstances brought about this tragedy? Although there were no survivors of the Fancher party who were old enough to tell what happened, it is possible to put the story together with some degree of accuracy.

In the first place, the Fancher party was probably the first to take the southern trail that season. There was no reason for parties to take this route unless they were too late for the northern one over the Sierra, and records of southern Utah make no mention of any before it.

With conditions in the southern settlements as described by George A. Smith, with the orders not to sell grain and the general feeling of animosity among the settlers toward all Gentiles, it is not strange that the company ran into trouble. The nature of the emigrants themselves was such as to sharpen and intensify the friction. It would seem that there were two parties traveling together, since both T. B. H. Stenhouse in his *Rocky Mountain Saints* and his wife in her *Tell It All* make this point. Mrs. Stenhouse quotes Eli B. Kelsey to the effect that he traveled with them from Fort Bridger to Great Salt Lake City, and that "the train was divided into two parts—the first a rough-and-ready set of men—regular frontier pioneers, the other a picked community, the members of which were all more or less connected by family ties."

Conclusive proof as to the full personnel of the group may never be found, in the face of the many different stories. For example, in the San Jose *Pioneer* of Saturday, April 21, 1877, is a letter from one P. K. Jacoby, who traveled with this party as far as Fort Bridger. He said that the company at that point numbered not more than a hundred persons and gave the names of the leading families as Bakers, Houghs, and Reeds. He insisted that because the train was composed of antagonistic elements, he and a few others left it at Bridger.

Perhaps the most reliable evidence comes from a letter from William C. Mitchell, special agent, which is now in the National Archives, and which lists the real names of all the surviving children and the names of all who left from four counties in Arkansas.[13] According to this list, the group from that state totaled 69

---

[13] An important source of information as to the personnel of this company is found in the National Archives among the papers of the Office of Indian Affairs, Utah Superintendency, a letter dated Crooked Creek, Arkansas, April 27, 1860. It arrived too late to be included in *Senate Document 42*, and is the only list of those from Arkansas known to be extant.

The letter proper gives the names of surviving children and an attached sheet gives the names of the company as follows:

"The following is the mames [*sic*] of those that was masacreed [*sic*] at the Mountain Meadows in September 1857

Capt. John T. Baker	From Carroll County Ark			
George W. Baker, Wife & 1 child	"	"	"	"
Abel Baker	"	"	"	"
Milum Rush	"	"	"	"
Allen Deskazo (Deskarzo?)	"	"	"	"
David W. Beller	"	"	"	"
Melissa Ann Beller	"	"	"	"
Robert Fancher	"	"	"	"
Charles R. Mitchell, wife & 1 child	"	Marion	"	"
Joel D. Mitchell	"	"	"	"
Lawson Mitchell	"	"	"	"
William & John Prewett two brothers	"	"	"	"
Jesse Dunlap, wife & 6 children	"	"	"	"

45

persons, of whom 17 children were saved. Since the number slain was something over 120, it would seem that another company must have been involved. A number of Mormon writers spoke of this twofold nature of the company, as though their being from Missouri might be in some way tied up with the bitter Mormon attitude toward them.

That this group began to have trouble soon after they left Salt Lake City there can be no doubt. Much of this grew out of the belligerent attitude of the Mormons and their steady refusal to sell supplies, but some of it also must be attributed to the conduct of the travelers themselves. Reports of their boastful and hateful remarks come to us from many sources; little things like naming their oxen Brigham Young or Heber C. Kimball and then cursing them roundly as they passed through the Mormon villages, or trying to buy provisions and, upon being refused, popping the head off a chicken with a long bull whip or turning their cattle into the Mormon fields.

As tensions grew, there were those who boasted of having participated in the Missouri outrages and the Haun's Mill massacre. One man even claimed to be carrying the gun which shot "Old Joe Smith." Wait until they reached California and told the people there what was going on in Utah! They'd come back with an army from that direction, too, and then these traitorous Mormons would literally be between the hammer and the anvil. They

L D Dunlap, wife & 5 children	"	"	"	"
William Wood	"	"	"	"
Solaman Wood	"	"	"	"
Richard Wilson	"	"	"	"
Milam Jones, wife & 1 child	"	Johnson	"	"
Pleasant Tacket, wife & 2 children	"	"	"	"
Cintha Tacket & 3 children	"	"	"	"
Josiah Miller wife & 3 children	"	"	"	"
William Camron wife & 5 children	"	"	"	"
Alexander Fancher wife & 4 children	"	Benton	"	"
Peter Huff wife & 3 children	"	"	"	"

The above is correct as far as we have any information

"WM. C. MITCHELL
Special Agt."

46

would learn what it meant to defy the United States of America!

After the deed was done, the Mormons tried to find all the justification possible, one of their favorite stories being that of a poisoned spring at which at least one Mormon died. This evidently stemmed from an incident told by Thomas Waters Cropper and written by him in his later life. At the time, he was just fifteen years old and was living at Fillmore. The part of his story pertinent here follows:

"In company with several other boys I was up on the benches when we saw the unusual sight of an emigrant train. We ran down to where they were. . . . They dared us to ride one of their wild steers and I got on it, and it dashed into Cattelin's Mill pond, which caused them a lot of merriment. . . .

"There appeared to be two companies of them joined together for safety from the Indians. One company which was mostly men called themselves the Missouri Wild Cats. I heard one of them make the brag that he helped to mob and kill Joe Smith, and he further said, 'I would like to go back and take a pop at Old Brig before I leave the territory.' They moved on over to what was known as the Big Spring on the Corn Creek Sloughs. A lot of the Kanosh Indians came to their camp to beg and trade. One man insisted on examining an Indian's bow and arrows but the Indian refused and jabbed an arrow into the man's breast. The man whipped out a revolver and shot the Indian dead.

"They poisoned the spring and a number of cattle died around the spring. The Indians ate some of the meat and several Indians died from the effects.

"I went over and saw the cattle dead around the spring. Proctor Robinson son of Joseph Robinson had been skinning some of the cattle. He went back with me as far as Meadow and insisted on my going on to Fillmore with him (I was staying at Barrows) He was on a poor rhone mare and I was afraid she would not carry us both, but we started for Fillmore about eight miles distant. When about 2 miles out it began to rain. He complained of his eye and kept rubbing it. It swelled shut and the rain came down in torrents. I slipped off from behind him and told him to

47

whip the old mare through and get home, for his face was getting very swollen.

"I trudged on until I finally reached Fillmore. I was almost perishing with the cold and rain. I stopped in to warm and got something to eat at Theodore Rogers. Bro Rogers went part way home with me and I succeeded in getting home all right.

"Next morning early I went down to see Proctor. He was so swollen and bloated I would not have recognized him. He died that night. Next day I went on the range and saw a lot more dead cattle.

"This same company moved on South and met a sad fate at the Mountain Meadows."[14]

Here is evidence of cattle dead from evident poisoning, which might have been the result of loco weed or other poison plant as well as polluted water. Proctor Robinson died of some infection from rubbing his eyes with hands that had been skinning animals too long dead. But this all provided a fact upon which it was easy to hang a growing line of accusations. Because of the Mormon tendency to exaggerate the offenses of the emigrants, reports from non-Mormons, and especially from men not friendly to the Mormons, take on added significance.

George Powers of Little Rock, Arkansas, made a statement which was read at a public indignation meeting in Los Angeles on October 12, 1857, and which was widely reported in California papers. Describing conditions in Utah, he said:

We found the Mormons making very determined preparations to fight the United States troops, whenever they may arrive. On our way in, we met three companies of 100 men each, armed and on the road toward the pass above Fort Bridger. I was told at Fort Bridger, that at Fort Supply, twelve miles this side of Fort Bridger, there were 400 armed Indians awaiting orders; they also said that there were 60,000 pounds of flour stored at Fort Bridger for the use of their army. We found companies drilling every evening in

[14] Handwritten original owned by J. W. Tippetts, Orem, Utah. Typescript at Utah State Historical Society.

the city. The Mormons declared to us that no U. S. troops should ever cross the mountains; they talked and acted as though they were willing to take a brush with Uncle Sam.

We remained in Salt Lake City five days, and then pushed on, hoping we might overtake a larger train, which had started ten days ahead of us, and which proved to be the train that was massacred. We came on to Buttermilk Fort, near the Lone Cedar 176 miles, and found the inhabitants greatly enraged at the train which had just passed, declaring that they had abused the Mormon women, calling them w——s, &c., and letting on about the men. The people had refused to sell that train any provisions, and told us they were sorry they had not killed them there; but they knew it would be done before they got in. They stated further that they were holding their Indians in check until the arrival of their chief, when he would follow the train and cut it to pieces.[15]

From Mormon evidence, this picture of activities in Utah during August, 1857, is accurate. The Buttermilk Fort is now called Holden, and was then one day's drive north of Fillmore, so that the Fancher company, to have been at Corn Creek on August 25, must have passed here two days earlier, while Jacob Hamblin and his Indians arrived on the 27th to take the local chieftain with them on to the city. When Powers passed the place, about the first of September, Hamblin had not returned from his conference with Brigham Young. Since the emigrants, having a large herd of cattle, must of necessity move more slowly than the ordinary train, and the Indians on horseback would travel faster, it would be possible for them to overtake the emigrants by the time they arrived at the Meadows (Haslam made the ride from Salt Lake City to Cedar City in a little more than three days.)

The point to be made here is that travelers immediately following the Fancher train found the citizenry incensed against them as far north as Holden, so that it is safe to conjecture that relationships did not improve as they moved on south. P. M. Warn, who was a few days ahead of Powers, made a similar report of con-

15 *Daily Alta California* (San Francisco), October 27, 1857. From a letter by its Los Angeles correspondent dated October 24, 1857.

ditions and commented that the trouble was, in part at least, the fault of the travelers:

> The men were very free in speaking of the Mormons, their conduct was said to have been reckless, and they would commit little acts of annoyance for the purpose of provoking the Saints. Feeling perfectly safe in their arms and numbers, they seemed to set at defiance all the powers that could be brought against them, and they were not permitted to feel the dangers surrounded them, until they were cut off from all hope of relief.[16]

Warn traveled in company with the Mormon train of Matthews and Tanner, which was the first to bring news of the disaster into California, and he "at various places heard the same threats of vengeance against them for their boisterousness and abuse of the Mormons and Mormonism." These accusations take on importance in showing that animosities grew out of all proportion to their importance.

Although Andrew L. Neff, in his *History of Utah*, maintained that this company of emigrants had passed down the length of the territory where "their peaceful contacts with the Saints had been frequent," there is evidence that they had trouble all the way. William B. Ashworth, in his "Autobiography," tells of their difficulties at Beaver, and of the intervention of the bishop there to prevent bloodshed:

> The bishop then advised the emigrants to protect themselves as best they could, as the town would not help them on account of all the women and children whose safety depended on the friendliness of the Indians. He urged the men not to come up into the town, as that would jeopardize, not only themselves but the people of Beaver. I was by my father's side and listened to every word with interest.[17]

[16] *Ibid.*

[17] A typescript of this "Autobiography" is in the library of the Brigham Young University. The whole excerpt on this subject follows:

"I remember when the unfortunate company came through Beaver. They came in about noon and passed on about a mile to a nice patch of meadow grass. In

At Parowan, the next settlement of any size on the road, the company was not allowed to pass through the town, but was forced to break a new road around it. This village was enclosed

the afternoon some boys and myself were up on the east edge of town and saw a man from the camp coming through the sage brush. He had a gun and was apparently hunting rabbits. There were some strange Indians in town, and one of them fired a shot at this man, but did not seem to hurt him, as he turned and ran back towards the camp.

"This incident caused quite a commotion in the town. The bishop and a number of the other men were gathered to learn the cause of the trouble. They met the Indians who were from Corn Creek; this seemed to be the headquarters for the Indians in that part of the country. The Indians said, 'The men of the Mericats (this term was generally used to designate what the Mormons called Gentiles), while encamped at Corn Creek, poisoned a mule that had died, and also a spring, and the Indians had been made sick by eating the mule and drinking the water, and they were heap mad!'

"Bishop, who was pretty well versed in Indian lore, sympathized with them, but told them they must not harm the emigrants, as there were lots of innocent women and children in the company, but with all the reasoning and persuading the Indians were determined to revenge themselves. They were offered an animal for beef, this being the policy of Mormons all through the early days, being the advice of President Young, 'It is better to feed them than to fight them.' But this offer had no effect.

"About this time a delegation from the camp came up to learn more about the trouble. They were told what had been done to dissuade the Indians from making further trouble, but that all their efforts had been to no avail. The bishop then advised the emigrants to protect themselves as best they could, as the town would not help them on account of all the women and children whose safety often depended on the friendliness of the Indians. He urged the men not to come up into town, as that would jeopardize, not only themselves but the people of Beaver. I was by my father's side and listened to every word with interest.

"Fortunately, just about sundown, Chief Walker and some others of his tribe came into town, and he was persuaded to let the emigrants proceed on their way. They, however, not realizing the danger they were in, manifest a very bitter spirit against the Mormons, and some of them were reported to have said they would like to go back to Salt Lake and help hang 'Old Brigham and the church leaders.'

"The Indians all disappeared the day after the emigrants left and it was surmised that they had followed the emigrants. This was at the time when there was a great bitterness against the Mormons. Buchanan's U.S. army was even then on its way to Utah for no good purpose."

While the above excerpt does show the conditions at the time, it has the weakness of all reminiscences. In this case, the writer did not remember his Indians well, for Chief Walker had died in January, 1855, nearly three years earlier.

in a wall, with gates to the east and west. It would seem that the reputation of this particular company had moved ahead of it so that the town gates were ordered closed, and the people there had no dealings whatsoever with the emigrants.

What happened at Cedar City comes to us largely from tradition, but there are some significant bits of evidence. Here also much of the friction was due to the refusal of the people of the town to sell provisions. The sentiments that were expressed by the stake president, Isaac C. Haight, and recorded in the minutes of the ward meeting held on September 6, seemed to be shared by many of his listeners:

> They [the Missourians] drove us out to starve. When we pled for mercy, Haun's Mill was our answer, and when we asked for bread they gave us a stone. We left the confines of civilization and came far into the wilderness where we could worship God according to the dictates of our own conscience without annoyance to our neighbors. We resolved that if they would leave us alone we would never trouble them. But the Gentiles will not leave us alone. They have followed us and hounded us. They come among us asking us to trade with them, and in the name of humanity to feed them. All of these we have done and now they are sending an army to exterminate us. So far as I am concerned I have been driven from my home for the last time. I am prepared to feed to the Gentiles the same bread they fed to us. God being my helper I will give the last ounce of strength and if need be my last drop of blood in defense of Zion.[18]

In this speech, the reference is clearly to the Fancher party, which just the day before had pulled south toward Pinto and from thence to Mountain Meadows, where they expected to let their cattle rest and recuperate. It seems that here, at the last settlement of any size on the road, the last possible source of supplies, the emigrants had met with active hostility. When the citizens would not accept their money in exchange for food, when they

---

[18] "Cedar City Ward Records," now reported to be in the archives of the Latter-day Saints church historian.

refused to barter on any terms, some of the men of the company felt free to help themselves. Worse still, they were loud in their abuse of the Mormons in general and the leaders in particular. They boasted of what they would do when the army came to set these people straight.

Immediately following the regular church service, a special meeting was called of the Stake High Council. Isaac C. Haight, as the highest in religious authority and the one in command of the military organization in the town, was in charge of this indignation meeting. The local officers wanted the help of the militia to enforce the law, and various members expressed themselves freely as to what should be done with regard to the emigrant company. Some felt that the travelers should not be allowed to get away with such defiance.

A resolution was presented and passed to the effect that "we will deal with this situation now, so that our hands will be free to meet the army when it comes." After it was passed, Laban Morrill and others began to ask questions. What, specifically, did the brethren mean by dealing with this situation now? Arrest and punish the offenders? Some felt that this would do no good; it would only mean men to guard them and food to feed them, and no one any better off.

So it was suggested that they be "done away with." Ever since the days of Missouri and Nauvoo, ever since the martyrdom of their prophet, the Saints had been taught that they should never cease to importune the Lord to avenge the blood of the prophets. Now here were the men who had boasted openly and defiantly that they had helped to kill Joseph Smith and his brother Hyrum. One had displayed the pistol which fired the fatal shot. All had laughed to scorn the attempts of the local officers to arrest them. Should they forget the oaths of vengeance which they had taken and sit back weakly while such as these taunted them?

Years later, Laban Morrill wrote in his journal:

> My opponents claimed that there were among the emigrants men who had assisted in the crimes of murdering and driving from

their homes our people in Missouri and that one of them had openly boasted that he had helped to kill our prophet. Other claims
brought against them by my opponents (among them were many
redmen) were that they had poisoned the springs of water, etc., as
they passed through the territory, and had proclaimed that they
would help to kill every damn Mormon off the earth.[19]

It seems that the discussion went on at some length, those favoring the killing of the emigrants being very heated and eloquent,
while those opposing it were very determined. Finally a second
resolution was passed, that they would send an express to Brigham
Young to inform him of conditions and ask for his directions, and
that no further action should be taken until the messenger returned. Another resolution was adopted that a messenger should
go to the home of John D. Lee at Harmony and request him to
come and manage the Indians, some of whom had followed the
company from as far north as Fillmore. Since January 1, 1856,
John D. Lee had been the official "Farmer to the Piedes," and
hence would be the logical one to take charge of them, especially
in the absence of Jacob Hamblin.

Remembering the waves of patriotic fervor that sweep nations
during wars, it is not hard to understand how the Mormons of
southern Utah might consider as traitors any who spoke out in
defense of this group of emigrants, or in any way befriended
them. In the Morrill record, quoted above, a daughter told one of
the family legends, giving the impression that her father's life was
endangered because of the firm stand he took against the killing
of the emigrants.

That night after the council meeting in Cedar [before the deed]
Father felt impressed to go a different way home—to Johnson's
Fort. He did so, giving the horses the reins, and going in a hurry.
Later he found that two men had been sent out to waylay him. He
said that he noticed the two men leave the meeting before it was out.

As has already been stated, the local officials combined the

[19] Typed copy in the Brigham Young University library.

54

authority of church and state, a fact which made any opposition to their orders doubly serious. Perry Liston's record suggests that it was not safe for a man to be too outspoken or vigorous in his stand against them:

> 1857. In the fall of this year, a large company of emigrants partly from Missouri, passed through our quiet settlements. They made threats, and swore that Johnston's Army was coming from the East and they from the South and they would kill every Mormon in Utah. These words I heard myself—but there was some good people among them, consequently I did oppose killing them. So much so that I did not have a thing to do with it and my life was at stake for refusing. But the Lord showed me my way, and I walked in it.[20]

The inference that since the company was partly from Missouri they would be natural enemies brings up again the motive of revenge. His followers had loved Joseph Smith with an intensity almost past understanding; they not only held him as a prophet second in greatness only to Jesus Christ himself, but they felt toward him great personal love and tenderness. In their eyes he was one so far above the sinful generation among whom he lived that his very goodness brought against him all the powers of evil. Diaries and records are full of statements by devoted followers that they would gladly have given their lives to have saved him: he was a martyr whose death God would wish avenged.[21]

This feeling was so widely shared by those who had known the Mormon Prophet personally and who hoped to be able to carry

[20] Typed copy in the Utah State Historical Society files, also in the Washington County library.

[21] The feeling of many Mormons regarding the death of Joseph Smith is expressed well by Joseph Allen Stout. He wrote: "Their dead bodies were brought to Nauvoo, where I saw their beloved forms reposing in the arms of death, which gave me such feelings as I am not able to describe. But I then and there resolved in my mind that I would never let an opportunity go unimproved of avenging their blood upon the heads of the enemies of the Church of Jesus Christ. . . . I hope to avenge their blood, but if I do not I will teach my children and children's children to the fourth generation as long as there is one descendent of the murderers on the earth."

out God's will in avenging him, that any man who came into a Utah community and boasted that he was one of the mob at Carthage jail would have taken his life in his hands, even in times of peace. With the feeling running high as it was at this time, such behavior was almost certain suicide.

William R. Palmer of Cedar City, Utah, one of the best students of the history of this area, has taken great pains to collect facts surrounding the massacre. He says:

> Ed Parry has told me many times that he was working with a group of young men on the irrigation ditch at the time the company which was later killed at Mountain Meadows came into Cedar City. [He was seventeen years old.]
>
> He told me how two men came up to the crowd on horseback; one riding a large gray mare seemed to be spokesman. He tried to get some of the crowd to buy him a gallon of whiskey, but none would do it. Then he became abusive, swore at us all, said that he had the gun that had killed Old Joe Smith, and that his company would go on to California and get an army and come back and wipe out every —— —— Mormon.
>
> Ed Parry has told me this not once, but a number of times. He said that he would make an affidavit to that effect also, but I neglected to make it out, a thing that I have regretted ever since.

Then, too, there was the problem of the Indians, newly impressed with the fact that the Mormons and Mericats were at war, and that they must help the Mormons. The stories of the poisoned seeps and the poisoned meat were told and retold, and grew with the telling. The herds of cattle and the fine outfits of this company would be a fair reward for doing away with people who so definitely deserved to be killed. The Indians, being "the battle-ax of the Lord," could logically do the work, for they had no qualms about shedding blood, even innocent blood. Since the Big Mormon Chief wanted them to help with this war, here was a good place to begin. So the natives had followed and annoyed the company, happy in the sense of Mormon approval; they sent out runners to other bands for reinforcements in this exciting and thrilling game.

It should be remembered also that at this time the whites in the area were outnumbered more than four to one by Indians, so that the business of maintaining friendly relations was important. In 1855, the inhabitants of Paragoona had moved to Parowan for safety; in 1856, all the families on the Santa Clara had been called back to Cedar City until a fort could be built for their protection. In all their dealings with the Indians, both before and after the massacre, the people of the area were careful to avoid frictions lest they lead to attacks upon the scattered ranches and smaller villages.

Among the Mormons many factors joined to increase the growing hate. Whether all the reports were true is not so important as the fact that the people believed that they were true. It was said that among the emigrant party were some who had assisted in the massacre at Haun's Mill, where seventeen Mormon men and boys had been killed and fifteen wounded. The brothers and sisters of those slain were living in this very locality—William Leany, whose brother Benjamin had been killed and thrown into an old well; Isaac Leany, who was wounded in four places and had twenty-seven bullet holes in his clothing; Tarleton Lewis, who was left for dead.

No less poignant was the assassination of their beloved apostle, Parley P. Pratt, who had so recently been stabbed to death in Arkansas. He had been the first of their people to explore this southern country; he had been in charge of the first Indian mission, a man mighty in the work of God. Many Mormon writers, among them B. H. Roberts and Leland H. Creer, have insisted that word of Pratt's death was not known in southern Utah at this time, and hence could not have had any influence upon the feelings of the people. This is a mistaken idea, for word had gone out immediately. Andrew Sproul, on the plains in charge of church cattle, wrote in his pocket diary on May 26, 1857, that "E. Snow tells me that P P Pratt is in trouble and that McLean has got him prisoner also woman and children. God deliver him if this is true."[22]

Jesse B. Martin, en route to the valley with a company of converts, recorded the word of Pratt's death on June 17.[23] John Stillman Woodbury, on his way to the Hawaiian Islands, saw in the papers "the account of Elder P. P. Pratts death (massacre) by the blood-thirsty hands of McLeane."[24] This was on July 2, at Genoa, Nevada, high up on the Carson River.

On June 23, 1857, the "Journal History of the Church" noted that the mail arriving that day brought news of the murder. Wilford Woodruff made a notation on the same date in his "Journal": "Eastern mail arrived bringing the sad news of the assassination of Elder Parley P. Pratt who had been killed near Ft. Smith in Arkansas by a man named McLean." Hosea Stout also promptly recorded on that day: "Accounts are current in the papers that Elder Parley P. Pratt has been assinated [sic] some eight miles from Van Buren Arkansas by one Hector H. McLean, that he was shot and lived some two hours. The truth is not known."[25]

The story was at once published in the Deseret News, and, with the semimonthly mail running regularly from Salt Lake City to San Bernardino, it is idle to suppose that in more than two months' time it should not have reached the settlements in southern Utah.

The people of southern Utah, most of whom had lived through the persecutions of Missouri and Nauvoo, found themselves recounting their past miseries and sufferings. Here were men who had survived the Haun's Mill massacre; here were others whose homes had been burned at the Morley settlement. James W. Huntsman's back was still scarred with the lashes it had received when he was whipped by a mob. If they now should use violence

---

[22] Original diary owned by Andrew Sproul, Jr., Washington, Utah.

[23] Photostat at Henry E. Huntington Library.

[24] Original at the Brigham Young University library; photostat at the Henry E. Huntington Library.

[25] Photostat at the Henry E. Huntington Library; typed copies in the Brigham Young University library and the Utah State Historical Society files.

in the defense of their homes, their own scripture would offer justification. True, they were counseled to bear all in meekness and not to retaliate, but ". . . thine enemy is in thine hands; and if thou rewardest him according to his works, thou art justified; if he has sought thy life, and thy life is endangered by him, thine enemy is in thine hands and thou art justified."[26]

So the wind grew into the whirlwind. Exaggeration, misrepresentation, ungrounded fears, unreasoning hate, desire for revenge, yes, even the lust for the property of the emigrants, all combined to give justification which, once the crime was done, looked inadequate and flimsy indeed.

[26] *Doctrine and Covenants*, Section 98, verses 23–32. This appears in the 1844 and 1845 editions published in Nauvoo on pages 335–446. For other religious implications which may have contributed see Juanita Brooks, *John D. Lee, Zealot–Pioneer Builder–Scapegoat*, 208–209.

4

Misunderstood Covenant

Before proceeding finally to the account of what happened on that fateful September afternoon, it might be well to point out how difficult it is to reconstruct with any degree of accuracy all the conditions—the various contributing factors, the many differing personalities involved. It has been compared to an attempt to disentangle a great snarl of multicolored threads, but such a comparison leaves out the emotional element. The fervor generated by the eloquence of George A. Smith, the rehearsals of past sufferings and indignities, the imagined threat of being again driven from their homes, the repeated vows to avenge the blood of their martyred prophet had set the fires smoldering even in the calmest heart. It would take little to fan them into a flame.

Mass murder, even in the name of war, is a highly complex act, requiring the creation of a mass mind and a powerful psychic contagion of great intensity. Among the Mormons of southern Utah, hatred for the mobocrats of Missouri was still keen. Along with the strict military authority was a small group of strong men, each of whom had his own influence in helping to shape events. The varying degrees of guilt of these men may remain always a subject of controversy, for later every participant steadfastly argued his own innocence.

Since John D. Lee has had to bear the special opprobrium of the massacre, it is only fair to point out that he was *not* present at the Sunday afternoon meeting where the fate of the emigrants was discussed, the gathering in which the idea of the massacre was first suggested. Neither was he in any way responsible for, or connected with, the death of Aiden, the first of the emigrants to be murdered—a crucial event which will be discussed later in its relation to the final decisions of the leaders.

Present at the massacre and guilty of participation as he admittedly was, Lee was not the initial force in stirring up the Indians, since it was Jacob Hamblin who took the chiefs north, and Brigham Young who counseled with them directly. They were already gathering to plunder the emigrants when the messenger was sent requesting Lee to come and help to manage them. Much of the actual massacre was carried on by a unit of the Iron County militia, over whom he had no command. He was brought into the picture and became a part of the general plan after the forces of destruction had been set in motion.

Any study of mob psychology will reveal the same pattern—men catching fire from each other, uniting under strong emotional stress, carrying out lynchings or burnings or mass murder, which in times of sanity and calmness every one would condemn individually. It is this elusive spirit and temper of the times, suggested by George A. Smith in his report, which must be taken into account—this interplay of personality and circumstance, this complexity of motives, which makes it difficult to measure individual responsibility.

Out of this grows naturally the question of greatest concern. To what extent were Brigham Young and the other general authorities responsible? Did the people of the south only take their threats and preachments too literally? Certainly all the plans were for real and deadly warfare; the collecting of guns, the storing of grain, the attitude toward all "Gentiles."

Claims have been made that this particular company, because of the "enemies" from Missouri, had been marked for destruction before it reached the borders of the territory, that the visit of George A. Smith to the south had for its purpose their ultimate destruction. No real evidence of this has been found, nothing more than the general resolution to withstand the approaching army.

One of the points of argument which has arisen out of the controversy regarding the possible guilt of Brigham Young concerns the date upon which the massacre occurred. Some students of the subject insist that the Mormon church moved the date ahead in an effort to clear Brigham Young of any taint of suspicion.

It is a fact that, among the many writers on the subject, many different dates have been used. At the trials of John D. Lee almost twenty years later, the witnesses seemed certain only that the council meeting at Cedar City was held on Sunday afternoon, and the massacre occurred on the Friday following. California newspapers first reporting it spoke of the massacre as being on September 10 or 12, though one put it on the twenty-second, adding in a footnote that it was fifteen days earlier. John D. Lee, writing about a year later, said that it was on September 25, which would be after he had gone to Salt Lake City. There is, therefore, some reason to consider the subject seriously.

The implications are clear. If the massacre took place before September 13, it was done before the messenger from Brigham Young returned, and so without his order. If it happened after that date, then the orders which Haslam carried must have said to go on with it, for it is inconceivable that the leaders in the south would have acted in defiance of their commander in chief.

The date of the arrival of James Haslam, the express rider who carried the messages to and from Great Salt Lake City, at Brigham Young's office is established by an entry in the "Journal History of the Church": "September 10, 1857 About noon an express arrived from Iron County and left at 1 P.M."

Although this gives no hint as to the reason for the express, the hasty return, or the nature of the messages, Brigham Young's answer carries evidence of the questions which he was answering. At the time of the Lee trials, many years later, one question asked of President Young concerned this message from Haight and his answer to it. Brigham Young admitted that an express did arrive on September 10, but said that the letter had been lost, and though he had searched diligently, he could not find it. His answer was paraphrased: "It was to let this company of emigrants, and all companies of emigrants, pass through the country unmolested, and to allay the angry feelings of the Indians as much as possible." The letter itself reads as follows:

PRESIDENT'S OFFICE
GREAT SALT LAKE CITY
SEPT. 10, 1857

Elder Isaac C. Haight:

DEAR BROTHER:— Your note of the 7th inst. is to hand. Capt. Van Vliet, Acting Commissary, is here, having come in advance of the army to procure necessaries for them. We do not expect that any part of the army will be able to reach here this fall. There is only about 850 men coming. They are now at or near Laramie. A few of their freight trains are on this side of that place, the advance of which are now on Green River. They will not be able to come much if any further on account of their poor stock. They cannot get here this season without we help them. So you see that the Lord has answered our prayers and again averted the blow designed for our heads. In regard to the emigration trains passing through our settlements, we must not interfere with them until they are first notified to keep away. You must not meddle with them. The Indians we expect will do as they please but you should try and preserve good feelings with them. There are no other trains going south that I know of. If those that are there will leave, let them go in peace. While we should be on the alert, on hand, and always ready, we should also possess ourselves in patience, preserving ourselves and property, ever remembering that God rules. He has overruled for our deliverance thus once again, and He will always do so if we live our religion and be united in our faith and good works.

All is well with us. May the Lord bless you and all the Saints forever.

Your Brother in the gospel of Christ.

BRIGHAM YOUNG[1]

This interesting document will bear closer scrutiny, both because it is so characteristic and because it bears internal evidence

---

[1] "Church Letter Book, No. 3," pp. 827–28.

of the letter to which it is an answer. A study of the letters of Brigham Young will show that very often he does not come to the point immediately; he begins with generalities and ends with them, and inserts the real message in a single terse sentence or two in the very heart of his letter. Here, after acknowledging receipt of the question, he proceeds to talk of other things before he answers it directly. He evidently knew well the emotional tension in the south, and was trying to quiet it by minimizing the immediate danger of the army.

On August 4, he had written to Jacob Hamblin that there were 2,500 soldiers on the way, besides teamsters for 1,100 wagons; on August 15, he had told the Carson Saints that there were from 2,500 to 3,500 soldiers and from 1,000 to 1,200 teamsters; on September 4, he had written John R. Young to say there were two regiments of infantry, one of dragoons, and two batteries of artillery; now, less than a week later, he assures Haight that "there is only about 850 men coming" and "they will not be able to come much if any further on account of their poor stock." This is surprising in view of the fact that he knew better, for his missionaries in the East had passed the troops and reported 2,500; his armed and mounted reconnaissance units kept him constantly informed that the army was drawing nearer daily. Tensions in and about Great Salt Lake City were actually mounting at the time that he declared, "They cannot get here this season without we help them."

His counsel that "we should also possess ourselves in patience" shows that he was well acquainted with the impetuous nature of his subordinates in the south, who, from the report of George A. Smith, he knew to be "alert, on hand, and always ready." His answer to Haight's question is direct: "In regard to the emigration trains passing through our settlements, *we must not interfere with them* until they are first notified to keep away. *You must not meddle with them*" (italics supplied). Yet, in almost the same breath, he suggests that should the Indians annoy the emigrants or prey upon them, he would assume no responsibility—but the people of the south must keep the good will of the natives: "The Indians we expect will do as they please but you should try and preserve good feelings with them." This sounds as though he might not condemn an Indian massacre.

Haight's letter is referred to as of September 7; the answer is dated September 10; Haslam arrived back in Cedar City on September 13, after the massacre had been committed. This should in itself definitely fix the date, but there are other bits of supporting evidence.

In a report to Jacob Forney, dated Fort Bridger, December 6, 1857, embodied in *Senate Document* 42, 36th Congress, 2d Session, 92–98, the Indian agent, Garland Hurt, wrote:

> On the 10th day of September last, George W. Hancock, a merchant in the town of Payson, came to the Indian settlements to look at some fat cattle that I proposed selling, and in the course of conversation, said that he had learned that the California emigrants on the southern route had got themselves into a very serious difficulty with the Piedes, who had given them to understand that they could not pass through their country, and on attempting to disregard this injunction, found themselves surrounded by the Indians, and compelled to seek shelter behind their wagons. He said he had learned these facts from an express man, who passed his house that morning with a message from the Indians to *President Young*, inquiring what they must do with the Americans. The express man had been allowed one hundred consecutive hours in which to perform the trip of nearly three hundred miles and return, which Mr. Hancock felt confident he would do.

It would seem that the clerk of the Parowan Ward did not enter his accounts of the ward doings daily, or perhaps did not at once copy them from his small pencil notebooks into his permanent record; nevertheless, the entry following is of some value in establishing the date. It also gives some body to the persistent stories of a child who was saved at the time of the massacre and then destroyed because he was old enough to remember what went on, a point which will receive consideration later.

Monday, Sept. 7 [1857]   This morning at daylight the Indians attacked a company of emigrants going to California, about 4½ miles beyond the Mountain Meadows, and the entire company was destroyed, except 18 small children, which the Saints took charge of. Report of Indians says they besieged them until Friday noon when all was finished.[2]

Perhaps the most conclusive evidence comes from the diary of Rachel Lee. Brief though it is, it does give the date of her husband's leaving home, his return, and his leaving for Great Salt Lake City. The record begins on February 17, 1857, and continues, with at least weekly entries, all through that year. From the end of 1858 until May of 1860, entries continue, but not regularly. Meetings are reported, speakers are listed, and the subjects discussed are often summarized. On top of the page where the following entry is made, there is a penciled note in a different hand, put there evidently to call attention to the date when Lee "went south." The diary itself is written in ink, and this penciled note was clearly made by a different writer at a later date.

Sept. 6 the thrashers have completed thrashing all the wheat at this place which amounted to 1000 bushels. Sunday the thrashing machine ret [Page torn and word not legible]. . . .

Bro J. D. Lee went on an expedition south Sunday at 2 o'clock meeting was held. Singing Prayer by H. Barney. Bro Phream, E. H. Groves & A. G. Ingram spoke from the stand on the test that was near at hand, aluding to the troops &c. A good spirit prevailed. Ben. by E. H. Groves.

13th   *this morning a great number of Indians returned from an expidition Southwest Also Bro. J. D. Lee.*

20th   The Bishop and J. D. Lee went to conference at S. L. City. In the afternoon meeting was held only a few of the Saints convened many being absent.[3]

This has an interest beyond the amount of wheat threshed and

2 "Parowan Ward Record Book," now reported to be in the archives of the Latter-day Saints church historian's files.
3 See note 8, chapter three.

the dates of the comings and goings of Lee; that there is no mention made of any company of emigrants who have been committing depredations might indicate that the stories which later were so widely told had not reached Harmony. The speakers discussed the threat of the approaching army and the test that was near at hand, but evidently did not know of the hostile emigrant company that was camped within thirty miles.

This brief entry is beyond question so far as the date of the massacre is concerned: Lee left home on Sunday, September 6, and returned on Sunday, September 13; he started for conference in Salt Lake City the very next Sunday, September 20. (Incidentally, this shows the accuracy of Lee's published account. He says he left home a week or ten days after the massacre and was nine or ten days on the road; his wife says he left on September 20, and Wilford Woodruff records his interview with Brigham Young on September 29. The dates fit perfectly. This is pointed out only because of the persistent efforts of many to discredit the writing of Lee.)

From all these citations, it seems that the date which was established by the court, September 11, is accurate. This clears Brigham Young of any direct responsibility for the massacre. His frequent cautions against shedding blood are evidence that he would not approve, much less order, a massacre.[4] Aside from the humanitarian aspects of the case, he knew it would be poor military strategy.

Since the massacre occurred without his knowledge or approval, and at a time when he was completely occupied with more urgent problems at home, he could do nothing more than send counsel by letter. Though his leaders had made a tragic mistake, they were still his strongest and best men in the south, and their error had been one of mistaken zeal for his cause.

---

[4] In the manuscript file of the Bancroft Library, there is a dictation by Dr. John Ward Christian of Beaver, Utah, which says, in part: "Wm C. Stewart, one of the participants in the massacre, when arrested employed me to defend him and he has often told me he did not think the Church ordered it or knew of it until after it occurred but he considered it a natural result of doctrines that had been promulgated."

His responsibility after the war was over and his possible guilt as accessory after the fact are points to be considered later in this study.

5

"This Horrid Story"

WHILE THE COUNCIL at Cedar City was debating the fate
of the Fancher company, that group of emigrants was climbing
up the winding trail to Mountain Meadows, at the rim of the
Great Basin. Where they entered the long green valley, a trickle
of water drained to the north, but about eight miles farther on,
over an almost imperceptible rise, a spring that bubbled forth ran
southward. On both sides of the divide, the grass was deep and
luxuriant, watered by innumerable seeps; on either flank, sage and
low brush stretched to gnarled and scattered junipers on the top
of rolling hills, and, in the washes and draws, the patches of scrub
oak had been touched lightly by fall. Here, at an elevation of six
thousand feet, the nights were crisp, but the days were sunny and
warm; here was an ideal place for an extended rest.

Except for Jacob Hamblin's cabin up the valley a few miles
and out of sight behind the hills, there was no habitation within a
day's journey of this place. Behind them thirty-five miles was
Cedar City; ahead of them nearly twenty miles was the rock fort
at Santa Clara, where a dozen families lived. Beyond that, they
would drop down quickly to the long desert, barren of feed and
scarce of watering places. They would rest here long enough to
prepare their cattle for the scanty feed ahead.

They chose their camp site wisely, leaving the upper valley
where the sage and junipers grew thickly enough to provide ambush for Indians and not going down into the place where the
valley narrowed sufficiently to shelter the natives. Here the grass

stretched in undulating beauty on all sides, far enough to be well out of range of Indian arrows; here the growth on the nearest hills was low and scant enough to make any skulking redskin clearly visible.

They did not encircle the spring, because it had washed out a narrow channel just below, and because the ground near it was damp enough to be almost swampy. Also, a loose camp would give more privacy to families. Far away as they seemed from the irritations of the Mormon villages, they could not have guessed that runners had gone out to collect the Indians at this place.

Some writers say that the first attack was made on the company early Monday morning; John D. Lee says that it was on Tuesday, and then the natives did not wait to carry out the original plans, but charged the camp before they were ready. They made their attack just before daybreak, running down the slope of the hills on the east, yelling and shooting. Taken completely by surprise, the men took a little time to rally, gather their arms, and return the fire, which they did with such effect that several of the Indians were killed and the others retreated. Lee says that seven of the men of the company were killed and three others were badly wounded, but there is now no way either to refute or verify this.

The emigrants immediately gathered their wagons into a close circle for defense and threw up embankments behind which to conceal themselves. During all the week following they were besieged by the Indians, though not in another so determined attack. The natives remained concealed and shot at anyone who ventured outside the barricade.

On Wednesday evening, three men decided to go back to Cedar City and ask for help. Whatever wrongs the Mormons thought they had committed, whatever the scores held against them, surely Christian people would help each other against savages. One of these men was young William Aiden, who had joined the party at Provo, and who, having had some previous association with the Mormons, felt that he could secure their co-operation. But young Aiden was ambushed, shot from his horse, and instantly killed by

70

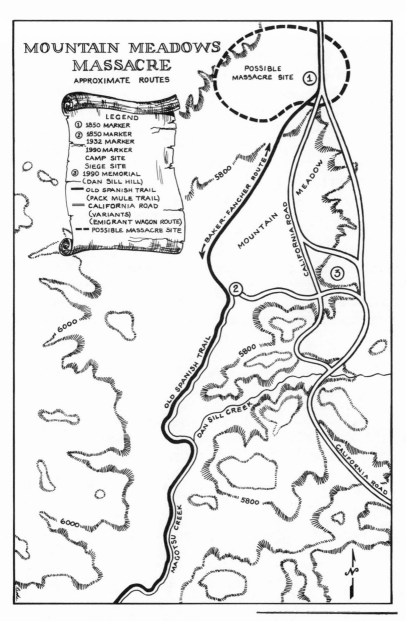

Site of Mountain Meadows Massacre

a white man. His two companions, both wounded, apparently escaped to the California road, to be followed by Indians and killed also.

Many writers have thought that the death of young Aiden was the immediate cause of the massacre, the reason why local leaders felt that they could not wait for the messenger to return from Brigham Young and argued that the whole company must be exterminated: first, because now the emigrants would know that their assailants were white men, and that would mean that an army from California would have a real cause to come against them; and second, because the local Indians, angry over the loss of their braves and determined upon revenge, would turn upon the Mormons if they could not get the emigrants.

Through it all, messengers hurried back and forth between Isaac C. Haight, at Cedar City, and his superior military officer, William H. Dame, at Parowan, and between Lee at the Meadows and Haight, his immediate superior. Every account mentions these express riders without naming them, but Jesse N. Smith, mentioned earlier, identifies himself as one:

Tuesday September 8, 1857. Was harvesting at Paragoonah when a boy brought me word that Col. Dame wished to see me. Went home at once and Col. Dame informed me "that he had word by an Indian that the Indians had attacked the Emigrant Company at Mountain Meadows, and he wished me to proceed to Cedar City and ascertain the truth about the matter." Edward Dalton accompanied me. At Cedar City asked Isaac C. Haight if he had any information about the matter; he had heard the same rumor but had heard nothing further.

Wednesday September 9, 1857. Dalton and myself rode on to Pinto, where hearing the word unmistakably confirmed, we returned to Cedar, and after resting awhile returned to Parowan and made report to Col. Dame. Returned to my work at Paragoonah. Another company of Emigrants having been attacked by the Indians at Beaver, Silas went over with some men to assist them.

The inference here is that young Smith went only to learn

what the situation was, and that whatever orders were sent out from the military headquarters at Parowan went out later. All the accounts secured from participants agree that the military officers were kept informed of developments.

With the death of young Aiden, the decision was made that the emigrants, all who were old enough to talk, must be "put out of the way," and a detachment of the military was sent to assist in carrying out the order. They were under command of Major John M. Higbee, and they arrived at the rendezvous in the night, Wednesday. According to Lee, there was a council meeting held on the ground, and other messages were sent back and answers received before the final plans were perfected and the fate of the emigrants decided. Lee was to decoy them from their stronghold; each member of the militia was to be responsible for the dispatch of one emigrant man, and the Indians were to take their revenge upon the women and children. Thus, they reasoned, no Mormon would be forced to shed innocent blood.

After the details were worked out, William Bateman, carrying a white flag, accompanied John D. Lee across the open country toward the camp, where a white flag had already been hoisted. Two men from the enclosure came out, and after a short conversation, the four went back to the camp.

Whatever arguments Lee offered to persuade the company to accept so unreasonable a plan must have been convincingly presented. Perhaps after a siege of five days, the emigrants were ready for anything; perhaps their stock of ammunition was getting low. Though they could hardly have suspected such treachery, yet a plan so utterly mad should have aroused suspicion. What could have been more unreasonable than to ask them to give up their arms, abandon their wagons, and start on a thirty-five-mile hike for protection? Their condition must have been desperate indeed for them to have considered it. The argument was that the cattle and wagons would appease the Indians, and that, with the red men temporarily drawn off, the Mormons would protect them all if those against whom they had complaints would come back and stand trial.

The terms were finally accepted, after a messenger had ridden up in haste to tell them that they must hurry, as it was getting late. Two wagons were driven up. Into the first, driven by Samuel McMurdy, were loaded the young children, along with some clothing, bedding, and guns; into the second, driven by Samuel Knight,[1] were placed one woman and two or three wounded emigrant men. The two wagons pulled out, with Lee walking between them. A short distance behind, in an unorganized and irregular group, walked the women and the older children. After these had proceeded nearly a quarter of a mile, the men came, single file, each unarmed emigrant beside an armed Mormon "guard." Major Higbee, on horseback, commanded the whole.

It all worked out according to plan. The horses, walking fast, were soon ahead, and, after they were out of sight beyond a knoll, the women came into the decline where the scrub oak grew thickly on both sides of the road. At the command "Halt! "Do your duty!" each Mormon man was to shoot the emigrant at his side, the Indians hiding in the brush were to kill the women and older children, and Lee and the drivers were to finish off the wounded in the wagon. Those of the Mormon men who protested the killing were to shoot into the air, and then sit down and remain quiet while the Indians killed their men.

All accounts agree that it was quickly over. Most of the emigrant men fell at the first volley, and those who started to run were quickly shot down by Mormons or by Indians. The sav-

---

[1] Samuel Knight lived at Santa Clara, but had come to Mountain Meadows some time previous to bring his wife for the birth of her first child, in order to get her away from the heat of the lower country and to have her where Rachel Hamblin could care for her during the confinement. The child had been born on August 8, with the covered wagon for the bedroom. Since the mother had not recovered well, and since the weather in Santa Clara was still very warm, she was still there. Knight had been hired by Hamblin to work on a house. Legend says that when Knight returned to the ranch after the massacre with blood on his clothes, bringing the crying children, one badly wounded in the arm, his wife had a nervous collapse from which she did not recover for a long time.

An affidavit from Samuel Knight, giving his version of the massacre, is on file in the Latter-day Saints church files, office of the first presidency, but was not made available for this study.

74

ages, far outnumbering the women and children, leaped from the brush on both sides of the road at once and, stimulated by the shrieks and screams, fell upon their victims with knives and hatchets and soon quieted them. At the wagons, the three men shot the wounded at close range and pulled the wagons off the road a short distance before they unloaded the bodies.

In these essentials, all accounts agree. The points of difference come in placing the responsibilities for giving and executing the orders. For many years it was all so secret—the whispered stories told and retold, modified to suit the whim or imagination of the narrator, rape added to murder, details supplied so generously— that it has been difficult to sift out facts. One thing should be kept in mind in considering all accounts: once the massacre was a horrible reality, no one wished to accept the responsibility, or any part of the responsibility for it; each man tried to clear himself at the expense of someone else. The modern student, weighing various accounts, finds himself so often between accusations and denials that it is difficult to determine which most nearly approximates the truth.

Since John D. Lee's name has been most persistently connected with the massacre, and since his account of it is most complete, we will briefly consider his story before passing on to the affidavits of other participants. Quotations are all from *Mormonism Unveiled, or the Life and Confessions of John D. Lee*, first published in 1877.

There is some evidence that rumors of this party had reached Harmony earlier, for Benjamin Platte, a convert from England who was working for Lee at the time, said that "a few days before Lee started, I heard some Indians talking to Lee and asking him to go and help them fight them, but he refused to do so."[2]

[2] The whole reference made by Benjamin Platte to the Mountain Meadows Massacre and Lee's connection with it is as follows: "In September the famous Mountain Meadows Massacre was committed I saw John D. Lee leave Harmony Fort on Sunday morning to go to meet the Emigrants at Mountain Meadows as they were campt there and the rumer was that they were very mean on the road to the people and had poisened an Ox at corn creek and given it to the Indians with intent to poison them and this enraged the Indians so that they

Lee himself says that he was summoned to Cedar City:

About the 7th of September, 1857, I went to Cedar City from my home at Harmony, by order of President Haight. I did not know what he wanted of me, but he had ordered me to visit with him and I obeyed. If I remember correctly, it was on Sunday evening that I went there.[3]

His wife, Rachel, agrees that he went on Sunday and gives the exact date, September 6. Since other participants say that they, too, were ordered to come in, we may well believe that this was the case with Lee also. He goes on:

When I got to Cedar City, I met Isaac C. Haight on the public square of the town. Haight was then President of that Stake of Zion, and next to Wm. H. Dame in all of southern Utah, and as Lieutenant Colonel he was second to Dame in the command of the Iron Military District. . . .

When I met Haight, I asked him what he wanted with me. He

___

were on there trail to massacre them at the first opertunity and they wanted the Mormons to help them and a few days before Lee started I heard some Indians talking to Lee and asking him to go and help fight them but he refused to do so, saying that the Indians had killed a good man meaning Captain Gunison of the United States surveying party he was killed at Gunison Sanpete County [*sic*] but on Saturday night he went to Cedar City to get his horses shod and came back with orders to gather up Indians and go to the Imagrants camp and commence an asalt on them as I was told by Don Carlos Shirts his son in law and the next Sunday morning he came back with a company of Indians loaded with plunder such as beds and tinwair and in about three days after there were a large heard of cattle brought to Harmony and he branded them with JDL I think on the right hip I think there were about 300 and some horses and some wagons perhaps 3 or 4; When he came back he road around half way of the fort inside about aposet the well and made this exclamation Thanks to the Lord God of Isriel that had delivered our enemies into our hands, the Indians following in single file after him with there plunder He afterwards made a statement of the affair in meeting in the afternoon;

"In the afternoon he told a great deal of what was done in a meeting called for that purpose."

Photostat of the above diary is in the Henry E. Huntington Library.

[3] John D. Lee, *Mormonism Unveiled, the Life and Confessions of John D. Lee* (hereafter cited as Lee, *Confessions*), 218.

said he wanted to have a long talk with me on private and particular business. We took some blankets and went over to the old Iron Works, and lay there that night so that we could talk in private and safety.

Here again all the offenses of the emigrants, real and imagined, were gone over; here again was summarized all the evidence that those in authority in the church would approve of the destruction of the emigrant train, if it could be done by the Indians. Lee had accompanied George A. Smith in his travels through the southern settlements, and, from the various conversations along the road as well as from the public speeches, convinced himself that this action would be in harmony with the course to be taken in the approaching war.

There are some reasons to believe that Lee would have fallen in with these ideas, although he might well have weakened when it came to carrying them out. He had been with the church nearly twenty years; he had held responsible positions in helping with the westward trek. He often made it clear that he had no love for the "Christians who drove us from their midst";[4] at one time he publicly rebuked a brother who preached kindness to their enemies, saying that "he himself would not hesitate to steal from the Gentiles who had so often robbed the Saints."[5]

As a result of the conversation that night, it was agreed that they would stir up the Indians further and encourage them to attack the company and rob them of their cattle and goods. At this point there was no decision to exterminate them. Everything was to be done by the Indians under the direction of a few white men. Lee goes on:

> I must here state that Klingensmith was not in Cedar City that Sunday night. Haight said he had sent Klingensmith and others

[4] John D. Lee to Brigham Young, January 10, 1852, in the "Journal History of the Church" for that date.

[5] Thomas D. Brown, "Journal of the Southern Indian Mission," dated March 18, 1855, p. 128. This interesting document is in the files of the Latter-day Saints church historian.

over towards Pinto, and around there, to stir up the Indians and force them to attack the emigrants.

On my way from Cedar City to my home at Harmony, I came up with a large band of Indians under Moquetas and Big Bill, two Cedar City chiefs; they were in their war paint, and fully equipped for battle. They halted when I came up and said they had had a big talk with Haight, Higby and Klingensmith, and had got orders from them to follow up the emigrants and kill them all, and take their property as the spoil of their enemies.

These Indians wanted me to go with them and command their forces. I told them that I could not go with them that evening, that I had orders from Haight, the *big Captain*, to send other Indians on the war-path to help them kill the emigrants, and that I must attend to that first; that I wanted them to go on near where the emigrants were and camp until the other Indians joined them: that I would meet them the next day and lead them.[6]

Lee left his little Indian boy, Clem, who had ridden behind him on the same horse, as hostage, and went to carry out his orders. Growing impatient during his absence, the Indians attacked the emigrant train early Tuesday morning, but were repulsed with some loss of life. A messenger to Lee urged him to hurry, so, cutting across the mountains by trail, he arrived at the scene on Wednesday.

When I reached the camp I found the Indians in a frenzy of excitement. They threatened to kill me unless I agreed to lead them against the emigrants, and help them kill them. They also said they had been told that they could kill the emigrants without danger to themselves, but they had lost some of their braves, and others were wounded, and unless they could kill all the *"Mericats,"* as they called them, they would declare war against the Mormons and kill every one in the settlements.

I did as well as I could under the circumstances. I was the only white man there, with a wild and excited band of several hundred Indians. . . .[7]

[6] Lee, *Confessions*, 226.
[7] *Ibid.*, 227.

That day the group was reinforced by other Indians from the south, accompanied by fourteen white men. After reviewing the situation, they decided to send a messenger to Haight to acquaint him with conditions.

> We knew that the original plan was for the Indians to do all the work, and the whites to do nothing, only to stay back and plan for them, and encourage them to do the work. Now we knew the Indians could not do the work, and we were in a sad fix.
>
> I did not then know that a messenger had been sent to Brigham Young for instructions. Haight had not mentioned it to me.[8]

There is reason to believe Lee's statement here, for had he known of the messenger, he would not have been so eager for orders from Haight; he would have tried to hold the situation in hand until word came from his chief. Few men in all the church looked with as much genuine affection upon Brigham Young as did John D. Lee. Through the religious rites of the church, Lee had been adopted as a son by Brigham Young, to be a member of his family, both in this world and the next. Because of this, Lee's love and loyalty shine out through every page of the many letters which he wrote to his adopted father. At one time, bitterly disappointed at a reversal of orders for carrying out one of his pet projects, Lee accepted the decision without question. Acknowledging his willingness to comply, he wrote:

> ... I am now as I always have been in your hands and in the hands of the Lord, ready according to the best of my skill and abilities to do for the best. I have no hesitancy in saying that I believe that I shall be able to accomplish whatever you in your wisdom may require at my hands, the God in whom I trust being my helper. . . . I am as clay in the hands of the potter. . . . With feelings of reverence, I subscribe myself your son and brother in the seal of the covenant forever.[9]

[8] *Ibid.*, 228.
[9] Letter, John D. Lee to Brigham Young, November 5, 1851.

Lee certainly would have carried out no orders which he thought would be contrary to the wishes of Brigham Young. With the repeated advice to conciliate the Indians, and in view of the fact that they far outnumbered the whites of the region, he might well have felt that to appease them was of first importance, for he insists that there were fully three hundred of them present, perhaps four hundred, all threatening and angry. In spite of his efforts and those of Oscar Hamblin to prevent it, the Indians made a second attack upon the emigrants, but were again repulsed, again with some losses. This was on Wednesday, the same day that Jesse N. Smith returned to Dame with his report; on the evening of that day, young Aiden was killed.

Wednesday night Lee sent another express to Haight, and on Thursday a group of men arrived from Cedar City, evidently sent out before Lee's messenger arrived and before word had reached there of Aiden's murder. Late Thursday night a second detachment of the Iron County militia arrived, under command of Major John M. Higbee. With this group were Philip Klingonsmith, the bishop of Cedar City, and Nephi Johnson, the best Indian interpreter for the southern Paiutes. Altogether, the white men on the ground now numbered fifty-four.

It would seem that, during Thursday night, Haight and Higbee had ridden to Parowan for a council of war with Dame because of the complications arising from the death of Aiden. In a number of accounts this is mentioned, and legends regarding it persist. Charles Adams, later bishop of Parowan, after he was an old man, told how, as a boy of thirteen, he was sent to prepare the horses for the return ride. As the men came out of the house and walked toward the stable where he stood with the animals, Higbee said, "You know what the council decided," referring to the decision of the Sunday before to hold the situation until orders came from Brigham Young. To this Dame answered, "I don't care what the council decided. My orders are that the emigrants *must be* done away with."

Lee says that:

As soon as these persons gathered around the camp, I demanded of Major Higbee what orders he had brought. I then stated fully all that had happened at the Meadows, so that every person might understand the situation.

Major Higbee reported as follows: "It is the orders of the President, that all the emigrants must be *put out of the way*. President Haight has counseled with Colonel Dame or had had orders from him to put all of the emigrants out of the way; none who are old enough to talk are to be spared."[10]

Lee insists that from the first assault of the Indians upon the emigrants he had tried to get the natives to take the cattle and go to their homes; only with great danger had he and Oscar Hamblin succeeded in calling off the Indians. He had reported the failure of the attacks to Haight and suggested that the Indians withdraw and let the emigrants go. Now with the militia present, he was subordinate to Higbee. The discussion went on, he says, until at last the Mormons knelt in a circle amid the sage and asked God for guidance and strength to do the thing that was required, or to give them some sign that they might know what to do.

After prayer, Major Higbee said, "Here are the orders," and handed me a paper from Haight. It was in substance that it was the orders of Haight to *decoy* the emigrants from their position, and kill all of them that could talk. This order was in writing. Higbee handed it to me and I read it, and then dropped it on the ground, saying,

"I cannot do this."

... The order was signed by Haight, as commander of the troops at Cedar City.

Haight told me the next day after the massacre, while on the Meadows, that he got his orders from Colonel Dame.

I then left the council, and went away to myself, and bowed myself in prayer before God, and asked Him to overrule the decision of that Council. I shed many bitter tears, and my tortured soul was wrung nearly from my body by the great suffering. I will

10 Lee, *Confessions*, 232.

here say, calling upon Heaven, angels, and the spirits of just men to witness what I say, that if I could then have had a thousand worlds to command, I would have given them freely to save that company from death.

While in bitter anguish, lamenting the sad condition of myself and others, Charles Hopkins, a man I had great confidence in, came to me from the Council, and tried to comfort me. . . .

At the earnest solicitation of Brother Hopkins, I returned with him to the Council. When I got back, the Council again prayed for aid.[11]

Finally convinced that he was doing what had to be done, Lee accepted the decision and helped to make the plans for the execution without further protest or weeping. He says that he gained his Indian name of "Yauguts" at this time, because he wept in his pleadings with the Indians. Certain it is that the Indians called him Yauguts, or "Crybaby," the rest of his life; he himself often referred to the name as meaning a tender-hearted man and sometimes signed his letters with it. Jacob Hamblin refers to it as though it were gained at this time, but William Rogers, writing in *The Valley Tan*, says that it was derived earlier. His spelling is slightly different also.

These Indians called Bishop Lee "Narguts," which in their language means a crying man. The name was given to Lee they stated, because he once cried when he lost some stock or had it stolen. They stated that "Narguts" was there but would not venture near, being, like themselves, afraid.[12]

Lee tells how the people of the camp welcomed him as their deliverer, how trustingly the women and children came to him. They accepted his terms and co-operated to fit into his plans. After the company was all on the road, and the signal was given, he says of his part in it:

[11] *Ibid.*, 234.
[12] William H. Rogers, account published in *The Valley Tan*, February 29, 1860.

John Doyle Lee at age thirty-eight (1850). From a print in the possession of Lee's grandson, Elwood Lee, of Virgin City, Utah.

The memorial atop Dan Sill Hill is a simple slab of gray Vermont granite (nine pieces formed into one long curved shape) onto which are etched a simple text and the names of the victims (left side), surviving children (first double column on the right side) and other possible victims (single column on the far right). It is set into the hillside, and landscaping will fill in the cut to give it a crown of hardy shrubbery. Behind the people to the left are other texts explaining the California Road and Old Spanish Trail. Courtesy Museum of Church History and Art, Salt Lake City, Utah.

... It was my duty, with the two drivers, to kill the sick and wounded who were in the wagons, and to do so when we heard the guns of the troops fire. I was walking between the wagons; the horses were going in a fast walk, and we were fully half a mile from Major Higbee and his men, when we heard the firing. As we heard the guns, I ordered a halt and we proceeded to do our part.

I here pause in the recital of this horrid story of man's inhumanity, and ask myself the question, Is it honest in me, and can I clear my conscience before my God, if I screen myself while I accuse others? No, never! Heaven forbid that I should put a burden upon others' shoulders, that I am unwilling to bear my just portion of. I am not a traitor to my people, nor to my former friends and comrades who were with me on that dark day when the work of death was carried on in God's name, by a lot of deluded and religious fanatics. It is my duty to tell facts as they exist, and I will do so.[13]

Both McMurdy and Knight later testified that Lee did the killing, though McMurdy refused to answer any question as to his own guilt. Lee says he himself intended to help, but was so excited and nervous that his shot went wild and almost wounded McMurdy. After the bodies were thrown out, Lee sent the teamsters with the wagons and the eighteen children on to Hamblin's ranch, while he walked back past where the women had been killed to join Higbee and the militia.

In attempting to place responsibilities, we can do no better than to consider affidavits and accounts of others who participated. Of those presented here, only one has been heretofore printed. They agree essentially as to what went on once the emigrants had been betrayed into leaving their shelter, but each gives his own interpretation as to the men at whose orders the killing was done.

THE STORY OF NEPHI JOHNSON

At the time of the massacre, Nephi Johnson was a young man of twenty-four, the father of one little daughter and with his first

[13] Lee, *Confessions*, 241.

son to be born within two months. For years before his marriage he had been an Indian interpreter and guide among the southern Paiutes; few men in the vicinity could speak their language as well. The Paiutes in turn had great confidence in him.

At the second trial of John D. Lee, Johnson testified that he was present at the massacre, but since his horse got away, he had gone to catch it and watched the proceedings from the top of a nearby hill. Legends say that he was one of a number of mounted scouts placed to pick off any who chanced to escape the first attack. In the court his memory was too short to remember any name except Lee's; he seemed sure only that he saw Lee kill two men and one woman.

This affidavit was made in the presence of, and was notarized by, Judge David H. Morris of St. George, Utah, in 1906. It is reproduced in full in Appendix I. He says, in part:

> During the year 1857 I was living at Enoch, Iron County, then Territory of Utah; that during the month of September I was working in the harvest field when two men came to my place and stated that Isaac C. Haight had sent them to request me to come to Cedar City immediately. I went to Cedar City and there Isaac C. Haight told me he wanted me to go to the mountains and settle a difficulty between John D. Lee and the Indians, as the latter had threatened to kill Lee. Haight also said that Lee and the Indians had went to the Meadows to kill the emigrants, and had made three attacks on them, but had found the emigrants better fighters than they had expected and as some of the Indians had been killed and quite a number had been wounded they were getting tired of it and Lee had suggested that they withdraw and let the emigrants go, and Haight sent word to Lee to clean up the dirty job he had started, and that he had sent out a company of men with shovels to bury the dead, but they would find something else to do when they got there.
>
> In company with John M. Higbee and others I went to the Mountain Meadows. We arrived at the springs where the Meadows or Hamblin [Hamblin's ranch] is situated about 10 o'clock at night where we found John D. Lee and the principal Indian chiefs were gathered. After discussing the trouble between Lee and the Indians,

Lee stated that they would try and get the emigrants to leave their camp and give up their arms after which they would kill them. That satisfied the Indians. I acted as interpreter between Lee and the Indians when the above arrangements were made.

Johnson's statement that Lee had suggested that they withdraw and let the emigrants go, that the Indians had threatened to kill Lee, and that he, too, was on the ground because he was ordered to be there, are in harmony with Lee's story. He infers that it was necessary to pacify the Indians, though his estimate that there were only one hundred fifty natives on the ground places the number at less than half of Lee's estimate, and only one-third as many as Higbee says were there. That some men, who would find something else to do when they got there, had gone out with shovels to bury the dead, also confirms other accounts. His description of the line of march is the same as that given in other statements. As to the actual killing, he says:

After marching along for some time, the signal Halt was given, at which each white man was to kill the emigrant man at his side. The Indians were in ambush at the place where the signal was given, and at the signal quite a number of the posse failed to kill his man, for the reason that they did not approve of the killing.

The plan was for the Indians to kill the women and children and wounded and the white men of the posse to kill the men of the emigrants, but owing to some of the white men of the posse failing to kill their men, the Indians assisted in finishing the work. There were about 150 Indians present.

In his testimony in the court, Johnson said that a good many of the men present objected to the plan, but, being a part of the military organization, were forced to help carry it out. As soon as it was over, Johnson and two others were sent to prevent the Indians from looting the wagons of the emigrants. They remained on guard until Isaac C. Haight arrived the next morning.

Haight asked me what I would do with this property. I asked

85

him if he wanted to know my real feelings about it and he said yes. Then I said you have made a sacrifice of the people, and I would burn the property, and let the cattle roam over the country, for the Indians to kill, and go home like men.

Johnson evidently did not want it said that they had murdered the people for their property, but the leaders could not stand to let so much be destroyed. The wagons and their loads, even the bloody clothes, were taken to Cedar City, stored in the tithing office, and later sold at auction.

THE STORY OF JOHN M. HIGBEE

At the time of the massacre John M. Higbee was also a very young man, not yet thirty years old, and a counselor to Isaac C. Haight in the Stake Presidency as well as a major in the military organization. Following the massacre, he went into hiding along with the others; later he moved to Arizona. He did not return to Utah to live permanently until after the execution of Lee. His account was written in 1894, and is signed "Bull Valley Snort," but there is no question as to its genuineness, for it has been carefully kept in the family with the understanding that it should be used when the truth of the affair could finally be told. It is reproduced in full in Appendix II.

In the Mormon temple at St. George is an affidavit with a long list of signers to the effect that since the life of John M. Higbee had been above reproach both before and after the tragedy, and since he was sent to the scene under false pretenses and was forced to participate against his will, he should be absolved of all blame and reinstated in full fellowship in the church.

His story, which covers seventeen handwritten pages in an ordinary notebook, makes the excitement aroused by the army the basic cause of the trouble, with the demands of the Indians and their threats to attack the Mormons the immediate cause of the massacre. He begins with a general picture of the excitement which prevailed, lists the offenses of the emigrants, and enlarges upon the threat of the Indians. He goes on:

About this time Indian Farmer Lee was heard of as being with Savages who reported to him that they had killed all the emigrant company and if Mormons wanted to bury them they could. Accordingly Lee sent an express to Cedar City asking for help to come and bury the dead. The bell was rung. The people came together; the express was read from Lee in regard to emigrant company. After which a dozen or more of as honorable good citizens as lived in the country volunteered and started at once to go and bury the dead.

Since this account and that of Nephi Johnson were far apart, both in time and location, the story of the deception takes on greater weight. Johnson says that it was Haight who was sending out men to bury the dead; Higbee says it was Lee who sent in the false report. Klingonsmith, on the other hand, says it was a purely military move in which the men were ordered out, armed and equipped as the law directs. Yet the story that many of the men were deceived as to the real purpose for their going to the Meadows has been widely and often repeated.

Higbee's description of conditions is graphic:

> Upon our arival a terible picture met our gaze   the valey was strewn with carkuses of catle and horses which the Indians had shot down through revenge. Indians were painted like devils, as though they had just arived from the Infernal regions & Howling with rage over some of their braves being wounded. All tending to make everything as hideous and deamon like as could be imagined. Lee was trying to Pasify them and have them Scatter and go away and let the Emigrants go. So he said to us.
>
> The Savages then came to Lee and said if he and the Mormons did not help them to kill the Merry Cats they would join the Soldiers and fight the Mormons. The Number of Indians there were variously estimated at anywhere from three to six hundred all determined it seemed to accomplish the destruction of the company if they had to fight all the Mormons in the Southern Country. J. D. Lee being a Major in the Nauvoo Legion and Commander over Kane [Washington] County where we were then said we dare not

make war with Indians   He then ordered all men Present to Join his Command for Self Preservation.

The whole group of white men held another council to decide what should be done, and:

> It was agreed to Send Higbee to Inform Col. Wm. H. Dame Commander of Iron Military District the condition of things at M. M. [Mountain Meadows]. Higbee proceeded at once to Cedar about thirty five miles and reported to Major Haight that Emigrant Company were not killed as Lee Express had stated the day before But were fortified and were under a State of Siege Surrounded night and day by Savages who were blood Thirsty and crazy because some of their number had been Wounded. To all appearances and attitude of Indians there were not Men enough in Southern Utah to Protect Company with force against the Savages.
>
> Under these circumstances Col. W. H. Dame was asked to Say what Should be done. I. C. Haight went to Parowan in the night and Made the report to Col Dame and returned next morning with orders which Higbee Caried Same day to Lee.

Here again is evidence that the military leaders were kept constantly aware of developments. Since the writer of this was also the messenger, he might be expected to know what the orders which he carried were. Whether or not he had the original document from which to copy them, we cannot know; he only quotes the orders as though they were verbatim:

> . . . When Mesenger returned he Said Col. Dames Orders given to Haight for Higbee to Carry to Major J. D. Lee were
> Compromise with Indians if Possible by letting them take all the Stock and go to their Homes and let Company alone but on no Conditions you are not to precipitate a war with Indians while there is an army Marching Against our People. As Indian Farmer and a Major in the Legion I trust you will have Influence enough to restrain Indians and Save the Company. If not Possible save Wimen and Children at all Hazards. Hoping you will be able to give a good account of the Important duty Entrusted to your

Charge I call upon all good Citizens in that Part of the District to
help you Cary out the above Orders. In helping to Make Peace between the two Parties.

by WM. H. DAME *Col Comanding Iron Millitary District*

This is far from the written orders which Lee says he received
from Haight, which were to decoy the emigrants from their shelter. Dame might well use such a document as this to clear himself
of a part of his responsibility, though the orders are contradictory.
On the one hand, Lee is ordered to save the company if possible
and the women and children at all hazards, and on the other, he is
told positively that "on no condition are you to precipitate a war
with the Indians while there is an army marching against our
people."

Another report of these same orders, passed down by word of
mouth, is to the effect that Lee should "keep the friendship of the
Indians at all costs, as in case of war, they will be our most valued
allies or our most dangerous enemies."

Higbee explains it all as a matter of appeasing the Indians; they
were too numerous and too threatening to be disregarded. Encouraged to begin by promises of great booty, they would be
satisfied with nothing less.

> Lee said he and Clingensmith had desided there was onley one
> way to Stop having an Indian war and Save wimen and children.
> After all this Talk we have agreed that we would Get the Men of
> the Company out where they could get at them without their
> Loosing any more of their Men on the following Conditions that
> they would let the Wimen and Children go to Cedar City un-
> molested and they take all the Stock and other Property. Indians
> agreeing to Perform there part of the Compact. Lee Said then to
> whites as Major in Command of this County I call on all of you in
> the Interest of Humanity and the liberty of the Scatering and Help-
> less condition of our Setlements to help Me to Carry out our Part
> of this agreement.

The arrangements for getting the emigrants out of their enclosure, the lining up of the militia, the loading of the wagons, and the order of march are all described. At the place appointed, the order "Halt!" was given.

Some say Clingensmith gave Order who was at head of company. One thing is Known by all Persons out there   It was Major Lee's Orders whoEver gave them. That was the Signal for guns to fire. Lee said those that are too big Cowards to help the Indians can Shoot in the air then Squat down So Indians can rush Past them and finish up their Savage work begun Many days Since.

It is said Most of our Company were nervious and afraid of Indian Treachery and Kept their guns loaded for their Own Protection   no doubt Each Individual knows more about that than any other Person Living and How they felt at that Particular Moment when Some Guns were fired and the Men Squated down and Indians Seemed to be there the Same Moment as they jumped out of the Brush, and rushed like a Howling tornado apast us. And the Hideous Deamon like yells of the Savages as they thirsting for blood rushed Past to Slay their helpless Victims it Seemed to chill the Blood in our veins.

The fleeing men ran up among the women and children, and the Indians following them killed all. Higbee's account closes with a plea that the truth of this should be told, so that men who had been deceived into going to the Meadows in the first place and forced to participate in the butchery after they got there might be cleared of responsibility. These men, he insisted, had been done a grave injustice.

That some of the Mormons in the ranks did not approve of what was done is generally admitted. A legend is told of young Tom Pierce, who refused to have anything to do with the affair and turned to walk away. When his own father, who was an officer, ordered him into the ranks and he still did not return, the father shot at him. The bullet grazed the side of Tom's head, leaving a permanent scar just above his ear.

The Mormon teaching of unquestioning obedience to authority, added to the strict military law then in force in the territory, would, in the eyes of their neighbors, relieve the men in the ranks of responsibility. For this reason, only a few went later into permanent hiding, and they were the men who had been in positions of command.

THE AFFIDAVIT OF DANIEL S. MACFARLANE

This statement, made June 26, 1896, is very similar to the one made by Higbee, except that it is brief. It is given in full in Appendix III.

There are some merciful men that volunteered to go out there and bury the dead; for John D. Lee had sent an express from the Mt. Meadows to Cedar City, stating that the Indians had killed all the Immigrants Co. and asking for volunteers to come out and help bury the dead. I was one of the Co of volunteers, who went on that humane errand. When we reached "the meadows" the Indians were still fighting the Imigrants.

About this time Lee got an express from Col. Wm. H. Dame telling him to treat the Indians in some way and let the Immigrants go and the natives take part of their stock and go to their homes. When we came to where Lee was, he and Klingon Smith were talking to some of the chiefs who seemed very much excited. . . .

Higbee asked Lee what the Indians were saying. He answered, "They say—I Lee told them we were at war with the Mericats, and you sent for all of us to come and bring our warriors and help you fight them, and now you want us to take part of their stock and go home and let them go and you know some of our men have been shot and my warriors are mad and their blood is up.

"Some of you want to take their part. We will fight you as well as them if you don't help us to get them out of their Fort."

Lee said further that himself and Klingon Smith had talked the matter over and come to the conclusion, under the circumstances that we had to make our appearance of helping them or we must fight them and the latter we cannot think of doing.

John M. Higbee said, "Is there no way that the women and children can be saved?" Lee said, "The Indians agreed not to molest the women and children if he (Lee) would get the men out so they could get at them." Then Higbee said, "Is there no way to satisfy the Indians and save the Imigrants." Klingon Smith said, "No we have got to do as Lee says." Then Lee spoke up in an important slurring manner and said, "If any of you are too big cowards to appear to help the Indians you need not shoot nor anything else. Only form a line, single file and march down to where I will call a truce and get the men out of their Fort and I will send the women and children ahead. The Indians will let them past a half a mile or more, they the Indians will rush past you when the signal is given and take the men." Lee then said to Higbee and Klingon Smith "You will see that my orders are strictly obeyed." So the line was formed and marched down to the road and up as he directed. After women and children had passed a half mile or more. Then Klingon Smith gave the word "Halt" signal agreed upon by Lee and Smith. When Klingon Smith fired his gun, our men dropped to the ground. Then Indians rushed past them yelling and like a tornado, they pounced upon their helpless victors [sic] and all was over in a few minutes, and still as death, and not till then did we realize that treachery had been practiced when only a few small children had been saved.

No one knew of the treachery before hand unless Lee and Smith. Perhaps they did not as Lee said it was the young bucks and the old ones could not stop them.

I always felt it was a base insult thrown at Higbee and volunteers by Lee and uncalled for at the time.

When Higbee asked Lee if there was no other way to dodge the issue and he (Lee) said or used the word "Cowards" as thru brute force he would brow beat us all. For we all felt as Higbee had expressed himself to avoid such a result and being also deceived in the object for which we consented to go to the "meadows."

Neither Higbee nor Macfarlane mentions Haight as being in any way connected with the massacre. They refer back to Colonel Dame at Parowan for issuing the orders which Lee interpreted and executed. Perhaps the fact that Macfarlane married one of Haight's daughters, and Higbee was one of his counselors in the Stake Presidency, accounts for their leaving out his name.

"This Horrid Story"

At the time of the massacre, Philip Klingonsmith was the bishop of Cedar City, but was released from this office on July 31, 1859, almost two years later. He remained a faithful member of the church more than ten years longer, filling some difficult assignments at the lead mines at Las Vegas and establishing settlements on the upper Virgin. About 1870, he moved into Nevada, and by April, 1871, had become estranged and was considered an apostate. His affidavit, made that year, three years before the arrest of John D. Lee, was published in *Rocky Mountain Saints*, by T. B. H. Stenhouse. It is here reprinted in Appendix IV.

This account differs materially from the others in that it does not even mention the Indians or any part they might have played in the affair. It was, instead, a military operation, directed by the military officials. After the company had passed through Cedar City, the militia was called out for the purpose of committing acts of hostility against them; but he was not among the number to go at the first call.

. . . about two days after said company had left said Cedar City, Lieutenant-Colonel I. C. Haight expressed in my presence, a desire that said company might be permitted to pass on their way in peace; but afterward he told me that he had orders from headquarters to kill all of said company of emigrants except the little children; I do not know whether said headquarters meant the Regimental Headquarters at Parowan, or the Headquarters of the Commander-in-chief at Salt Lake City. . . .

. . . after the fight had been going on for three or four days, a messenger from Major Lee reached Cedar City, who stated that the fight had not been altogether successful, upon which Lieutenant-Colonel Haight ordered out a re-enforcement; at this time I was ordered out by Captain John M. Higbee, who ordered me to muster, 'armed and equipped as the law directs;' it was a matter of life or death to me to muster or not, and I mustered with the reenforcing troops; it was at this time that Lieutenant-Colonel Haight said to me that it was the orders from headquarters that all but the little children of said company were to be killed; said Haight had at that time just returned from headquarters at Parowan, where a military council had been held.

He mentions the meeting wherein Lee called all the men together to read his orders, but claims that he was so far away that he did not see the paper in Lee's hands. The plans were carried out, and the emigrants surrendered to their death. He was with the militia, a mile or so behind the wagons and out of sight of them, when the slaughter took place, so he knew nothing of Lee's activities at the time. As for his own part in it, he says:

> . . . at the time of the firing of the first volley I discharged my piece; I did not fire afterward, though several subsequent volleys were fired; after the first fire was delivered I at once set about saving the children; I commenced to gather the children before the firing had ceased.

He says that he was responsible for placing the orphaned children in good homes, and that he gave no orders except those given as a Mormon bishop for the care of these children. His story of the quarrel between the leaders over who had issued the orders for the massacre supports the one told by Lee. In his opinion, the responsibility lay between Haight and Dame; all the others were doing only what their place in the military organization forced them to do.

> . . . on the evening of the massacre, Colonel W. H. Dame and Lieutenant I. C. Haight came to Hamblin's, where I had the said children, and fell into a dispute, in the course of which said Haight told Colonel Dame, that, if he was going to report the killing of said emigrants, he should not have ordered it done. . . .

In his testimony in court later, when questioned about the Indians and their part in the massacre, Klingonsmith admitted that he saw some one hundred of them, but made no mention of the necessity of appeasing them nor of their part in killing the women and children. Since his station was with the militia, and his business was to kill one emigrant man and then to supervise the surviving children, he omits all other phases of the slaughter. From his point of view, Lee and all others present were acting under definite orders from their military superiors.

Perhaps at this point we should recapitulate briefly in order to note variations in the different accounts. While both Higbee and Macfarlane emphasize the threat of the Indians and insist that the final massacre was carried out in order to appease them, Klingonsmith pictures it as a strictly military affair, conducted by the officials of Cedar City under orders from William H. Dame of Parowan. Nephi Johnson likewise places the blame upon the Mormon military leaders, but admits that the Indians were getting out of hand and he was called to help manage them. Lee's statement that the original plan was to stir up the Indians to the attack seems to be true. The Mormons were brought in later when it became evident that the Indians alone could not commit the crime. Certainly the final responsibility must rest squarely upon the Mormons, William H. Dame as commander, and those under him who helped to form the policy and to carry out the orders.

All accounts agree in the major particulars of the massacre; all say that it was quickly over. Some say it took five minutes, others say fifteen minutes, while Jacob Hamblin's Indian boy estimated that it was nearly a half hour before it was over. In that short time the last fleeing man had been shot, the last hysterical, shrieking woman quieted, and the limbs of the last youth had ceased to twitch and jerk. Now the Indians and some of the white men went among the slain, pulling off shoes and other clothing which might be worn, searching for money, watches, knives, or other valuables. The Indians began looting the wagons, throwing out dishes, scattering feathers from pillows—ransacking like gleeful, mischievous children.

Nephi Johnson says that he was one of three mounted men sent to guard the wagons. They allowed the Indians to keep what they had already taken, but would not allow them to take any

95

more. Others of the party were detailed to round up the cattle and guard them from the natives, or hold them until some decision could be made for their disposal.

So the evening fell over the scene of blood and carnage; a short distance away, at their camp by the spring, some fifty grim, silent men awaited the arrival of their commanding officers. They had to agree upon a number of things, the most important of which were the story they would tell to their shocked neighbors and the stand they would take before an outraged nation.

6

Questions Answered

Some questions with regard to the massacre itself arise so consistently that it may be well to consider them here before moving on to later developments.

DID ANY PERSONS OR WRITTEN RECORDS SURVIVE?

John D. Lee's account says:

> Three of the emigrants did get away, but the Indians were put on their trail and they overtook and killed them before they reached the settlements in California. But it would take more time than I have to spare to give the details of their chase and capture. I may do so in my writings hereafter, but not now.[1]

C. P. Lyford, whose account, quoted from a Chicago paper, seems to be a combination of well-established facts and a vivid imagination, tells how:

> Thursday night the emigrants drew up a petition or an humble prayer for aid. It was addressed to any friend of humanity, and stated the exact condition of affairs. It told that on the morning of the 10th the train was attacked by Indians, and that the siege had continued uninterruptedly. There was reason to believe, it stated, that white men were with the Indians, as the latter were well supplied with powder and weapons. In case the paper reached California, it was hoped that assistance would be sent to their rescue.

[1] Lee, *Confessions*, 244.

Then followed a list of the emigrants' names, each name was followed by the age, place of nativity, latest residence, position, rank, and occupation of its owner. . . . The paper, also, contained an itemized list of their property, such as wagons, oxen, horses, etc. . . .

Volunteers were called for, and three of the bravest men that ever lived stepped forward and offered to attempt to dash through the enemy, and across the wilderness and desert. . . . In the dead of night they passed the besiegers, but Indian runners were immediately placed on their track.

Fleeing for their lives, they traveled until completely exhausted. An Indian chief, named Jackson, boasts of having killed the first, having found him lying on his back asleep, between the Clara and the Rio Virgin. . . .

In after years my informant was taken by Jackson to the remains. . . .

The letter was found on a divide, near the murdered man. Jackson discovered it, and gave it to my informant, who kept it safely for months. Happening to show it one day to a man who was a leader in the massacre, he promptly destroyed it. The honest old Mormon, however, is perfectly acquainted with the nature of its contents, and has no sympathy with the tragedy or its perpetrators.[2]

The writer goes on to tell how the other two emigrants traveled forty miles farther to the Virgin Hills, where they too were overtaken by Indians, surrounded, and one was killed. The other escaped and made his way across the desert, fifty-four miles, where he met some Indians who were kind to him and helped him to reach Cottonwood Springs.

"Here he met two young gentlemen from California, Henry T. Young and Cau Young. They gave him a horse and some clothing, and bade him Godspeed to California," the account goes on. The emigrant evidently feared to face the long road to California alone, preferring to accompany these friendly travelers back to Great Salt Lake City. On the Muddy, the group met Ira Hatch and a band of Indians, who recognized the fugitive and demanded

[2] C. P. Lyford, *The Mormon Problem*, 296–99.

"Lonely Dell," Lee's home at the mouth of the Paria. In 1872 he established "Lee's Ferry" on the Colorado River, and operated it until he was taken into custody in late 1874. His wife, Emma Batchelder, lived here until 1879, assisting Warren Johnson with the ferry. Until 1928 this was the only crossing for Mormon colonists into Arizona.

Stone fort erected during the winter of 1874–75 by "missionaries" called from the settlements, as a protection and camping place for emigrants. It is on the bank of the Colorado River about two miles below the "Lonely Dell" home. The state of Arizona authorized a monument, located some six miles downstream from this fort, commemorating Lee's role in the colonization of Arizona.

that he be killed, while "the Young brothers had all they could do to preserve their own lives."

This story leaves no doubt that the informant is Jacob Hamblin, who is several times referred to as the "honest old Mormon" who was "the owner of the ground then and now." Since Hamblin had been granted Mountain Meadows as a herd ground, and since he was on the most friendly terms with Indian Chief Jackson, it could mean no one else. From his own writings we learn that Hamblin immediately set about to get the details of the massacre from the Indians.

J. H. Beadle wrote the story of the escaping emigrants more briefly, but was forthright in naming names. Although he visited the locality and gathered his material in 1872, his book did not appear in print until 1880, after the trials and execution of Lee. His account is so similar to that of Lyford that it is clear that both had the story from Jacob Hamblin. He says:

Three men escaped the general massacre. The night before the closing scene the party first became convinced that white men were besieging them. They drew up a paper addressed to the Masons, Odd Fellows, Baptists, and Methodists of the States, "and to all good people every-where," in which they stated their condition, and implored help if there was time; if not, justice. To this were attached the signatures of so many members of various lodges and churches in Missouri and Arkansas. With this paper three of their best scouts crept down a ravine and escaped, starting on foot for California. The next day Ira Hatch and a band of Indians were put upon their track. They came upon them asleep on the Santa Clara Mountain and killed two as they slept. The third escaped, shot through the wrist. He traveled on and was relieved by the Vegas Indians, on the Santa Clara. After a day's rest he started on, but meeting John M. Young and another, they told him it would be madness to attempt the Ninety-mile Desert in his condition, and promised to try and smuggle him through to Salt Lake City. A few hours after, they met Hatch and his Indians on the hunt for the fugitive. . . .

The Indians promptly killed the man, while:

> The paper dropped by the fugitive was given by an Indian to Jacob Hamblin, Church Indian Agent, who kept it many years; but one day showing it to Lee, the latter took it from him and destroyed it.[3]

A third account comes from P. M. Warn, a member of the first group to reach San Bernardino after the massacre. His affidavit, read in the mass meeting at Los Angeles on October 12, was published widely in the California press. He tells how, just two days before they reached San Bernardino, his company was overtaken by the mail. With it was traveling one Bill Hyde, who gave a description of the scene of the massacre and told him again of meeting Hatch and the Indians. He evidently saw the paper written by the emigrants or some diary or record book. Since it too was held by Chief Jackson, it could well have been the same one referred to by Lyford and Beadle. Warn said regarding it:

> Hyde also related to his Mormon brethren that on arriving at the Santa Clara, where formerly there was a Mormon settlement, and is now occupied by chief Jackson, he saw in the hands of that chief, a little book or journal of one of the emigrants in which was written the name, "William B. Jones, Caldwell County, Missouri." He offered to purchase it, but the chief refused to part with it. This is the first intimation that will in any way identify the train.[4]

Since witnesses at the Lee trial all agree that none escaped the general massacre, it would seem that these men left the camp earlier. Perhaps they were the group of which young Aiden was the first victim. That there were records found which would have given pertinent and valuable information as to the personnel of the company, and that these were destroyed by the Mormons would seem evident. This would fit well into the general policy of keeping the matter quiet.

[3] John H. Beadle, *Western Wilds and the Men Who Redeem Them*, 500–501.
[4] *Daily Alta California*, October 27, 1857. This was quoted from a Los Angeles correspondent of October 24.

HOW MANY CHILDREN SURVIVED?

So many legends have grown up around the fate of the surviving children that it is almost impossible to determine where the truth lies. The Parowan Ward record, already quoted, was definite in its statement that "the entire Company was destroyed, except 18 small children, which the Saints took care of." Of these, only seventeen were finally delivered to the government officers to be returned to relatives in the East.

Klingonsmith, in his testimony in the court, told how he left his post with the militia as soon as the emigrant men were killed, walked a quarter of a mile to the wagons, and assumed management of the children, whom he took immediately to the Hamblin ranch. "I had my hands full with the children," he said, "seventeen of them, from two to seven or eight years of age; two were wounded, and one died on the way."[5]

In the spring of 1859, Jacob Forney visited southern Utah for the purpose of investigating the massacre and locating these children. When he arrived at the fort on the Santa Clara, he found that Jacob Hamblin had collected thirteen of them there, according to his orders. One other was in Pinto, and two were at Cedar City. With the sixteen thus located, he was led to believe that there was but one more to be found in order to have them all.

"Mr. Hamblin has good reason for believing that a boy about 8 years, and belonging to the party in questions, is among the Navajos Indians, at or near the Colorado river," he wrote in his report.[6]

As he moved toward Great Salt Lake City, Forney was told by the Indian Chief, Kanosh, that there were two more children saved than Hamblin had collected, verifying again the statement that eighteen had originally been saved. William H. Rogers was accordingly detailed to accompany Hamblin back to search further for these two. Rogers tells how they passed through a small settlement and made inquiries, but no one seemed to know any-

[5] Beadle, *Western Wilds*, 508.
[6] Jacob Forney, letter to Kirk Anderson, May 5, 1859, published in *The Valley Tan* for May 10, 1859.

thing about any children other than the ones who had already been found.

I told them that if the children were in the country at all, every house would be searched if they were not given up. At this, one of the men present, but who did not live in the place, but had arrived just before me, stated that his wife had one of the children besides those that Mr. Hamblin had collected and that he lived at Pocketville [Virgin] named from its location in the mountains. He stated that the child was very young, and that his wife was very much attached to it, and that it would give me much trouble if I took it away, and seemed by all his reports to be anxious to retain it. . . . Mr. Hamblin went over and brought this child away in a few days after I discovered where it was. This child was a bright eyed and rosy cheeked boy, about two years old, and must have been an infant when the massacre occurred.[7]

With seventeen children safely in the hands of the superintendent of Indian affairs, Hamblin arranged to make a trip across the Colorado River in search of a child who might be missing. The motive behind this is clear. For some time Hamblin had been discouraged with his work among the Paiutes; in letters and in recorded speeches he had expressed an eagerness to labor among "the nobler branches of the race." He had heard that the Hopis, across the Colorado, were a peaceful, agricultural people who had many skills. Surely they would be more amenable to his teachings. Here was an opportunity to do something he had long wanted to do, and at government expense. Thus, while his letters to Brigham Young and George A. Smith speak of this as a bona fide "mission" for the church, the records in the General Accounting Office in Washington, D. C., show that he was paid $318 for expenses incurred while conducting a search for the purpose of finding a child said to have been among those saved in the massacre.[8]

[7] William H. Rogers, *The Valley Tan*, February 29, 1860.

[8] Jacob Hamblin has received some severe criticism because, while he took pains to learn the facts of the massacre, and while he always deplored and con-

Although Jacob Hamblin knew well that no child had ever
been in the hands of the Indians, his search for one would imply
that not all had yet been given over to the proper authorities.
In the first trial of John D. Lee, a Mrs. Ann Eliza Hoge testified
that a certain boy said of an Indian, "He killed my pa—he's got on

demned it, he would not tell anything that might involve any of his people.
Although he did discuss the affair fully with his superiors in the church, it was
not until the second trial of Lee, almost twenty years later, that he gave any
pertinent information to officers. He testified then only upon order of Brigham
Young.

The following letter shows the amounts which he received from the government during the years he was connected with the Office of Indian Affairs:

"GENERAL ACCOUNTING OFFICE
WASHINGTON 25

"RECONCILIATION AND
CLEARANCE DIVISION
"In reply please quote
RT-1264367-JMcN

"SEPTEMBER 30, 1944

"JUANITA BROOKS
ST. GEORGE, UTAH
"MADAM:

"In reply to your letter of August 14, 1943, requesting information concerning
payments made to Jacob Hamblin while he was connected with the Office of
Indian Affairs, Utah Territory, during the years from 1858 to 1872, you are advised that the records of this office show that he served as follows:

"From September 10, 1857 to April 18, 1859, Mr. Hamblin was paid $600.56
for the care and supervision of Sarah, Rebecca, and Louisa Dunlap, who were
children saved from the 'Mountain Meadow Massacre.' He was also paid $318.00
for expense incurred while conducting a search for the purpose of finding a child
said to be among those saved in the 'Massacre.'

"Subject man was paid $350.00 for the period from December 1, 1858, to June
30, 1859, for the care and supervision of children saved from the 'Mountain
Meadow Massacre'; and $1,693.20 for the period from August 1, 1858 to April 18,
1859, for the board, clothing, and schooling of children saved in the 'Massacre.'

"From September 15 to September 19, 1865, Jacob Hamblin was paid $25.00
as a special interpreter and for the service of collecting certain Indians at Pinto
Creek for the purpose of making a treaty in pursuance of an act of Congress approved February 23, 1865.

"No further information in connection with this matter is on record in this
office. . . .

"Respectfully
"P. D. FALLON
*Asst. Chief, Reconciliation
and Clearance Division*"

my pa's clothes," and that the boy was taken away by John D. Lee and never seen again. Variants of this story are told in many places. Some say that it was a boy; others insist that it was a girl. "That is my father's pocket knife"; "That woman is wearing my mother's shawl"; "He is the man that killed my mamma"; "That man is riding our old gray horse"—every one of these was given as the expression of the child who disappeared. Some make Lee responsible, especially after it became popular to make him responsible for the entire affair; others say the child was taken to Haight at Toquerville. Even from Pioche, Nevada, comes a similar story, laying the blame to Klingonsmith after he moved into that area, though he did not go into Nevada for ten years after the massacre.

That some of the children did remember the incident was reported by James Lynch, who said that "when the Mountain Meadows Massacre children were gathered in 1859, there was among them a ten-year-old girl, Mary Dunlap, who identified some of the Mormons in the attack, and also the clothes and jewelry worn by John D. Lee's wife and others as plunder in the massacre."[9] Although this child evidently talked, she was spared.

Another story of the missing child is that the people who had taken her into their home did not give up one little girl to the officers, but kept her and raised her as their own without telling her of her parentage. Zera P. Terry, aged ninety-one (1948), insists that he knew the woman and her parents, and that she grew up, married a Morman, and lived in Cedar City much of her life. A lawyer in Salt Lake City says that he taught school in Cedar City in 1900 and established to his own satisfaction the fact that one little girl had been kept there, had grown to maturity, and had married a man named Urie. From a tiny village on the banks of the Colorado River comes the same story. Kumen Jones, of San Juan, also insisted that a girl was saved.

In the twelve years that have elapsed since the first publication of this book, so much evidence has come in that a baby girl saved

[9] *Union Vidette*, July 28, 1866.

from the massacre grew up a Mormon and married a Mormon husband that it seems now an established fact.

A granddaughter of Ann Chatterly McFarlane said, "Why do you give this as a question? My grandmother told often of the girl whose family lived in Cedar City. I thought everyone knew. We all certainly did."

A lady schoolteacher said, "I am a descendant of the girl who was saved. I always knew that there was some mystery around my grandmother, but did not know what it was until after her death. Your book, *The Mountain Meadows Massacre*, brought it into the open for us all."

A practicing physician, attending a reception in Salt Lake City, told the author, "While I wouldn't want it published, I am a descendant of the missing child."

In each case the informant asked that his name not be used; each seemed unwilling to give full genealogical information, but all agreed that a child had been saved, grew up, and became the mother of a respectable family.

THE TWO GIRLS LEE IS SAID TO HAVE KILLED

Another story which was modified with time and telling was that two teen-age girls broke away from the group of women and ran to John D. Lee for protection, falling at his feet and promising to serve him all their lives if he would spare them. The story which was finally developed, and even suggested at the trials, was that Lee first violated them and then cut their throats.

Although there have been cases where man has committed murder after rape, the circumstances surrounding the massacre make such an action highly improbable. In the midst of wholesale murder, surrounded by excited Indians, with more than fifty Mormon men in the immediate vicinity, such an incident seems fantastic. Such use of bleeding corpses is beyond the realm of the probable. In fact, the whole suggestion of rape in this incident seems to be another example of how repeated suggestion and whisperings may grow into more and more impossible tales, which are then passed on as fact.

Lee himself denied the whole story, of course. He said that he saw a girl some ten or twelve years old running toward the wagons, but "an Indian shot her before she got within sixty yards of us. That was the last person I saw killed on that occasion." He then went on to tell how he saved the life of a little boy just as an Indian had clutched him by the hair and was ready to cut his throat. Later he adopted this boy and kept him until he was taken by Dr. Forney to be sent east to his relatives. So well was the boy treated in the Lee household that after a few years he returned to visit them.

In the second trial of Lee, Jacob Hamblin testified that his Indian boy, Albert, had told him of the two girls who had hidden in the bushes and were discovered and killed by Lee and the Indians, and that the Indian boy had shown him the bodies of the two a little apart from the general massacre. He testified further that the Indian chief had told him of the murder of the girls, saying that Lee ordered it because they were too old to spare, though he himself thought they were too pretty to kill. Hamblin's final statement was that soon after the massacre he had met Lee in Fillmore and heard from him the story of the death of the two girls. This, he said, was when Lee was on his way to Great Salt Lake City to make his report to Brigham Young.

The original of "Military Orders No. 5," dated at Great Salt Lake City, September 14, has come into the hands of the writer recently. At the bottom of the handwritten page is a note in lead pencil by William H. Dame stating that these orders should be implicitly obeyed, and on the back another note, evidently by the filing clerk, "Rec'd Sept. 26/57 fr. Jacob Hamblin."

Since Lee had left his home in Harmony on September 20 and arrived in Salt Lake City on September 29, and since Hamblin, returning from the north, delivered this document in Parowan on September 26, they might well have met at Fillmore. Working as they did among the same bands of Indians, Lee as Indian farmer employed by the government, and Hamblin as president of the

Indian mission appointed by Brigham Young, it is natural that they would have discussed the massacre. The temperament of the two men was such that they had never, from the time the Indian missionaries first arrived, been on cordial or too friendly terms, so it is doubtful that Lee would have made an admission of murder to Hamblin. He would more naturally have blamed it to the Indians.

Lee denied ever having discussed the massacre with Hamblin. He had called him "dirty fingered Jake," and later was to brand him an "old fiend of hell," adding, "such a thing I never heard of before, let alone committing the awful deed."[10]

Perhaps the most reliable story is the one which was told by Jacob Hamblin's Indian boy, Albert, when he was questioned by Brevet Major J. H. Carleton in May, 1859. Albert was, at the time, about sixteen years old, and had lived in the home of Jacob Hamblin for nine years. His story of what happened at the massacre is vivid, but makes it entirely an Indian affair, with but few white men in the vicinity. He watched the killing along with Sam Knight's Indian boy, John, who, with him, was in charge of Hamblin's sheep. Regarding the murder of the two girls, he said:

> John and I could see where the Indians were hid in the oak bushes and sage right by the side of the road a mile or more on their route; and I said to John, I would like to know what the emigrants left their wagons for, as they were going into "a worse fix than ever

[10] John Doyle Lee, *Journals of John D. Lee,* (ed. by Charles Kelly), 242. Lee was writing to his wife Emma from the jail at Beaver on September 21, 1876, and said in part: "Six witnesses testified against me, four of whom perjured themselves by swearing falsehoods of the blackest character. Old Jacob Hamblin, the fiend of Hell, testified that I told him that two young women were found in a thicket where they had secreted themselves, by an Indian chief, who brought the girls to me and wanted to know what was to be done with them That I replied that they was too old to live and would give evidence and must be killed; the Indian said they were too pretty to kill, that one of them fell on her knees and said, Spare my life and I will serve you all my days, that I then cut her throat and the Indian killed the other. Such a thing I never heard of before, let alone committing the awful deed. The old hypocrite thought that now was his chance to reek his vengeance on me, by swearing away my life."

they saw." The women were on ahead with the children. The men were behind. Altogether 'twas a big crowd. Soon as they got to the place where the Indians were hid in the bushes each side of the road the Indians pitched right out onto them and commenced shooting them with guns and bows and arrows, and cut some of the men's throats with knives. The men run in every direction, the Indians after them, yelling and whooping. Soon as the women and children saw the Indians spring out of the bushes they all cried out so loud John and I heard them.

The women scattered and tried to hide in the bushes, but the Indians shot them down; two girls ran up the slope toward the east about a quarter of a mile, John and I ran down and tried to save them; the girls hid in some bushes. A man, who is an Indian doctor, also told the Indians not to kill them. The girls then came out and hung around him for protection, he trying to keep the Indians away. The girls were crying out loud. The Indians came up and seized the girls by their hands and their dresses and pulled and pushed them away from the doctor and then shot them. By this time it was dark, and the other Indians down by the road had got nearly through killing all the others. They were about half an hour killing the people from the time they first sprang upon them from the bushes.[11]

Whatever the details, the fact remains that the entire company was betrayed and murdered, an ugly fact that will not be downed. Certainly, when the facts are marshaled, there is not justification enough for the death of a single individual. Certainly, too, once it was over, all the participants were shocked and horrified at what had been done; somehow they had not taken into account how sickening human slaughter can be.

Perhaps all that happened that fateful afternoon can never come nearer to being understood than can some of the atrocities that were committed during the last war, not only among enemy nations, but, if one is to trust the reports of some of our finest boys, by our own soldiers in the heat of battle or under the strong emotional tensions caused by hate and revenge.

[11] 57 Cong. 1 sess., *House Document 605*, p. 6.

This is not an attempt to palliate the crime that was committed on Mountain Meadows, nor to condone it. In trying to understand it, one is led to think of other mass killings through the ages, most of them done in the name of God and in defense of religion. Even in free America, such groups as the Vigilantes of California and the Ku Klux Klan of the South have carried on lynchings and burnings, for what seemed to them to be the public good. If examples from the past were lacking, the recent world war would furnish others.

The people in southern Utah thought that they were at war and were in a state of extreme war hysteria. They believed, evidently, that it would be good strategy to strike the first blow. That their "enemies" were innocent civilians instead of soldiers was not important until after the deed was done. Scarcely was the massacre over before every man connected with it was ashamed of his part and certain of public condemnation. Criminal and innocent alike, each man wanted to save his own life and, if possible, his reputation as well.

7

Misgivings after the Fact

O NCE THE DEED was done, the dead stripped, the cattle rounded up and placed under guard, the Indians sent to their camp with some loot and beef, the participants had to devise ways to make this appear to have been an Indian massacre; that seemed the only way out.

Sometime during the night following, the commanders, William H. Dame and Isaac C. Haight, arrived together at Hamblin's ranch, where the sight of the crying, orphaned children made them more conscious of the enormity of the crime. Now neither of them wanted to assume the responsibility; each was determined to place the blame upon the other.

Klingonsmith's statement that they quarreled, and that "Haight told Colonel Dame, that if he was going to report the killing of said emigrants, he should not have ordered it done," is further borne out by the account of John D. Lee. The protest against reporting to their leader would indicate that Brigham Young did not know about, much less order, the massacre.

Lee makes a point of the fact that Haight seemed to be the dominating personality, in spite of Dame's superior military position. There was no suggestion that morning that Lee was the one upon whom the blame should rest; he was only carrying out orders. He records the incident of the quarrel thus:

> I soon learned that Col. Dame, Judge Lewis of Parowan, and Isaac C. Haight, with several others had arrived at the Hamblin Ranch in the night, but I do not know what time they got there.

Misgivings after the Fact

After breakfast we all went back in a body to the Meadows, to bury the dead and take care of the property that was left there. When we reached the Meadows we all rode up to that part of the field where the women were lying dead. The bodies of men, women and children had been stripped entirely naked, making the scene one of the most loathsome and ghastly that can be imagined.

Knowing that Dame and Haight had quarreled at Hamblin's that morning, I wanted to know how they would act in sight of the dead, who lay there as the result of their orders. I was greatly interested to know what Dame had to say, so I kept close to them, without appearing to be watching them.

Colonel Dame was silent for some time. He looked all over the field, and was quite pale, and looked uneasy and frightened. I thought then that he was just finding out the difference between giving and executing orders for wholesale killing. He spoke to Haight and said:

"I must report this matter to the authorities."

"How will you report it?" said Haight.

Dame said, "I will report it just as it is."

"Yes, I suppose so, and implicate yourself with the rest?" said Haight.

"No," said Dame. "I will not implicate myself, for I had nothing to do with it."

Haight then said, "That will not do, for you know a d——d sight better. You ordered it done. Nothing has been done except by your orders, and it is too late in the day for you to order things done and then go back on it, and go back on the men who carried out your orders. You cannot *sow pig* on me, and I will be d——d if I will stand it. You are as much to blame as any one, and you know that we have done nothing except what you ordered done. I know that I have obeyed orders, and by G——d I will not be lied on."

Colonel Dame was much excited. He choked up, and would have gone away, but he knew Haight was a man of determination, and would not stand any foolishness.

As soon as Colonel Dame could collect himself, he said:

"*I did not think there were so many of them, or I would not have had anything to do with it.*"

I thought it was now time for me to chip in, so I said:

111

"Brethren, what is the trouble between you? It will not do for our chief men to disagree."

Haight stepped up to my side, a little in front of me, and facing Colonel Dame. He was very mad, and said:

"The trouble is just this: Colonel Dame *counseled* and *ordered* me to do this thing, and now he wants to back out, and go back on me, and by G——d he shall not do it. He shall not lay it *all* on me. He cannot do it. He must not try to do it. I will *blow him to h——l* before he shall lay it all on me. He has got to stand up to what he did like a little man. He knows he ordered it done, and I dare him to deny it."

Colonel Dame was perfectly cowed. He did not offer to deny it again, but said:

"Isaac, I did not know there were so many of them."

"That makes no difference," said Haight, "you ordered me to do it, and you have got to stand up for your *orders*."[1]

In spite of Haight's accusations, it seems that Dame was able to clear himself, in part at least, of the responsibility. If the orders quoted by Higbee are genuine, and if he kept a copy, or if the original were preserved for the time of reckoning, he could show that he had ordered them specifically to "compromise with the Indians if possible by letting them take all the stock and go to their homes and let the company alone," and further, "I trust that you will have influence enough to restrain the Indians and save the company. If not possible, save the women and children at all hazards." The statement that they were not to precipitate a war with the Indians, he might argue, was only the same kind of advice that had been repeated to the missionaries since they first came to this section. If the orders seemed contradictory, he had not meant them to be, and his subordinates had misinterpreted them.

Sickened as he was by the sight of the dead on the field, Dame was more disturbed to arrive home the very next day and get the word carried back from President Young by James Haslam.

"Go in haste, and do not spare horseflesh," Haslam quoted his

[1] Lee, *Confessions*, 245–47.

leader as saying. "The emigrants must be protected if it takes all the men in southern Utah." He told his story to the people along the way where he changed horses, and is reported to have let some read the open letter which he carried. This letter, discussed at some length in chapter three, was definite in its orders not to meddle with emigrant trains.

With this word, Colonel Dame on Monday issued the following orders for trying to quiet the Indians:

HEADQUARTERS IRON MILITARY DISTRICT
PAROWAN, SEPT. 14, 1857

*To Majors, Commandants of Posts
and Captains of Companies*

You are required to use your influence to allay all excitement with the indians which they may have toward the emigrant and traveler, and assist in passing through the trains now upon the road, affording them what assistance may be necessary to secure a safe journey. They, of late, have manifested many signs of hostility toward the whites and passers-by. You will therefore send forward the best interpreters and clear the way by sending the Indians off the road, and guarding them through the different tribes now showing signs of hostility, and any property found among them should, if possible, be secured and returned to the owner which they have taken.

(Signed)   WM. H. DAME
Colonel Commanding Iron Military District.[2]

This indicates the problem facing the local Mormon leaders. Having been used as "the battle-ax of the Lord," having once been stirred up to kill and loot, the Indians knew no restraint. Every company on the road was in jeopardy, no matter how friendly they wished to be. Perhaps by following the accounts of those immediately behind the fated group, we can better understand conditions.

The account of George Powers, which was published in the

[2] "Parowan Ward Records" now in the files of the Latter-day Saints church historian. Entries are made by date.

Daily Alta California for October 24, 1857, after describing the general unrest and excitement throughout the territory, and the bitterness he had often heard expressed against the Fancher party, goes on to say:

> We laid by at Beaver several days, as the Bishop told us it was dangerous for so small a company as ours to go on. Our train consisted of only three wagons, and we were hurrying on to join the larger one.
>
> While waiting here, the train of Wm. Matthews and Sidney Tanner of San Bernardino came up, and I made arrangements to come on with them. We came on to Parowan and here we learned that the train ahead had been attacked by the Indians at Mountain Meadows, fifty miles from Parowan, and had returned upon their road five miles, to a spring, and fortified themselves. We then drove out of Parowan five or six miles and camped at what is called Summit.
>
> Next morning an express arrived from Mr. Dame, President of Parowan, requesting us not to proceed any further that day, if we pleased; also that Matthews and Tanner should returned to Parowan and bring me with them. We returned and a council was held, at which it was advised by Mr. Dame that I should go back to my own train, as they did not wish to have any strangers in their train. He also stated that at two o'clock that morning he had received an express from the train ahead saying that they were surrounded by Indians who had killed two or three of their number and asking for assistance.

This is another evidence that the military leaders were in close touch with what was going on at Mountain Meadows. Could the express which Powers reported have been the one carried by Haight and Higbee? Could it be that the decision to destroy all the train ahead was the reason for holding this one back until it was accomplished? The massacre happened the next day.

The Powers report continues:

> While we were talking, an express came from Beaver, saying that the Indians had attacked my train in the streets of that place, and were fighting when he left. One reason given was that ten miles the

other side of Beaver an emigrant train had shot an Indian, which greatly enraged them; that the people of Beaver went out in the night and brought the emigrants in and were followed by the Indians, who made the attack after their arrival.

A dictation given by Philo T. Farnsworth, of Beaver, and placed in the manuscript collection of Mormon material at the Bancroft Library gives an account of this episode which verifies the Powers report:

I was for several years captain of the militia and held that position at the time of the Mountain Meadows Massacre. When the Arkansas Company passed through Beaver I was in Salt Lake City and returned as the company that followed them was going through. This company had trouble and divided and its Captain Duke with a portion were left camped just below Beaver and a portion were left back in Indian Creek about six miles. After I got home that evening an Indian . . . came to me and told me the Indians intended to attack the company that was back on Mill Creek. I went to the captain of the company and told him of the intended attack and urged him to go back and bring the rest of the company and protect them. About 9 o'clock that evening he [sent?] the Captain to me and said his Company were so demoralized he could do nothing with them. I then got out ten men and finally five of his men joined them and I sent them under command of R. R. Rogers and before [they] had got to their camp the Indians had attempted to drive off their cattle and one of the guards had shot an Indian. My men helped them to hitch up and the company started for town. . . . About 2 o'clock in the morning some Indians came to me and wanted me to join them and get revenge. I told them to send their chief and I tried to pacify him. . . . when I was eating breakfast I heard shots and rushing out I saw the Capt. Duke, Turner, & Collins who had just passed my house and Turner and Collins were both wounded. I spoke to the Indians and ran between them and the men. . . . Later I got the Indians out of town and sent to Parowan for ten men to escort them on their way. . . .[3]

[3] From Utah Notes, a collection in the Bancroft Library, collected in 1884 under the supervision of Franklin D. Richards.
Another entry from this same collection is the dictation of Dr. John Ward

In the Los Angeles *Star* for October 24, 1857, is a story of this company written by a member of it, who concluded his account with the statement, "Two men in a train that joined them, Capt. Turner and Mr. Collins, were shot and seriously wounded while in the Mormon town of Beaver, by the Indians."

On the day before the massacre was consummated at the Meadows, the clerk of the Parowan Ward made the following entry in the "Ward Record Book":

Thursday Sept. 10, 1857   This day the Indians attacked a company of California emigrants at Beaver, wounding two of them. David Carter, who is a young man traveling with them from Provo, started for Parowan on a mule belonging to the emigrants, and got here (Parowan) in three hours, a distance of 35 or 40 miles. A company of nine men started from Parowan to the scene of the disturbance, but on arriving at Beaver found all quiet, the emigrants having made a treaty with the indians. They accordingly returned to Parowan the next day. When the emigrant train arrived at Parowan, Pres. Dame gave permission for trading provisions &c and they remained a day for that purpose. The emigrants were very much frightened for fear of the indians, and placed themselves almost entirely under the counsel and direction of Pres. Dame, seeking his counsel in everything.[4]

In the meantime, the Matthews-Tanner train, with the Powers group of three wagons, had been detained first in Parowan and then in Cedar City until after the massacre. They heard rumors

---

Christian. With reference to this company, he says: "My father-in-law, Wm Matthews was in a train of which Sidney Turner was capt. that contained some 20 men and they were stopped at Parowan by W. H. Dame Col of Militia, and told not to go beyond Summit until further orders on account of Indian troubles and when they were permitted to go they were ordered to go through Mountain Meadows in the night.

"The real reason of this was there were several Gentiles in the train and they did not want them to know what had occurred. This has been told me by several but some of them might deny it now."

4 See note 2 above.

of it and saw wagons hauled into Cedar City and Indians riding about with loot of tinware and clothing tied to their saddles. About a week after the massacre, they started for California, but saw nothing of the scene of carnage because they were guided past it in the night and ordered to stay with their wagons and keep moving. They rested two or three hours after they had passed the place, according to the Powers story, and hurried on to camp on the Santa Clara River the next night, near the village of Chief Jackson, who had taken such an active part in the recent massacre.

Since both Matthews and Tanner were Mormons who had carried on a regular freighting business between Great Salt Lake City and San Bernardino, the Indians knew them and were friendly toward them. But Powers and Warn they called "Mericats" in such a threatening manner that Matthews advised them all to get out of there as soon as possible. Tanner, however, said that he would not go a step without Ira Hatch as guide, since he had more influence with the Indians than anyone else in that part of the country. Hatch agreed to go ahead and pacify the Muddy Indians. Here the company met him again, in company with the two Young brothers, and here they learned that the Indians had killed the two men who had left the emigrant company before the massacre at Mountain Meadows.

At Las Vegas they found another band of Indians, also eager to join in the war. "The chief asked our interpreter whether our captain had brought him no word from Brigham Young, whether he was nearly ready to fight the Americans yet; adding that he was ready, had got his arrows poisoned, etc.," Powers reported.

Two days before they reached San Bernardino, they were overtaken by the mail and with it the Mormon, Bill Hyde, who told the story of the emigrant record book in the hands of Chief Jackson, already mentioned. This whole group arrived in San Bernardino on the first day of October, and immediately the clerk of the Mormon mission, Richard R. Hopkins, recorded that:

They reported a dreadful massacre of about one hundred and

eighteen emigrants by the Indians at Mountain Meadows. The party from the states were enroute to California. The brethren were afraid it would create an influence against the Saints as the massacre would be attributed to them.[5]

The word spread like wildfire; delegations were sent to Los Angeles and El Monte, and public indignation meetings were held to decide whether or not to do anything about it. On October 5, the mission clerk reported that apostates and other enemies were trying to get volunteers to go back and learn the particulars, a threat which spent itself in angry talk. The news spread throughout California, renewing itself in waves of horror as succeeding companies brought in added detail. Within two months, word had reached the cities of the East; the Washington *Globe* of November 19 made reference to it as having been published earlier.

The second company to pass over the southern route after the massacre was the one already referred to as being attacked by Indians at Beaver. It has been variously called the Duke train, the Collins-Turner company, the Duke and Turner train, and the Honea and Davis train. From their own account, the company had divided into three units before it arrived at Beaver; but after the trouble there, they joined forces for mutual protection, to separate again in crossing the desert. They arrived in San Bernardino in several sections, a few days apart.

This company, about a week behind the Matthews and Turner wagons, was piloted by the Mormons on a new route which bypassed Mountain Meadows. By this time, not only the sight of the disinterred bodies, but the stench which permeated the whole area would be reason for avoiding the road, especially with so large a group of non-Mormons. The route traveled approximates the present highway from Cedar City to Santa Clara, but this was the first wagon train to go over it, and the first company of any

[5] George William Beatty and Helen Pruitt Beatty, *Heritage of the Valley*, 280. The *Los Angeles Star*, October 9, 1857, made the first published report.

size since Parley P. Pratt and his exploring party had marked it out during the winter of 1849–50.

Thus, having missed the scene of the massacre, the Duke companies added little to the knowledge of the Californians on that score, but they had their own troubles and losses to relate.

By this time, Colonel Dame's orders to quiet the Indians had gone out, and there was some effort made to put them into effect. The natives, however, thought the war with the Mericats was just getting well underway, a war which might yield much loot for them. The Mormons had taken such pains to impress them with the fact that a war was on and that they were to be a part of it that they viewed every emigrant train with expectant interest. An abrupt change of policy would be hard for them to accept.

On September 14, the very day that Colonel Dame issued the orders to send the Indians off the road and "any property found among them should, if possible, be secured and returned to the owner which they have taken," Brigham Young wrote a letter outlining the plans of operation for the next spring. With it he sent also the governor's official declaration of martial law. The order "to save life always when it is possible, we do not wish to shed a drop of blood if it can be avoided," was perhaps made more emphatic because of Haslam's visit just four days earlier and his report of the then threatened massacre.

The plan outlined by the Mormon leader was one of guerrilla warfare, of hiding food and moving families to the mountains, of burning everything before the approaching army; "waylay our enemies, attack them from ambush, stampede their animals, take the Supply trains. . . . To waste away our enemies and lose none, that will be our mode of warfare," the letter advised.[6]

[6] The full text of Brigham Young's letter to Willam H. Dame follows:
"GREAT SALT LAKE CITY
SEPT. 14, 1857
"COL. WM. H. DAME
"PAROWAN, IRON CO.
"Herewith you will receive the Governor's Proclamation, declaring Martial Law. You will probably not be called out this fall, but are required to continue

According to legend, Jacob Hamblin carried this letter also, but again we are faced with a difference of dates. As has been noted earlier, Hamblin's handwritten diary says that he arrived at the Meadows on September 18. In his interview with Brevet Major J. H. Carleton two years later, Hamblin gave the same date for his arrival home. Being a man with a reputation for veracity, he might be expected to tell the truth here. As other evidence, Mr. Charles Kelly claims to have an original diary in which the writer notes that on September 19, "Mr. Hamblin" passed from the Meadows toward Cedar City with a wagonload of loot. There is

---

to make ready for a big fight another year. The plan of operations is supposed to be about these. In case the U. S. Government should send out an overpowering force, we intend to desolate the Territory and conceal our families, Stock, and all our effects in the fastnesses of the mountains, where they will be safe while the men, waylay our enemies, attack them from ambush, stampede their animals, take the Supply trains cut off detachments, and parties sent to the Kanyons for wood, or on other service. To lay waste to everything that will burn, houses, fences, trees, fields, grass, that they cannot find a particle of any thing that will be of use to them, not even sticks to make a fire for to cook their suppers. To waste away our enemies and lose none, that will be our mode of warfare. Thus you see the necessity of preparing, first secure places in the mountains where they cannot find us, or if they do where they cannot approach in any force; and then prepare for our families building some cabins cacheing flour and grain. Flour should be ground in the latter part of winter or early in the Spring in order to keep. Sow grain in your fields early as possible this fall so that the harvest of another year may come off before they have time to get here. Conciliate the Indians and make them our fast friends.

"In regard to letting people pass, or travel through the Territory, this applies to all strangers and suspected persons. Yourself and Bro. Isaac C. Haight in your district are authorized to give such permits. Examine all such persons strictly before giving them permits to pass, Keep things perfectly quiet and let all things be done peacefully but with firmness and let there be no excitement. Let the people be united in their feelings and faith as well as works and keep alive the spirit of the Reformation, and what we said in regard to saving the grain and provisions, we say again let there be no waste, save life always when it is possible, we do not wish to shed a drop of blood if it can be avoided. This course will give us great influence abroad.

"BRIGHAM YOUNG

"DANIEL H. WELLS

The above letter is from the "Church Letter Book, No. 3," pp. 858–60. It is reproduced in the court records at Beaver, Utah, in the transcript of the trials of John D. Lee in the Huntington Library, and in Lee's *Confessions*, 315.

the possibility, however, that this could refer to Jacob's brother, Oscar Hamblin, who was with Lee at the massacre.

On the other hand, Jesse N. Smith, in a carefully-kept daily diary, records that he was on his way from Parowan to Great Salt Lake City, "Friday the 25th [1857] Met Jacob Hamblin who had a copy of Governor Cummings Proclamation."

The original copy of "Orders No. 5," which bears on its back the notation that it was received in Parowan from Jacob Hamblin on September 26, has already been mentioned. That would put him at the Meadows on the twenty-eighth instead of the eighteenth.

The importance of the date lies in the fact that it bears upon the fortunes of the Duke company of emigrants, which was attacked in Beaver on September 10 and robbed of its cattle on October 7, on the crossing of the Muddy, or lower Virgin River. Just where these emigrants spent the four weeks between those two points is not known, but, having a large herd of cattle, they must have moved slowly and stopped whenever feed would justify it, perhaps for days.

Whatever the date, Hamblin arrived to learn that the natives were following the company with another massacre in mind. He at once dispatched two of the missionaries, Dudley Leavitt and Sam Knight, to overtake the Duke company and prevent another Indian attack. It is interesting to note that Hamblin's *Autobiography*, published in 1881, does not give the same picture of this venture as does his handwritten diary, now in the archives of the Latter-day Saints church historian. The manuscript account begins in the middle of a sentence, because of the one missing leaf just preceding.

> . . . with and, if possible get them to let the company pass uninterrupted. They told me that the Indians in the south were determined to have a spoil upon the first opportunity, and that several of the brethren of the mission had gone with the company but they thought it would be impossible to get them through with their stock. I told them to do the best they could. . . .

After describing conditions at his home and telling of his visit to the scene of the massacre, he mentions the Duke company thus:

... within a day or two bro. Dudley Levett came in from the Muddy and told me that the Indians had robbed the company (previously spoken of) of near 300 head of cattle. They made their descent upon the train 7 miles west of the Muddy by moonlight and by taking advantage of the deep ravines they completed the design. The missionaries went with the cattle and indians according to the instructions given bro. Levett to prevent further outbreaks. The breathren saved nearly 100 head of cows from being destroyed and wasted by the indians, and brought them to the Mountain Meadows.

This policy of robbing the passing emigrant was clearly a part of the general war tactics, since, for the time being, all "Mericats" were considered enemies. It was the same thing Lot Smith and his men were doing to the government trains in the north. Although Brigham Young's letter outlined the plan of procedure for the next spring, they might see no harm in proceeding at once to "waylay our enemies, attack them from ambush, stampede their animals." Besides, all the emigrant trains which passed through this section came in the late fall and winter.

Since the two accounts are quite typical of the suppressions in the writing of Mormon history, this episode deserves, perhaps, some attention. For while at the time Hamblin admits freely that "the missionaries went with the cattle and indians according to the instructions," his *Autobiography* says solemnly that "the brethren remained with the company, determined to assist in its defense, should the Indians attempt anything more than they had agreed." Nor is any mention made of cattle being brought to his ranch at Mountain Meadows. The inference, instead, is that all the stock remained in the hands of the Indians and more than a hundred miles away on the Muddy, for the *Autobiography* says:

As soon as possible, I talked with the principal Indians engaged in this affair, and they agreed that the stock not killed should be given up. I wrote to the owners in California, and they sent their agent, Mr. Lane, with whom I went to the Muddy, and the stock was delivered to him as the Indian had agreed.[7]

A single sentence in the middle of a letter from Brigham Young makes one wonder how much that leader might know of this affair. The cattle were taken in late September, 1857; Jacob wrote, evidently asking advice as to what to do with them, on February 16, 1858; the answer from President Young was dated the following March 5. "In regard to the cattle you should control them and use them for the best interest of both the missionaries and the Indians," the letter reads.[8] What cattle? Those taken at the massacre were in the care of John D. Lee.

[7] The account as given by James A. Little, in his *Jacob Hamblin, Personal Narrative*, varies from the diary to the extent that it seems worth while to present the published version for comparison. Beginning on page 46, it reads:

"At Cedar City I found Brother Samuel Knight and Dudley Leavitt.

"As I was weary with hard riding and want of sleep, I hurried them on after the emigrants, while I traveled more slowly. I instructed these men to make every possible effort to save the company and their effects, and to save their lives at all hazards.

"They overtook the company one hundred and fifty miles from Cedar City, on Muddy Creek, in the heart of the Indian country. They found a large body of excited Indians preparing to attack and destroy them.

"Finding it altogether impossible to control the Indians, they compromised the matter. The Indians agreed to only take the loose stock of the company, and not to meddle with the teams and wagons, and not to make any effort to take their lives.

"The Indians took the loose stock, amounting to four hundred and eighty head, on the fifty mile desert, beyond the Muddy.

"*The brethren remained with the company, determined to assist in its defense, should the Indians attempt anything more than they had agreed* [italics supplied].

"The company continued their journey safely to California. Brothers Knight and Leavitt returned to Santa Clara.

"As soon as possible, I talked with the principal Indians engaged in this affair, and they agreed that the stock not killed should be given up. I wrote to the owners in California, and they sent their agent, Mr. Lane, with whom I went to the Muddy, and the stock was delivered to him as the Indians had agreed."

[8] Original owned by Mrs. Mary Hamblin Beeler, Mesa, Arizona. This seems another example of the habit of Brigham Young to insert the really vital part of a message in the heart of the letter:

Concerning the return of the cattle to their owner, a letter written by Zadok K. Judd, bishop at Santa Clara, makes one question Hamblin's statement that he took the initiative in contacting the emigrants and the Indians. Judd's letter bore the heading, "Ft. Clara, Feb. 10, 1859," and added as a postscript:

Mr. Lane, one of the emigrant stockowners that was robbed by the Indians just when leaving the Muddy (it was said by them that the Mormons had a hand in it) has been here and found 25 head of his cattle which the Indians left here a year ago last fall. Mr. Lane went away feeling well.[9]

"PRESIDENT'S OFFICE
GREAT SALT LAKE CITY
MARCH 5, 1858

"ELDER JACOB HAMBLIN
DEAR BROTHER:

"Your note of the 19th last month came to hand on the 3rd inst. I am happy to learn of the success and the general prosperity of the mission and trust that the genial and salutary influences, now so rapidly extending to the various tribes in that region, may continue to spread abroad until it shall pervade ever son and daughter of Abraham in their fallen condition; the hour of their redemption draws nigh, and the time is not far distant when they will receive a knowledge, and begin to rise and increase in the land and become a people whom the Lord will delight to own and bless.

In regard to the cattle you should control them and use them for the best interest of both the missionaries and the Indians [italics supplied]; the Indians should be encouraged in keeping and taking care of stock. I highly approve of your designs in doing your farming through the natives; it learns them to obtain a subsistence by their own industry and leaves you more at liberty to visit others and extend your missionary labors among them. A few missionaries to show, and learn them to raise stock and grain, and then not eat it up for them is most judicious, and you should always be careful to impress upon them that they should not infringe upon the rights of others; and our brethren should be very careful not to infringe upon their rights in any particular—thus cultivating honor and good principles in their midst by example as well as precept.

"I wish all missionaries to aid and assist Brother Amasa all they can in his explorations.

"As ever, I remain your Brother in the Gospel of Salvation

"BRIGHAM YOUNG"

The above letter, except for the part of the sentence in italics, is reproduced in Little, *Jacob Hamblin*, 51–52. The omission is possibly significant.

[9] This letter is found in the "Journal History of the Church," under date of February 10, 1859.

Twenty-five of more than three hundred head of cattle stolen is not a large proportion. Perhaps the missing animals had already been used for the "best interest of both the missionaries and the Indians," as the letter nearly a year earlier had advised.

After being relieved of their cattle, the Duke train made their way across the desert, again separating into a number of small units. The vanguard arrived at San Bernardino on October 17, and asked for relief to be sent back to the members on the road who were suffering for lack of provisions. While some loaded wagons with food and started back on their errand of mercy, their neighbors took statements from two of those first to arrive, S. B. Honea of Franklin County, Arkansas, and George B. Davis. Their report of conditions in Utah added fuel to the flame of anger in California.

Honea said that he passed through Great Salt Lake City on August 17, that he saw everywhere preparations for war, that the company were harassed by Indians all the way, that in southern Utah they hired Mormon guides and interpreters to the sum of

It is interesting also to compare the report of J. H. Carleton, brevet major, United States Army, of his interview with Hamblin in early 1859. In this, the number of cattle supposed to have been taken is much smaller than was admitted earlier:

". . . I [Jacob Hamblin] got a horse at Beaver about 8 o'clock that evening, and the next evening at Pinto Creek, 83 miles distant, I met Mr. Dudley Leavett, from the settlements on the Santa Clara.

"I told him what I had heard. He told me it was true, and that all the Indians in the southern country were greatly excited and "all hell" could not stop them from killing or from at least robbing the other train of its stock. He further stated that several interpreters from the Santa Clara had gone on with this last train. I told him to return and get the best animal he could find at my ranch and go on as fast as he could and endeavor to stop further mischief being done. That if the Indians ran off the stock of the train, for himself and all the interpreters to go and recover it, if possible, and prevent further depredation. He left me under these instructions. . . .

"The train I sent Leavett to protect had gotten as far as the canyon, 5 miles beyond the Muddy, when the Indians made a descent upon its loose stock, driving off, as the immigrants have since said, 280 head of cattle. Leavett and the other interpreters recovered between 75 and 100 head, which were brought back to my ranch. Of these, the Indians afterwards demanded and stole some 40 head, and last January I turned over to a Mr. Lane from California the balance."

The above is found in 57 Cong., 1 sess., *House Document 605*, p. 6.

$1,810, and then were robbed on the Muddy of 375 head of cattle. Davis described the Indians who stole the cattle as having among them some with light, fine hair and blue eyes, and light streaks where they had not used sufficient paint. He gave the number of cattle taken as 326 head, and mentioned the Duke and Turner train as one company. The advance group "consisted of 71 souls: men 22, women 17, children 32. The second division of this train, under the supervision of Capt. Nicholas Turner of Missouri, is expected to arrive here in the course of five or six days. It consists of 10 men, 5 women, and 14 children."

The next story to appear in California papers regarding the situation in Utah was signed by John Aiken. He said that he arrived in Great Salt Lake City on September 20, where he received a pass, dated September 21, 1857, from Daniel H. Wells to insure his safe passage through the territory. This pass was endorsed by William H. Dame in Parowan on September 28. Aiken traveled with John Hunt, the mail carrier, but with no assurance of protection. As they passed over the field where the bodies of the murdered emigrants lay in a state of nudity and putrefaction, he remarked that:

> I saw about twenty wolves feasting upon the carcasses of the murdered. Mr. Hunt shot at a wolf, they ran a few rods and halted. I noticed that the women and children were more generally eaten by the wild beasts than were the men.[10]

He noticed also the tracks of a large herd of cattle going up the Santa Clara creek bed toward the Mormon settlement, and judged that the herd contained upwards of three hundred head.

The third large group of emigrants to pass through the southern settlements was the train of Livingston and Bell, merchants. They were the first to view the massacre ground, since the Matthews-Turner train had been taken over the area in the night, and the Duke train had been guided around the place on a new route.

---

[10] Affidavit of John Aiken made before Marcus Kate, Notary Public, San Bernardino, California, November 24, 1857.

The experiences of this company were recorded by two different people: John L. Ginn, of the Livingston group, wrote a detailed account of the trip some forty-six years later, and Jacob Hamblin, the Mormon guide for the company, kept a brief diary of the journey.

Ginn says that Hamblin joined the train at Fillmore; Hamblin says that he acted as guide from Pinto, some three days' travel farther south:

> I started to Cedar City with a beef for the purpose of purchasing flour for my family that I with others, might visit the Moquitch Indians east of the Colorado river. At Pinto Creek I met Isaac C. Haight with Mr. Bell of the firm of Livingston, Kinkead & Co. and other merchants enrout for California.
>
> Br. Haight had instructions from Gov. Young to call on me as a guide for the company, requesting me to use my best endeavors to get them and their effects safe through.[11]

Isaac C. Haight made a journal entry which would seem to bear Hamblin out:

> November 1857. . . . at the request of Prest. Young went and employed an Indian interpreter to go to San Bernardino with some gentile merchants and apostates to see them safe through to California.[12]

Ginn's story reads like a Wild West thriller. He tells how at Fillmore they were accosted by a tall, blanketed Indian who scrutinized them closely and then struck off across the country in a long trot. A little later they were stopped by "some 400 Indians all well armed, nearly every man having a gun of some sort," and, but for the intervention of the son of a Mormon bishop and a friendly Indian named Canosh, they might have been extermi-

[11] Original diary of Jacob Hamblin in the archives of the Latter-day Saints church historian, Salt Lake City, Utah.

[12] Diary of Isaac C. Haight. Copies are in the Utah State Historical Society files and in the Washington County library, St. George, Utah.

nated then and there. Certainly a band of four hundred well-armed Indians might have challenged any company on the road. Both writers describe the scene at the Meadows, though Hamblin's description is that made when he visited the place just a week after the massacre took place, whereas Ginn's description is based on what he remembered seeing in mid-November. Hamblin says:

> I went to the place of slaughter! Where those unfortunate people were slain. Oh! horrible, indeed was the sight—language fails to picture the scene of blood and carnage. The slain, numbering over one hundred men, women and children, had been intered by the inhabitants of Cedar City. At three places the wolves had disintered the bodies and stripped the bones of their flesh, had left them strewed in every direction. At one place I noticed nineteen wolves pulling out the bodies and eating the flesh.

This corresponds rather closely to John Aiken's story, already referred to, though Aiken passed the place early in October. But Ginn tells solemnly how:

> When we passed over the grounds, about three weeks after the slaughter, the bodies were still well preserved, and most of them lay just as they had fallen, each wound that had caused death being immediately over the corresponding pool of coagulated blood on the ground. The eye of all who had fallen upon side or back had been picked out by the crows, but otherwise none of the bodies has been mutilated or disfigured by decay, the weather being cold, with a few patches of snow on the ground.[13]

This, on the face of it, is the sheerest nonsense. By his own statement, Ginn's company did not leave Great Salt Lake City until November 7, nearly two months after the massacre, and from their own chronology they were ten or eleven days on the

[13] This manuscript is owned by Mrs. Emma Shepard of the Shepard Book Store, Salt Lake City, Utah. Copies also in the archives of the Latter-day Saints church historian and in the Coe Collection, Harvard University.

road. So instead of arriving at Mountain Meadows three weeks after the massacre, they were there really eight or ten weeks later. Anyone who knows anything at all of the progress of putrefaction in the human corpse knows that a body lying in the open sunshine for one day would become bloated and discolored; after eight weeks, it would be a fleshless skeleton, even if it were undisturbed by wild animals. In southern Utah, in September and October, the sun is bright and warm all day, and while the nights may see slight frosts in the upper areas, there would not be freezing sufficient to preserve bodies, even in midwinter. By November there might be snow on the ground, but only patches. Nor are the coyotes and wolves and buzzards so discriminating as to leave such fare untouched.

Ginn's description proceeds, clearly written for effect, with an account of a tall, handsome woman, a beautiful little girl whose hand still clasped her mother's, and a venerable old man, evidently the grandfather of the child, who all lay in this state of perfect preservation, exactly as they had fallen. Later he did admit that a number of bodies had been thrown into a pit, from which the wolves had dragged them, and in the process had mutilated them to some extent.

Both narrators tell of taking Chief Tutsegabit along to help control the Indians; both tell of the camp on the Santa Clara, where Jacob says there were about a hundred Indians and Ginn says there were one hundred and fifty. Both relate how stolen items were returned to the company by order of Hamblin.

On the Muddy, where the Duke company had lost their cattle, this group also seemed due for trouble. Ginn says:

... There were 500 warriors at the Muddy, and as they knew of our coming they had made every preparation to kill us before we reached the ford. This tribe had two chiefs, Isaac and Thomas, of apparently equal authority, and two Mormon missionaries were stopping there to instruct them in Mormonism and agriculture. The whole tribe, armed with buck-horn bows and arrows (with which they could shoot sixty yards with great accuracy and deadly effect), had been distributed for a mile or more along the roadside concealed in a jungle of tules and willows. Hamblin had reached there in time, explained matters to Isaac and Thomas, and they decided to let us pass, sending out runners to call the Indians in from their ambuscade. As we descended the mountain overlooking the valley we could see the runners darting from place to place through the tules, and every now and then a band of 40 or 50 Indians would rise up, strike the road and proceed on foot to the ford, to which we drove and encamped till the next forenoon.

. . . During the early hours, at least of that evening all of the 500 bucks and many of their squaws remained with us. We fed them well, and then got them to sing and dance for us.[14]

One wonders how a traveling train could have along enough provisions to feed five hundred hungry Indians "well" without seriously depleting its own stock. Hamblin's account speaks of "a few Indians" who were fed some mush. Of more significance is his suggestion of Mormon activity and general policy during the short time preceding, when there was serious talk of war. He says:

We persued our journey as far as the Muddy without molestation or interruption. Here I found two brethren from Cedar City who had been sent there to learn the Indians to cultivate the earth. For some cause a plan had been laid and matured in their minds to kill off this company and take the spoil. I told them the instructions I had from Gov. Young; but they held out the idea to me that there was secret instructions that I knew nothing of—we had much talk upon this subject—I felt vexed at the course that had been taken, and I told them that words were to convey ideas, and that I had written instructions from Brigham Young to take this company through safe, and that I would stand by them to the last.

A few Indians came to our camp that evening—we made them some mush and I got them to dance by joining with them.

Both writers tell of finding the two Mormon missionaries, Dud-

14 *Ibid.*

ley Leavitt and Ira Hatch, at Las Vegas; both relate how the Indians there tried to make Hamblin believe these men were killed. Hamblin's concern for them was genuine, since both were his friends, Leavitt his brother-in-law, and they had gone to visit these hostile natives upon the "call" of Hamblin himself. Ginn, on the other hand, pictures the Vegas Indians as ready for an attack upon his train and held in check only by the influence of these Mormon missionaries.

Hamblin accompanied the travelers as far as the Mohave, but did not go on to San Bernardino. He had been warned that with the feeling there, his life would be in danger, for his name was connected with the robbery of the Duke train, if not with the massacre. On his return trip, he stopped again with the missionaries on the Muddy, and again he registered a protest against the policies that were being carried out among the Indians. As president of the southern Indian mission, he was responsible for the conduct of Indian affairs; as military commander of the area, Haight had sent these men to work with the natives in carrying out the war policies. With Zion standing against the world, and with the Indians as allies, they were prepared to prey upon every passing emigrant company as part of their contribution to the war.

These men [the missionaries] had counseled the indians to gather to the road at the crossing of the Muddy but as they had no means of subsistence I considered it a poor policy.

I then hurried home and sent Bro. Hatch to manage the affairs at that place. Shortly after, I sent Bro. Haskel to assist Bro. Hatch on the Muddy as the indians were very troublesome, and as there was many travelling through there that were not acquainted with the indians, it was hard to restrain them from robbing and plundering. These two brethren remained at the Muddy until the last of February. This was a very arduous task and hard to be endured and it tried the faith and patience of these two men, but they endured it without a murmur. . . .

Hamblin does not give the names of the two missionaries from

Cedar City who were at the Muddy. Many writers concerned with this period speak of Hatch as being stationed on the Muddy during the time of the Indian depredations, but it is clear that he was not there until after the change of policy went into effect. Commodore Perry Liston tells that he himself was there, serving in a military capacity:

> 1857   Late in the fall I and Brother Jehiel McConnell were called to the Muddy or Ma-pat-pah river—meaning muddy water. Here we labored to get the Indians to cease killing the Americans, for they had become much infuriated at the abuse of this emigrant company [—] they threatened our lives. . . . We returned to our families in the spring. While we were wintering on the Muddy, Johns[t]on's army wintered in the deep snow at Fort Bridger. Many of our brethren were out in the snow, watching the troops and their movements. My brother-in-law M. F. Farnsworth was one who toiled in the north while we toiled in the South to pre-serve peace.[15]

The fact that an Iowan, William Clark, who passed through the area in late December and arrived at Las Vegas on New Year's Day, 1858, says definitely that "the Mormons had two mission-aries, McConnel and Liston," further identifies them. Amasa Lyman and other Mormons returning from San Bernardino reported how precarious the situation of Hatch was, there alone, and sug-gested that Haskell be sent to help him manage the natives. Hatch told his experiences of this "mission" to James A. Little, who wrote the official report of it for the church.[16]

The next account of the Indians of the south and their activities during this period comes from William Wall, a Mormon mission-ary who had gone to Australia in 1856 and was returning to Utah with a group of converts. They landed during the time of great-est excitement in California, and to judge from the reports in the

[15] Perry Liston, "Journal." Copies in the Washington County library and the Utah State Historical Society.

[16] This is on file in the office of the Latter-day Saints church historian under title of "Mission to the Muddy in 1858," by James A. Little.

California papers, there were some attempts to prevent their coming on to Utah.[17] They left San Bernardino with the mail carrier, Griff Williams, and arrived in Great Salt Lake City on December 3.

Wall reports that at Las Vegas they found a band of Indians who insisted upon knowing their religious affiliations before they would be friendly. At the Muddy Valley, the old chief Isaac said that "the Mormons could pass there whenever they pleased, but the Merikats had shot his men and killed them and he intended to kill the Merikats. He said 'Tell Brigham to speak to God for me, for I don't want to be sick. . . .' "[18]

[17] The Los Angeles correspondence of the *Daily Alta California*, October 27, 1857, says: "Just while we were greatly interested in the report of these outrages, there arrived at San Pedro, a vessel from Australia, with over seventy converts, the fruits of the labors of a fellow named Wall, who is recognized by persons here as a danite from Fillmore, and as they say, one of the biggest rascals alive. He came to town the night of the meeting and remained until morning, when he was waited upon by a committee (self constituted) who greeted him in such a decided manner that he was glad to escape, declaring that he had too much regard for his own life to endanger it by remaining here."

[18] "Journal History of the Church," December 12, 1857, quoting William Wall: ". . . Nothing of importance occurred until we reached Las Vegas, we found a few Indians there. We there fell in with 40 or 50 Indians, they seemed friendly as soon as they found who we were but they inquired very particularly into our religious tenets. As I could talk rather the best Indian in the crowd they directed their conversations more particularly to me. I had no difficulty in convincing them that Bros. Knowlton, Miles and myself were Mormons, but the balance they said might be Mormon papooses (children) but there was not much Mormon in them, showing on their fingernails how much.

"We then came on to the Muddy, the company went on ahead, leaving Mr. Williams and myself with the mail. They reached the Muddy a little before day, when the Indians discovered them, one got upon the hill and cried 'Merikats' (Americans). The squaws ran in every direction but we soon arrived with the mail an Indian also arrived there from the Rio Virgin; by that time they had surrounded the party and seemed pretty savage, but when they learned from this Indian who we were they treated us very friendly. Some of the children stole some few articles. One of the Indians stole a pistol from us and Isaac the chief of the Rio Virgin made him give it up. An Indian overtook us about half way across the desert with it. Isaac traveled with us about half way up the Rio Virgin to his home. He told us to tell Brigham that he had not stolen anything from the Mormons, he paused a little, and then said, rather reluctantly, nor from the Merikats neither, and that he did not intend to steal anything from the Mormons as they had never interrupted him. He said that the Mormons could

The mail carrier, Williams, prepared to return at once with the mail to the coast. With him went several Mormons, and at least three young Gentiles, Edwin Leach, Martin Sherwood, and William Clark. These young men had come west with the supply trains for Johnston's army, en route for Utah. Their employing company, Russell, Majors, and Waddell, had discharged them and paid them off when the winter weather forced the army into winter quarters. Despite all warnings and all orders to return to the East, the young men determined to make their way through Utah to California.

William Clark evidently kept a record of this trip, which was amplified and published in the *Iowa Journal of History and Politics* for April, 1922. He gives a good picture of conditions among the Mormon soldiers and their attitude toward the United States Army.

Colonel Johnston had forbidden anyone going into Salt Lake City, and had his pickets out five miles.

The Mormons had twenty-five hundred soldiers stationed between here and the city. There was no other way of going except through the Mormon camps. . . .

This was about the middle of November and very cold weather. . . .

After supper Captain Maxwell, a Mormon officer, with twenty-eight men came riding up, and ordered us to saddle up and go with them and be quick about it too. . . . So we packed our ponies, mounted, and rode six miles as fast as our ponies could go . . . to the Mormon camp where there were two or three hundred men. . . .

Here they amused us for some time by asking questions. We answered them as we thought best. Finally, when bed time came, they sang some of their Mormon songs and had prayer. But such a prayer I never heard before. They prayed for the destruction of Johnston's army and for the torture of all Gentiles—not excepting the present company even. . . .

---

pass there whenever they pleased, but the Merikats had shot his men and killed them and he intended to kill the Merikats. He said 'Tell Brigham to speak to God for me, for I don't want to be sick.' "

Next morning they sent five men with us to their big camp at the entrance of Echo Canyon. The road ran close to the rocks and wound along the stream. The Mormons had stone fortifications all along on top of the mountains. They could get behind these and shoot the soldiers as they passed through. It was a very strong position.

The Mormons were armed with every conceivable kind of guns from a toy pistol up.

They had prayer here also before retiring.

These were the poorest specimens of humanity that I had ever seen together, nearly all English, Danes, and Welch. And such clothing! It was impossible to tell what the original goods were.

Remnants of old bed quilts and blankets served as over-coats. They were a set of bigots—claimed that they could whip the whole world, and that Johnston's army would not be a breakfast spell for them, as they had the Lord on their side to help fight their battles.

Clark goes on to give details of the stop in Great Salt Lake City and the arrangements they made to go on through to California with the mail. Quite a number of teams from the settlements en route joined them, to travel together for their common safety on the road.

His account of the massacre might have been gathered from the group as they traveled or pieced together from subsequent information; like others, he claimed to be one of the first company to pass over the ground after the tragedy.

. . . We were the first train that ever passed over this ground after that wholesale murder, and we gentiles were ordered to stay close to our wagons and not be looking around, as it would not be safe for us if we did. But I counted eighteen skeletons close to the road, mostly of women and children with the hair still on their skulls. . . .

He named Bishop Higbee and President Haight, of Cedar City, and John D. Lee, of Harmony, as the leaders of the massacre and gave the number killed as 132, with 17 children saved.

After giving some details of the trip through Santa Clara and the sending of Indian runners ahead to the Muddy where "the Mormons had two missionaries, McConnel and Liston," Clark describes the journey on to Las Vegas. He tells also of the cattle-stealing episode, and, aside from the fact that he is not clear on his geography, gives it with fair accuracy.

> . . . This was the Crooks, Cooper, and Collin's train. They had been very careful not to arouse the Mormons, and had hired Ira Hatch and another interpreter, the two best in Utah, to guide them through and pacify the Indians. They piloted this train through by way of Old Harmony, instead of over the massacre ground.
>
> While that train was moving up this ravine the Indians charged down on them and drove off all of their loose stock, about one hundred head. The men were going to protect themselves, and their property, and there were enough to have done so, their being sixty in the train, but the interpreters ordered them not to or they would all be killed; but let the Indians have their stock and not get into a fight with them, and they would go and get the stock back. They took their advice and Hatch and the other man went off with the cattle but never returned. The Company paid the interpreters one hundred dollars apiece in advance, and now they had lost their stock in the bargain. . . .
>
> We arrived at the Vegas Springs on January first, 1858. Three or four of us took a bath in this spring on New Year's Day. . . .
>
> We drove into San Bernardino, arriving there on the thirteenth day of January, 1858.

Other companies may have passed through Utah over the southern route in the fall of 1857 of which no records were kept nor mention was made by the California papers. As was noted in chapter three, the "Journal History of the Mormon Church" lists companies arriving in Great Salt Lake City on August 3, 4, and 5, with the notation that the one on August 3 "had a large drove of cattle," and that the one on August 5 was "a very large company of emigrants." Others followed on August 10, 11, and 28. From those who passed over the southern route, word went in to California of the massacre and of conditions in the territory, drawing threats of violence from the citizens and suggestions that they raise an army to come against Utah.

These developments had a profound effect upon the military strategy of the Mormon leaders. Whereas during August and early September they had exhorted their people to *"Stand up and fight! Defend your homes and firesides! We have been driven for the last time, and with God's help we shall never be driven again!"* now quite suddenly they began to declaim, *"Flee to the wilderness! Hide in the fastnesses of the hills! Burn all before the enemy!"*

With this new policy, the status of the Indians in the war was entirely changed. No longer must they be used as "the battle-ax of the Lord"; they must be controlled for the safety of the Mormon colonists and restrained from molesting traveling parties. The work of the missionaries carried on so patiently for more than three years had been almost entirely undone, so that their efforts must now be redoubled. Although the communication between even the best of the Mormon interpreters and the natives was imperfect, it was effective enough when it was accompanied by patience. Such missionaries as Jacob Hamblin, Thales Haskell, and Ira Hatch had to exercise all their influence to turn the minds of the Indians back again to the more monotonous business of farming.

Transcontinental travel was limited to the summer season. By the next season, difficulties between the Mormons and the government had been adjusted, and the Indians ceased to be a problem on the road, except as they tried petty thieving or followed along to pick up a discarded animal. Even before the army passed through Salt Lake City the next spring, the war was over for the red men.

137

8

A Bloodless "War"

Having followed briefly the developments of the "Mormon War" as they affected the southern part of the territory, the emigrant trains on the road, and the Indians, let us consider the effect which the Mountain Meadows Massacre had upon the conduct of the war in the northern part of the territory. Perhaps to see this terrible event in relation to the over-all picture will be to understand relationships more clearly.

While John D. Lee connived with the band of Indians and Isaac C. Haight sent out for interpreters and marshaled the militia, Brigham Young had his eyes and his interest upon the approaching army. While he had said repeatedly and emphatically that "with God's help, they shall not come here," the fact remained that they were coming. His trusted emissaries were waiting in Angel's Camp in California for their $1,260 worth of ammunition to arrive from San Francisco. In every town and village throughout the territory, men were drilling and inspecting arms, and between towns expressmen shuttled back and forth with orders and messages. Throughout the territory the atmosphere was one of impending trouble.

Less than a month before, Major Haight had assured George A. Smith that in the event of a crisis, he would not wait for instructions, but would attack the enemy if they should appear. Now, while James H. Haslam was urging his horse back at full speed with the injunction to let the emigrants go on their way, the massacre had been committed. At that time, Captain Van Vliet of the quartermaster's corps of the army was in Great Salt Lake

City, and had been in conference several times with Brigham Young. Always the Mormon leader had insisted that the Mormons would resist any attempt of the troops to enter the territory.

"If the government dare to force the issue, I shall not hold the Indians by the wrist any longer," he had threatened on September 7. "If the issue comes, you may tell the government to stop all emigration across the continent, for the Indians will kill all who attempt it."

At about the same hour that Haslam rode into Cedar City on Sunday, carrying his letter intended to quiet the hysteria and save the emigrants, Brigham Young and other leaders were preaching their most fiery war sermons in the Salt Lake tabernacle and calling for a show of hands by those who would be willing to burn their homes and desolate the land rather than submit to tyranny. The whole service was intended to impress the visitor from the army with the resolution of the people of Utah—and succeeded very well, as his later report shows.

On the same Sunday morning, September 13, John D. Lee, with a large band of Indians loaded with loot from the massacre, arrived back at Fort Harmony. Entering the gates, they rode around the center of the fort, their tinware jangling and the bundles of clothing tied awkwardly; they rode around once and stopped while the Indians gave their whoop of victory, and Lee declared loudly, "Thanks be to the Lord God of Israel, who has this day delivered our enemies into our hands."

On Monday morning, September 14, Captain Van Vliet left Salt Lake City to return to the troops and the East, and Brigham Young wrote the military orders quoted in the last chapter, outlining the strategy to be used in the big fight the next year. If worst came to worst, they would desolate the land totally, leaving not even sticks to start a fire.

At almost the same hour, William H. Dame, sickened by what had already happened, was issuing orders to quiet the Indians and take them off the road.

Attempts to keep the Mountain Meadows Massacre quiet were, of course, futile. Not only had the travelers through the district carried the word out, but Mormons were full of talk of it. Despite the oath of secrecy among those who were on the ground, too many others knew that trouble was afoot—too many who looked with disfavor upon the whole affair, too many who might not publicly condemn but would whisper and collect damning evidence and repeat rumors. At Harmony, the entire population had witnessed the demonstration of Lee and the Indians, and he spoke in justification of what had happened in the afternoon meeting.

Brigham Young must hear of this sooner or later. How should they best break the news to him? As to the plan, Lee says:

> Haight then told me that it was the orders of the Council that I should go to Salt Lake City and lay the whole matter before Brigham Young. . . .
> He refused to write a report, saying:
> "You can report it better than I could write it. You are like a member of Brigham's family, and can talk to him privately and confidentially. . . ."
> I started about a week or ten days after the massacre, and I was on the way about ten days. When I arrived in the city I went to the President's house and gave to Brigham Young a full, detailed statement of the whole affair, from first to last.[1]

As has been stated earlier, Rachel Lee recorded the departure of John for Salt Lake City on September 20; Wilford Woodruff's journal entry shows that Lee made his report to Brigham Young on September 29, 1857. Under that date, Woodruff wrote:

> We have another express in this morning, saying that the army are rapidly marching toward us, soon will be at Bridger, and wish men immediately sent out. John D. Lee also arrived from Harmony with an express and an awful tale of blood. A company of California emigrants, of about 150 men, women and children. Many of them belonged to the mobbers of Missouri and Illinois. They had many cattle and horses with them, and they traveled along south. They

[1] Lee, *Confessions*, 251–52.

went damning Brigham Young, Heber C. Kimball and the heads of the Church; saying that Joseph Smith ought to have been shot a long time before he was. They wanted to do all the evil they could, so they poisoned beef and gave it to the Indians, and some of them died; they poisoned the springs of water, and several of the Saints died. The Indians became enraged at their conduct and they surrounded them on the prairie, and the emigrants formed a bulwark of their wagons, and dug an entrenchment up to the hubs of their wagons, but the Indians fought them five days until they had killed all the men, about sixty in number. Then they rushed into the corral and cut the throats of the women and children, except some eight or ten children which they brought and sold to the whites. They stripped the men and women naked and left them stinking in the sun. When Brother Lee found it out he took some men and went and buried their bodies. It was a horrid, awful job. The whole air was filled with an awful stench. The Indians obtained all the cattle and horses and property, guns, etc. There was another large company of emigrants who had 1,000 head of cattle, who was also damning both the Indians and the "Mormons." They were afraid of sharing the same fate. Brother Lee had to send interpreters with them to the Indians to help save their lives, while at the same time they were trying to kill us. I spent most of the day trying to get the brethren ready to go to the mountains. Brother Brigham, while Lee was speaking of the cutting of the throats of women and children, said it was heartrending; that emigration must stop, as he had said before. Brother Lee said he did not think there was a drop of innocent blood in the camp, for he had two of the children in his house, and he could not get but one to kneel down in prayer-time, and the other would laugh at her for doing it, and they would swear like pirates.[2]

This record will bear some study, since it was made at the time and left without correction or modification. For private consumption only, it was perhaps more detailed than it would have been, had it been a public record. The fact that he begins with the rapidly approaching army, so near to Bridger that the Mormon leaders

[2] The original journal of Wilford Woodruff is in the archives of the Latter-day Saints church historian.

must do something immediately, is of first concern. That this is vital is further shown by the fact that the writer interrupts himself in the midst of his tale of horror to say that he had spent most of the day trying to get the brethren ready to go out to the mountains, where already men were working feverishly to throw up fortifications against the approaching enemy.

It would seem that Woodruff gave a good reproduction of Lee's story, for the same grievances were listed that had been repeated all along. That the company, or some of them, belonged to the mobbers of Missouri and Illinois was one point; that they swore at the church leaders was another. The poisoned meat story was unlikely, while the poisoned springs was quite clearly fabrication; to poison a running stream of any size would take a great amount of poison, and if several of the Saints had died, their names and homes and other details would have been given.

From the first this was to have been an Indian massacre, and as such it was presented now. Brigham Young had heard already from Haslam that the emigrants had entrenched themselves and that the fighting was going on; he knew from the same messenger that the local Mormon officials had some responsibility in it all. Although he had sent orders not to interfere with travelers, he must have sensed the importance of his own interview with, and instructions to, the Indian chiefs of all the southern area. It might well have been heartrending to have his own teachings taken too literally.

Lee was evidently true to the pact made at the Meadows that no white man's name was to be mentioned, for if he had implicated any, Woodruff would likely have named them. The Mormon president could guess who some of them were, and if he could not, he would use his own method of finding out. But that must all come later, after the exigency of the present was met.

If Lee's report was doubted, there arrived soon the report written by the Indian agent, George Armstrong, of Provo, and dated September 30. From this, it is clear that word of the massacre had spread all through the territory. This account is occupied with the troubles of the Fancher company at Fillmore, and with the "shameful treatment which many of the Indians receive at the hands of emigrants passing to and from California." Here again is given in detail the story of poisoned meat, but no mention is made of the poisoned spring which was later said to have been in that vicinity. The massacre itself is condensed into one sentence: "The Indians followed them to a place known as Mountain Meadows where they attacked the camp and after a desperate fight they killed fifty-seven men and nine women."[3]

[3] Agent George W. Armstrong wrote from Provo, Utah, to Brigham Young, September 30, 1857. The original of this document is found in the records of the Utah Superintendency of the Office of Indian Affairs, in the National Archives. The part referring to the massacre is as follows: ". . . I beg leave to call your attention to the shameful treatment which many of the Indians receive at the hands of emigrants passing to and from California. One circumstance which especially deserves notice and which should for the future be guarded against as much as possible is that of poisoning a part of the band of Parvantes which occurred during the present month by a company of emigrants from the States to California. While the company were camped a short distance from Fillmore City for the purpose of recruiting their teams a number of the Parvantes visited the emigrant camp which is their custom for the purpose of begging. They asked for something to eat which was denied them, but was answered if they did not immediately leave that they would receive a volley of bullets. This answer displeased the Indians, when some of the citizens of the settlement interfered and to prevent bloodshed informed the camp that they had better give the Indians a small present which would settle the difficulty. The captain of the Emigrant train after consultation with his company told the Indians that they would give them a beef the next day but claimed the privilege of killing it themselves. The Indians then left but previous to their return . . . the beef was killed and poisoned and given to the Indians. They cut up the beef and packed it to their lodges several miles distant from the emigrant camp. After partaking of the beef four of the Indians died and a large number taken dangerously sick. When the cause of this unhappy circumstance was discovered by the Indians they held a council and determined to be revenged upon the camp. The citizens of Fillmore on learning what had been done as well as the determination of the Indians endeavoured to appease their savage vengeance but without the desired result. The Indians followed them to a place known as Mountain Meadows where they attacked the camp and after a desperate fight they killed fifty-seven men and nine women.

"I have always advised emigrants who have consulted me upon such matters to treat the Indians Kindly and wherever my advice was taken they traveled in safety.

"Other acts of cruelty have been practiced towards the Indians on the Northern rout[e] to California which have resulted in a similar manner, and until emigrants will learn to use wisdom and prudence in their treatment of the untutored savage they may expect to be severely handled by them. . . ."

143

Almost as soon as the word had reached Great Salt Lake City, the Matthews-Tanner train had carried it to San Bernardino. The news, as it echoed throughout the nation, carried always implications of Mormon responsibility.

That Brigham Young lamented the massacre, there can be no question, for it was a ghastly error from a military as well as from a humanitarian point of view. He was too good a general not to know that the repercussions would be immediate and violent. But at that time the very existence of his "Kingdom" was in jeopardy; his resolution to take a defensive stand against the United States must soon be put into action. If a mistake had been made in the south, this was not the time to admit it; though his leaders there had been over-zealous for his cause, they were still his strongest men and his best officers.

Nor did his problems decrease, for the army came nearer daily. His men, under Lot Smith, did what they could to impede its progress, but they were not much more effective than a swarm of mosquitoes trying to stop a buffalo. As the army approached, the scorched-earth policy was put into effect.

Jesse W. Crosby, one of the men who carried the torch, recorded this dramatic episode in some detail. Beginning under date of September 25, 1857, he tells of his trip out from Great Salt Lake City, through snow and cold. He was on horseback, riding almost night and day:

> I went to Fort Supply with a small company to help take care of the crops, and to make ready to burn everything if found necessary, but we were soon disturbed by the arrival of an express from Bridger, ordering everything destroyed.
>
> We took out our wagons, horses, etc., and at 12 o'clock noon set fire to the buildings at once, consisting of 100 or more good hewed houses, one saw mill, one grist mill, one threshing machine, and after going out of the fort, we did set fire to the stockade, grain stacks, etc. After looking a few minutes at the bonfire we had made, thence on by the light thereof.
>
> I will mention that owners of property in several cases begged the privilege of setting fire to their own, which they freely did,

thus destroying at once what they had labored for years to build, and that without a word.

Thence on the way a few miles we stopped and set fire to the City Supply—a new place just commenced—10 or 15 buildings perhaps, and warmed ourselves by the flames. Thus we laid waste in a few hours all the labor of a settlement for three or four years, with some five or six hundred acres of land all fenced and improved.

Our work of destruction was now finished and we moved silently onward and reached Bridger a little after daylight and found it in ashes, having been fired the night before. We joined our companions in arms, who with us, after some deliberation evacuated the place and moved back in the brush to await orders on the approach of the enemy.[4]

Fort Bridger had recently been purchased from Louis Vásquez —or his share of it was purchased—for eight thousand dollars in gold, made in two payments.[5] Fort Supply was valued at fifty thousand dollars because of buildings, land, and improvements. Thus this one expedition destroyed more in value than could be found in all southern Utah. The fact that the owners "begged the privilege of setting fire to their own" indicates that they, too, were full of zeal for the cause.[6]

[4] "History and Journal of the Life and Travels of Jesse W. Crosby." Typewritten copies at Brigham Young University and Utah State Historical Society. Printed in *Annals of Wyoming*, Vol. XI (1939), 147–221.

[5] Jim Bridger and Louis Vásquez had built Fort Bridger in 1843, and, when the Mormons arrived in 1847, were operating a trading post and a ferry. Soon after Brigham Young's appointment as governor of the territory in 1851, he proceeded to set up a ferry on the Green River near Fort Bridger. In 1852, he charged Bridger with selling ammunition to the Indians and inciting them against the Mormons. James Ferguson was sent with a posse to arrest Bridger and bring him in to answer the charge, but Bridger eluded the officers and fled to the east. Church representatives later negotiated with Vásquez for the property and made the purchase. Signed receipts are extant.

[6] The first company of colonists to go to Fort Supply went out in early 1852, but were recalled in October of the same year. In 1853, two companies were sent—John Nebeker with thirty-nine men and Isaac Bullock with fifty-three. Not all of them stayed, however, and the next year others were sent, of whom John Pulsipher was one. He named seventy men in the community.

The land was sterile, the growing season short, and the winters so long and severe that the settlers were glad to be released from this mission.

The emphatic descent of winter, on October 17 and 18, certainly could have been considered by Brigham Young as a direct intervention of Providence in his behalf. The army had already passed the marker which defined the boundary of the territory of Utah, the deadline which he had indicated. Had the weather permitted them to proceed, war would have been inevitable, for the Mormon army of twenty-five hundred men was stationed at strategic points, and reserves were all alerted for action at an hour's notice.

So extreme was the cold on October 17 that the cattle of the army began to die in herds, and with all they could do for shelter, the men were suffering severely. Forced to retreat and take up winter quarters, the soldiers postponed any potential battles until spring. Strangely enough, on the same day, October 17, the first members of the Duke train of emigrants arrived half-starved at San Bernardino with the story of the Mormon theft of their cattle to add to the tale of the massacre. So the lull in affairs in the north gave the leaders more opportunity to listen to the hue and cry which came up from California. The feeling against the Mormons as expressed by the San Francisco *Daily Evening Bulletin* was:

> The blood of American citizens cries for vengeance from the barren sands of the Great Basin. The insulted dignity of the nation demands retribution from their infamous murderers. Virtue, Christianity and decency require that the vile brood of incestuous miscreants who have perpetrated this atrocity shall be broken up and dispersed. And the tide of popular opinion, now rolling up from every end of the land, calls loudly upon the Government to let no longer delay ensue before beginning the good work.
>
> And even should the news of the Mormon massacre upon the plains not suffice to incite to full activity the entire power of the Federal Officers, the position now taken by Brigham Young must do so. He has not waited to be attacked, but has commenced offensive warfare. The Independence of Utah Territory has been declared, and the determination announced of adhering to no laws except such as the Mormons make themselves. This must bring

them into speedy conflict with the United States—and this insures their final extermination. For once the general detestation and hatred pervading the whole country against the Mormons is given legal countenance and direction, a crusade will start against Utah which will crush out this beast of heresy forever. From this state alone thousands of volunteers could be drawn, who would ask no better employment than the extermination of the Mormons at the call of the government.[7]

Every mail into Utah brought such threats and expressions of hatred, tirades made more bitter by the fact that there was a real offense to call them forth. With the army at the eastern door temporarily stopped by the weather, the more imminent danger seemed to be an attack from California. On October 30, Wilford Woodruff wrote:

> I went up in the evening to the President's office and learned that the California mail had arrived. I heard some letters read. One stated that the government had made arrangements to send light draft boats up the Colorado with men and arms against us at that point.

The rumor grew until the people of southern Utah began to be alarmed. The evacuation of San Bernardino had begun in November; by the twenty-third of that month, fifty-five families had taken leave, according to the *Daily Alta California* of that date. Within six weeks, all the faithful had started back to Utah, leaving behind their thriving farms and growing businesses and good homes. To them, nothing material was as important as standing with their people in this time of crisis. Ginn reported that his company passed many Mormon families along the Mohave Desert and about Cajon Pass, who had sacrificed their orchards and vineyards to comply with the order to return to Utah.

With the arrival of these refugees in the settlements of southern Utah the excitement could hardly abate, and the sense of emergency was everywhere in the air. The following brief extract

[7] *Daily Evening Bulletin* (San Francisco), October 27, 1857.

from a letter written under the heading of Fort Clara illustrates the spirit of the times:

Dec. 25 [1857] the mail just arrived, Orson Pratt, Ezra T. Benson, George Q. Cannon at San Bernardino. The road is crowded. Many bronchos. Bro Lyman is here and it is exciting times. No troops as yet in sight below. All right. In haste.

Respectfully your brethern

WILLIAM H. DAME   JAMES LEWIS[8]

Two days later Jesse N. Smith, writing from Parowan, reported:

We hear a rumor that there are a party of 300 U.S. troops ex-

[8] This letter is quoted in the "Journal History" of the Latter-day Saints church under date of December 23, 1857. Because it shows something of the temper of the time, it is quoted here in full:

"FORT SANTA CLARA, IN CAMP,
DEC. 23, 1857

"BRO. GEORGE A. SMITH,

"Expecting the mail today a line from this part of the territory might not be amiss Bro. Amasa Lyman's arrival in the south collecting teams on the way from Fillmore to assist the emigration from San Bernardino caused the boys to stir a little in the accomplishment of the desired object. Two teams from Fillmore and from Beaver arrived Friday evening Dec. 18 at Parowan. Six teams were baited at that point to roll Sunday to start on Monday morning from Cedar. Bro. Lyman, Wm. H. Dame and the judge started Saturday, 19th for Cedar on the way to meet the emigration and Cedar forwarded five additional teams. We arrived yesterday at this point, where we met Bros. Matthew's and Tanner's train with Bro. Amasa Lyman's family or a portion of them. Today another train arrived here and some of the teams from the south are preparing to return for those who are still behind and ox teams will be immediately on hand to forward their loading to the settlements. The spirit of the south is good and all are on hand to do what they can to roll forth the good work. Bro. Dame has put 60 bushels of wheat into your bin and has stopped the work upon the overshot wheel until orders from you. Your family is well; the spirit of the times suits the boys in the south, and things are progressing. If you have any orders pertaining to your business, please forward, so that we may be directed.

"Dec 25 the mail just arrived, Orson Pratt, Ezra T. Benson, George Q Cannon at San Bernardino. The road is crowded, many bronchos. Bro Lyman is here and it is exciting times. No troops as yet in sight below. All right. In haste.

"Respectfully your brethren

"WM. H. DAME,   JAMES LEWIS"

ploring the Colorado conducted by an old mountaineer who says there can be a more practicable road made up the head waters of the Virgin and down the Sevier than the one at present traveled. Whether this report is true or not I cannot say. . . .[9]

Among the Mormons, such an exploration could be only an evil omen. In order to learn the truth of the situation and to determine what action should be taken, Jacob Hamblin was called to investigate. It was not until March 16, 1858, that the Hamblin party and the Ives expedition met, or that a representative of the Mormon group was taken on board the ship. Here there was an exchange of formalities but little information, for each side wished to obtain all that he could regarding the activities of the other without disclosing those of his own party. A comparison of the two reports is an interesting diversion.[10]

[9] Letter from Jesse N. Smith to George A. Smith, dated Parowan, December 27, 1857. Quoted in the "Journal History" of the Latter-day Saints church under that date.

[10] In Little's *Jacob Hamblin*, the account of his examination of the Ives expedition is found on pages 52–53: ". . . In the spring of 1858 I took five men, and went by way of Las Vegas springs to the River Colorado, at the foot of the Cottonwood Islands, 170 miles from the Santa Clara settlements. . . .

"A small steamer lay at the head of the islands and a company of men, with animals, were making their way up the river, on the opposite side from us. I requested Brother Thales Haskell to hail the boat's crew from a thicket of willows, while the rest of the company remained secreted. If a boat were sent to take him over, he was to pass as a renegade from Utah, and learn who they were and their intentions. Brother Haskell was soon taken on board of the steamer.

"I prayed for him that night, for my mind was filled with gloomy forebodings. I dreamed that the officer in charge of the boat, offered the Indians a large reward for my scalp.

"Soon afterwards we saw the yawl from the steamer land Brother Haskell. He informed us that the company was of a military character, and exhibited very hostile feelings against our people; that the expedition had been sent out by the government to examine the river, and learn if a force could be taken into Southern Utah from that direction, should it be needed, to subjugate the 'Mormons.'

"We were soon on our way homeward.

"The first night out from the river, a Las Vegas Indian overtook us, and informed us that soon after we left the river, the steamer came down below the Cottonwood Islands, brought a large amount of blankets and other goods ashore, made some presents to the Mohaves and Piutes, and offered to pay well for the capture of any 'Mormon' they found in their country."

The massacre at Mountain Meadows, of course, was still conceived as a part of the military campaign rather than a brutal mass murder of civilians. John D. Lee had returned from making his report to Brigham Young on October 17, according to the journal of his wife, and on the next day, Sunday, he occupied the time in the regular meeting with a report of conditions in the north, the approaching army, and the fact that they must all prepare for the big fight in the spring.

On November 20, he made a written report of the massacre to

Joseph C. Ives, *Report upon the Colorado River of the West in 1857 and 1858,* described his meeting with the Mormons on page 88. Writing at Camp 52, thirty miles below the mouth of Black Canyon on March 16, 1858, he says:

"While steaming around the base of Mount Davis we overtook the expressman, who called out to us that there were fresh tracks of horses and mules on the west bank, leading down the river, that had been made only a few hours before. At the first wooding place the trail was searched for and examined. There appeared to be four persons; and we concluded that they were Mormons, from the Vegas, who came to look after our movements.

"This evening an individual called to us from across the river to send a boat over. As soon as the visitor made his appearance we perceived that he was a Mormon. A member of my party who had been in Utah said that he recognized him as one of their bishops. For some reason he chose to make a mystery of his personality and told a clumsily contrived and impossible story; representing himself and companions as California Emigrants *enroute* to Los Angeles. He said they had taken this detour of a couple of hundred miles to avoid meeting Indians; and, according to his own account, they had already passed all the Indians that were to be encountered on the regular trail, and by coming to the Colorado would be obliged to run the gauntlet of one or two thousand more. This and several similar discrepencies did not argue well for the bishops sanctity; but we gave him a nights lodging—that is, a pair of blankets to sleep upon—and entertained him as well as corn and beans would permit.

"The bishop departed with early dawn to join his companions, first extracting all the information he could concerning our expedition and the practicability of navigating the river. A reconnaissance is being made, under the guidance of Nah-vah-roo-pa, to connect the head of navigation with the Mormon road, and we have remained in the valley today awaiting the return of the absent party.

"The latter are extremely sensitive about the possibility of strangers invading their domains. I learned from Irebeta that the Mormons had on several occasions made friendly overtures, but that his tribe suspected them of looking with covetous eye on the beautiful Mojave valley. Certain zealous divines, eager to make proselytes, had baptized a number of the Indians. Irebeta told me, with a grin, that Cairook was among the number, and that the big chief was greatly disgusted when they tried to duck his head in the river."

150

Brigham Young. In it he detailed the offenses of the emigrants which caused the anger of the Indians to grow so intense that they had attacked the train and killed all the emigrants. Strangely, he did not give the number slain nor did he mention any children saved, but told how the Duke train following would have met the same fate had not the Mormon interpreters interfered to persuade the Indians to take only the cattle. All this was due to the fact that the white man had been the first aggressor, he said, and as if to give validity to his report, he charged the government for teams and wagons given to the various tribes through William H. Dame, P. K. Smith, Jacob Hamblin, and Henry Barney to the total of $2,200![11] Lee insists that this report was made at the re-

---

[11] The report of Lee was made a part of the records of the court at his trial, and is filed along with the complete minutes of both first and second trials at the Henry E. Huntington Library. Full text follows:

"HARMONY, WASHINGTON CO. U. T.
NOV. 20TH 1857

"TO HIS EXCELLENCY, GOV. B. YOUNG
EX-OFFICIO AND SUPERINTENDENT
OF INDIAN AFFAIRS
"DEAR SIR:—

"My report under date May 11th 1857, relative to the Indians over whom I have charge as farmer showed a friendly relation between them and the whites, which doubtless would have continued to increase, had not the white men been the first aggressor? as was the case of Capt. Fanchers Co of Emigrants passing through to California about the middle of Sept. last on Corn Creek 15 ms south of Fillmore City Millard County. The Co there poisoned the meat of an ox which they gave the Pahvant Indians to eat, causing 4 of them to die immediately besides poisoning a number more the Co. also poisoned the water where they encamped, killing many of the cattle of the settlers; this unguided policy planed in wickedness by this Co. raised the ire of the Indians which soon spread through the Southern Tribes, firing them up with revenge till blood was in their path and as the breach according to their tradition was a national one, consequently any portion of that nation was liable to atone for that offence, about the 22nd of Sept. Capt Fanchers and Co. fell victims to their wrath near Mountain Meadows, their cattle and horses shot down in every direction, their wagons and property mostly committed to the flames and had they been the only ones that suffered we would have less cause of complaint. But the following Co. of near the same size had some of their men shot down near Beaver City, and had it not been for the interposition of the citizens at that place, the whole Co. would have been massacred by the enraged Pahwants from this place they were protected by military force by order of Col. W. H. Dame through the Territory besides providing the Co. with interpreters to help them through to the lass vages on the

151

quest of Brigham Young, so that he in turn could complete his to the government officials over him. This Brigham Young did on the following January 6, quoting from Lee's letter and making the massacre entirely an Indian affair.

Early in January, John D. Lee returned to Great Salt Lake City to attend the legislature. His diary gives a detailed account of his varied activities while there, and of the general situation with regard to the army and the imminent war. Under date of January 4, 1858, he wrote:

Clear & fine. At 10 morning Legislative Assembly met in joint session, committee reports 1st, petitions & then the news. John Sheen [Gheen?] gave an account of the spirit & state of the people

Muddy some 3 to 500 Indians attacked the Co. while traveling and drove off several hundred head of Cattle telling the Co. that if they fired a single gun that they would kill every soul; interpreters tried to regain the stock or a portion of them by presents but in vain, the Indians told them to mind their own business or their lives would not be safe.

"Since that occurrence no Co. has been able to pass without some of our interpreters to talk and explain matters to the Indians.

"Friendly feelings yet remain between the Natives and the settlers and I have no hesitancy in saying that it will increase so long as we treat them kindly and deal honorably towards them, I have been b'lest in my labors the present year, much grain has been raised for the Indians.

"I herewith furnish you the accts. of W. H. Dame of Parowan for cattle wagons &c furnished for the benefit of the chief Owanup (SS) for two yoke of oxen $100.00 each, one wagon and chains $75.00 $275.00
Total $275.00
2 cows $30.00 each for labor $80   Total $140.00

$415.00

P. K. Smith, Cedar City, Iron Co. for 2 yoke cattle $100
   for Wms & Moqueeteses Bands $200.00
for 1 cow $35 do to 1 wagon $80 total $115.00
                                     Total $315.00
Jacob Hamblin acct for the benefit of Tatse gobbitts Band Santa Clara, Washington Co. (SS)
2 yoke of cattle $100 do 1 wagon 2 chains $100   Total $300.00
2 cows $35.00 each   Total $ 70.00

                                     Total $ 370.00

in California, said the road was lined from San Bernardino to Cedar City with Saints leveing California. . . . All hell is in commotion, government intends sending ten thousand troops by the south rowt and as many by the north rowt. . . . this evening I had an interview with the gov; he counseled me to bring Emma and he would seal her to me I also signed quite a no of vouchers, as claims against the government for servises among the Indians. . . .[12]

This last sentence seems significant indeed, for it gives evidence that Brigham Young discussed with Lee the report of November 20, in which so many wagons, oxen, and cows were listed as having been given to the Indians of the south by Dame, Klingonsmith, Hamblin, and Barney. For six weeks, Brigham Young had known of the massacre; from the message which Haslam had carried, he might have been sure of the fact that some of his people were implicated. Yet he accepted the report and signed the vouch-

Henry Barneys acct. for the benefit of Jemiquiches Band Harmony (SS)

for 2 yoke cattle $100		$200.00
" 1 wagon $100. do 1 plough $40.	Total	140.00
" 4 cows at $35. each	Total	140.00
labor in helping to secure crop etc		40.00
		$520.00
For my services the last six months and for provisions clothing &c		$600.00
	Sum total	$2220.00

"From the above report you will see that wants of the natives have increased commensurate with their experience and practice in the art of agriculture with sentiments of high consideration, I am your humble servant,

JOHN D. LEE
Farmer to Pahute Indians

GOV. B. YOUNG
EX-OFFICIO & SUPERINTENDENT
OF INDIAN AFFAIRS

ENDORSED:
Filed Dec. 20, 1876

JAMES R. WILKIN, *Clerk*

[12] This quotation and the one immediately following are from the handwritten diary owned by the Henry E. Huntington Library. The diary was published in 1955 as *A Mormon Chronicle: The Diaries of John D. Lee* (ed. by Juanita Brooks and Robert Cleland).

ers charging the government with material which came from the murdered emigrants.

Lee's diary gives details of each day's activities, his speeches delivered before the legislature, his business transactions, his social activities. On Sunday, January 24, just before his return to the south, he tells of the sermon of Ezra T. Benson, of the sealing of Isaac C. Haight's new wife, and goes on:

> . . . after which the prest. remained in his sealing room & conversed with me some hour or more, upon the moves of government against us & counciled me to encourage the manufacturing of powder & getting out of Lead; & to wake up the Saints in all the Southern settlements to their duty, thus reviving the spirit of the reformation &c—blessed & we parted.

Thus the winter passed. In the south, the first parties of explorers were out in the desert searching for places to hide their families and cache their grain; Jacob Hamblin and a few picked men were stalking the Ives expedition; local folk were raising teams and wagons to help the San Bernardino Saints across the desert. In the north, with the United States Army in winter quarters, all the Mormon army was sent home except a few guards and pickets and expressmen.

As spring approached, the Mormon leaders knew they must either make good their boasts of the fall before, or come to an agreement with the government of the United States, accept their officers and army, and adjust to more regulation from them. They had been fortunate in having the services of Dr. John M. Bernhisel and Col. Thomas L. Kane to defend their case in Washington, D. C., and to explain the Mormon attitude toward the army. A few eastern papers had written in their defense; some politicians were already beginning to make capital out of what they came to call "Buchanan's Blunder," and to question not only the wisdom of sending the army, but the graft connected with fitting it out.

Yet for Brigham Young the fact remained that the army was at his door, and with the warm weather it would be a real problem to try to stop it. On March 18, 1858, a council was held in Salt Lake City to decide what course to follow. Hosea Stout recorded the deliberations in his diary:

Attended a general Council at the Historians Office of the first Presidency and Twelve, and officers of the Legion   The object of which was to take into consideration the best plan of operations to be adopted to counter act the purposes of our enemies, whether to attack them before they come near us or to wait untill they come near, or whether it is yet best to fight at all only in unavoidable self defense or in case a large force is sent against us this spring whether to fight or burn our houses & destroy every thing in and around us and flee to the mountains, deserts &c &c &c   It appears that the course pursued hitherto by Gov Young in baffelling the oppressive purpose of Prest Buckhannan had redounded to the honor of Gov Young and the Saints and equally to the disgrace of the President & his cabinet   Mormonism is on the ascendency. If we whip out and use up the few troops at Bridger will not the excitement and sympathy which is now raising in our favor in the states, be turned against us. Whereas if we only anoy and impede their progress while we "Burn up" and flee, the folly, the meanness of the President will be the more apparant and he and his measures more unpopular &c   This is about a fair statement of the subject matter in council   There was no definite measures adopted   many people spoke on the subject and the council adjourned til 8" April at 2 p.m. at the Tabernacle.[13]

On Sunday following, March 21, Brigham Young presented the new plan to the people in a special session of conference, explaining the plan, and calling for a show of hands of all present who had never before been driven from their homes. These people, he said, might have the privilege of being the first to move.

By the time President Buchanan's proclamation of pardon was issued on April 6, the road south was lined with wagons and herds of cattle. Governor Cumming was on his way from Camp Scott

[13] Copies of the Hosea Stout diaries are in the Brigham Young University Library and the Utah State Historical Society.

to Salt Lake City, accompanied not by the army but by a small escort of Mormons under Porter Rockwell. He arrived to see the last of the Saints take leave, in spite of his assurances that the move was entirely unnecessary.

That Brigham Young did not know himself where this move was finally to take them is quite evident. In his instructions on September 14, he had told the leaders in the south to secure "places in the mountains where they cannot find us, or if they do they cannot approach in any force; then prepare for our families building some cabins, cacheing flour and grain."

Unacquainted with the geography of the Southwest himself, Brigham Young insisted that somewhere in its desert wastes there must be an oasis which would at once shelter and protect the Saints. With this in mind, he sent repeated orders for parties of explorers to go in search of this place, as evidenced in the journals of both Isaac C. Haight and John D. Lee. Haight says:

> March 10 [1858]   Received a letter from Prest Young to send a company to explore the White Mountains to find a place for the Saints to hide from the Gentiles. . . .
> April 14th   Bro. Dame arrived, and having orders from Prest. Young to raise another company to go west to explore for a place to hide from the fase of our enemies, called upon me to raise fifteen men for the expedition. I called a meeting and raised the requisite number of men and animals. . . .

John D. Lee's entries would indicate that President Young had almost lost patience at their failure to find the kind of place he wanted:

> . . . Spent the night at Pres. W. H. Dame, who had just returned from G. S. L. C. with instructions from Pres. B. Young to raise a co. of from 60 to 70 men 20 wagons with 4 mules to each wagon 2 teamsters & a horseman, with seed grain, tools &c to penetrate the desert in search of a resting place for the saints. Said that he hoped the Co. could find a desert that would take them 8 days to cross

but was affraid that it would take them only 3 days to cross it, counting this is the 4th attempt & if you cant find the place I will go myself when I get to Parowan.

Finally, after all the fruitless efforts, after all the exposure and hardships of the explorers, after considering Mexico and the islands of the sea, and writing on March 24 to tell John D. Lee that "it is at present expected to make Headquarters at Parowan for a time, when we arrive there,"[14] the Mormon leader decided that only those north of Provo should move at all, and then only as far south as Utah County. Such a gesture would validate his earlier threats at a minimum of inconvenience.

Through all this, the matter of the massacre at Mountain Meadows had been dismissed with a report made by Brigham Young to James W. Denver, commissioner of Indian affairs, wherein

[14] The following entry in the journal of John D. Lee shows the change in the Mormon policy as it might affect the southern settlements. The parentheses are all his. One might wish that he had copied also the circular which he is instructed to keep so carefully.

"Wed 31st [March 1858] about 4 morning an Express reached this city from Pres Young stating that the policy of this church is to desolate all the settlements north of Utah Co., inasmuch as government was determined to erect a military station or post at or near G. S. L. C. & give them up the city in ashes; by this express I received a letter from Pres Young & 2 copies of the circular accompanying the letters of instruction. A copy of the letter I will here insert.

'G.S.L.C. MARCH 24, 1858

'ELDER JOHN D. LEE

'DEAR BRO., You will learn by the circular two copies of which are now forwarded to you, that the policy has varied somewhat from the past. Please loan the circular to none except those who will (faithfully) return (to you again & keep the policy at home) You will understand that we shall need men teams for the present movement, and we expect Washington County to assist us, as much as they can conveniently, and to furnish covers & bows to the waggons they send to our aid, so far as they have them. You can begin to send teams here for families &c as soon as the weather and roads are sufficiently settled. As we shall not sow or plant any more north of Utah County this season you will (also) see the propriety of raising all the flax sugar cane, [word illegible] barley corn potatoes & other vegetables that (you) are able to. It is at present expected to make Headquarters at Parowan for a time, when we arrive there.

'Your brethren in the Gospel,

BRIGHAM YOUNG'"

the massacre was pictured as Indian revenge for the acts of emigrants.[15] With this official report, the matter was evidently dismissed, and in the uncertainty of "the move" and the discussions with the Peace Commission, it was not a pressing question.

[15] The following extract is taken from the Third District Court records:

"OFFICE OF SUPT OF INDIAN AFFAIRS
G.S.L. CITY U.T.
JANY 6TH 1858

"HON. JAMES W. DENVER
COMMISSIONER OF INDIAN AFFAIRS
WASHINGTON CITY, D. C.

"SIR:

"On or about the middle of last September a company of emigrants travelling the southern route to California poisoned the meat of a ox that died and gave it to the Indians to eat, causing the immediate death of four of their tribe and poisoning several others. This company also poisoned the water where they were encamped. This occurred at Corn Creek fifteen miles south of Fillmore City. This conduct so enraged the Indians that they immediately took measures for revenge. I quote from a letter written to me by John D. Lee Farmer to the Indians in Iron an Washington Counties.

"'About the 22nd of Sept. Capt Fanchers & Co. fell victims to the Indians wrath near Mountain Meadows; their cattle and horses were shot down in every direction; their wagons and property mostly committed to the flames.' Lamentable as this case truly is, it is only the natural consequences of that fatal policy which treats the Indians like wolves or other ferocious beasts. I have vainly remonstrated for years with travellers against pursuing so suicidal a policy and repeatedly advised the government of its fatal tendency. It is not always upon the heads of the individuals who commit such crimes that such condign punishment is visited, but more frequently the next company who follow their fatal path become the unsuspecting victims, though preadventure innocent. Of this character was the massacre of Capt. Gunnison and party in 1853. He was friendly and unsuspecting, but the emigrant company who immediately preceded him had committed a most flagrant act of injustice and murder upon the Indians, escaped unscathed causing the savage feeling and vengeance which they had so wantonly provoked to be poured upon the head of the lamented Gunnison. Owing to these causes the Indians upon the main traveler's roads leading from this Territory to California have become quite hostile so that it has become quite impossible for a company of emigrants to pass in safety. The Citizens of this Territory have frequently compromised their own safety and otherwise peaceful relations with the Indians by interposing in behalf of travellers, nor can they be expected to be otherwise than hostile so long as the traveling community persist in the practice of indiscriminately shooting and poisoning them as above set forth.

"In all other parts of the Territory except along the North and South route to California as above mentioned, The Indians are quiet and peaceful. It is owing

The "full and free pardon" issued by the President of the United States on April 6 was not accepted by the Mormon leaders until June 12, when they consented for the army to march through Great Salt Lake City, then deserted and ready for burning, en route to their headquarters some forty miles beyond ^ Camp Floyd. On June 14 Governor Cumming issued a proclamation declaring that "peace is restored to our Territory," and offering his congratulations "for the peaceful and honorable adjustment of recent difficulties."

But it was peace in name only. The Mormons were as suspicious as ever of the army, and the winter in the snow at Camp Scott had not increased the soldiers' love for the Mormons. Although open hostilities no longer existed, Saints and soldiers were still "enemies" in a very real sense.

to the disturbed state of our Indian affairs that the accounts of this quarter have been so considerably augmented. It has always been my policy to conciliate the native tribes by making them presents and treating them kindly, considering it much more economical to feed and clothe than to fight them. I have the satisfaction of knowing that this policy has been most eminently successful and advantageous, not only to the Settlements but the Government as well as the emigrants and travellers; but the most uniform judicious and humane course will sometimes fail in holding ignorant wild revengeful Indians by the wrist to be indiscriminately murdered. We trust hence forward such scenes may not be reenacted and that the existing bad feeling among the native tribes may become extinguished by a uniform consistent humane and conciliating course of superior acts by those who profess superior attainments.

"Respectfully I have the honor to remain Your Obedient Servant

BRIGHAM YOUNG

Gov. & Supt. of Ind. Affairs
U. T."

9

The Church Acts

Wiтн тне вrief "war" over, and the people of Salt Lake City back in their homes after the exodus to the south, affairs in Utah were able to run smoothly again. The full and free pardon granted by President Buchanan was received resentfully by most of the Mormons, who still felt that the sending of the army was a gross insult to them. It was they who should have pardoned the President, they thought. But it had worked out well for them, and Brigham Young had conducted affairs in a masterful manner; his word would be law to them, regardless of who the civil officers were.

Frictions between the Mormons and the military force were bound to develop—frictions made the more complicated because of the divided attitudes of the government officials. The army and the federal judges had only contempt for Governor Cumming, who, they thought, was a tool in the hands of Brigham Young. They had been sent out to clean up Utah and set the Mormons straight, and they meant to do it.

That the troops were bitter and vindictive was recognized by many of the eastern papers, the New York *Tribune* for July 3, 1858, saying, "If it be deemed proper or necessary to station troops in Utah, they ought to be a fresh corps, and not a body of men filled with such hatred and prejudice." On the other hand, many were free in their criticism of Governor Cumming, declaring that he always sided with the Mormons, and that he had proved himself utterly unfit for the position.

John Cradlebaugh, associate justice in charge of the southern district of the territory, set about at once to ferret out the truth of the affair at Mountain Meadows. He expected to fasten upon Brigham Young and his immediate associates the responsibility of this, as well as of most of the other crimes that had been committed in the territory. Such was the attitude that, even had he been disposed to, it would have been hard for Brigham Young to co-operate with the judges. Edward W. Tullidge insists that "the action of the Judges, at the very onset, made it impossible for ex-Governor Young or Governor Cumming to move far in the matter [of investigating the Mountain Meadows Massacre]. Though Brigham Young had been justice personified, had he proceeded he must have walked into the deathtrap set for him."[1]

In the meantime, before the civil authorities had been able to start an investigation, the church conducted a private one, if we are to trust their own records. The leaders had to know the truth of this affair, even though the group loyalty which they had always encouraged would not permit them to make public their findings. Through long years of experience they had developed the attitude that, right or wrong, they must stand together.

As has already been shown, the leaders of the Mormon church knew the tensions and emotional pitch of their people in the south; they had themselves fostered and encouraged the idea of conciliating the Indians and making them fast friends. They knew something of the frictions which had culminated in the massacre. Lee had come in with his story at once; Armstrong had reported what he had heard; practically every man high in authority in the south was in Great Salt Lake City during January, 1858, among them, Isaac C. Haight, Philip Klingonsmith, William H. Dame, Charles Hopkins, and John D. Lee. While each perhaps tried to shield himself, and all suppressed the names of their white companions, they did discuss the tragedy with their leaders.

Later, in his testimony at the first trial of John D. Lee, Klingonsmith insisted that he visited Brigham Young in company with Lee and Hopkins, and that the three discussed the disposition of the spoil. "Let John D. Lee take care of it, in as much as he is the

[1] Edward W. Tullidge, *History of Salt Lake City*, 243.

161

Indian Agent now. What you know of this affair, say nothing about it," he quoted Brigham Young as saying.

Under date of June 18, 1858, nine months after the massacre, the "Journal History of the Church" records that: "Jacob Hamblin called at the office and had a long conversation with George A. Smith in regard to the Santa Clara Indians. He also gave an account of the massacre at Mountain Meadows."

This man had visited the scene just a week after the massacre, had heard the details of it all from his adopted Indian boy, an eyewitness to the event, had presumably received from Chief Jackson whatever record or journal was left by the emigrants, and had heard that Indian's version of the three survivors. Bound by no oath of secrecy, he could tell what he knew without implicating himself, and tell it fully. This he did, if we are to trust his testimony in the Lee trial, where he admitted that he had told more to George A. Smith than he told in court "because I remembered it better."

The very next month after this conversation with Hamblin, George A. Smith visited the southern settlements. On July 28, accompanied by Amasa Lyman, James McKnight, and Nephi Johnson, Indian interpreter, he left Cedar City. At Pinto, they held a meeting at the home of Richard Robinson, where a large crowd had assembled, more than the house could hold.

"Elder Lyman and myself addressed the saints," George A. Smith wrote for the church records. "We recommended to them a line of policy, calculated to make us free from Gentile bondage."

The next day, July 29, they visited the scene of the massacre:

We visited the ground [Mountain Meadows] where the emigrants and Indians had their battle last year. The wolves had apparently torn all the bodies from their graves; their bones lying scattered all around were undergoing a process of rapid decomposition, an item which seemed singular, they having so recently enjoyed life. The hair of the women indicated the spot where most of them were buried and from appearances the men had run away and left the women, they having been shot chiefly by themselves; while the men, many of them, were killed beyond them and buried about where they were shot.[2]

Certainly some questions must have arisen in the minds of any who noted these things. Here were the entrenchments behind which the emigrants had defended themselves for five days. Why did they leave them? And if they must leave them, why did they choose to walk? Cedar City was thirty-five miles away. Would they not have done better to have loaded the women and children into two or three wagons around which the men could have maintained a strong guard? If they *must* walk, why would all the women and children have been alone, and the men a half-mile away? Even Missouri mobbers could be expected to defend their wives and babies.

In the face of all the external evidence, would not George A. Smith have asked questions? Would not Nephi Johnson have answered them in some fashion? Could the treachery be justified on the grounds that those who had resisted arrest in Cedar City and defied the officers there were going back to stand trial? Might not the militia have been there to protect them, and the Indians gotten out of control? Had Johnson tried to explain, or had he remained mute, might not Smith, in the light of his experiences the year before, have guessed what happened?

An investigation was made immediately after this visit to the scene. Although the church records proper make no mention of complaints among the people, some diaries fill in the gap. The official company visited Santa Clara, Heberville, and Washington, returning to Harmony on August 2. Under date of August 3, 1858, Lee wrote in his diary:

> . . . they requested me to go as far as Cedar with them, spoke of an investigation of something that was between Bro. Haight and Bro. J. Hamilton family & want I should attend with them—I ac-

[2] "Journal History of the Church," items recorded under dates specified.

cordingly did so. We all dined at Fort Sidon with Bro. Hamilton & the saints of this place. At 3 p.m. the investigation commenced in the 1st ward school house Cedar City. Quite a no. of complaints were entered against Prest Haight & Bishop Smith. I was also accused of having used an influence against Pres. Haight but was exhonerated from the charge, which was decided by the brethren of the 12 to be founded in blind prejudice only. At six evening the meeting adjourned to 8 o'clock tomorrow. Bro. E. Snow said that he wanted me to stay with him wherever he tarried. We accordingly went home with J. M. Higbee supped & lodged, promising to breakfast with Bishop Smith.

Sat 6th the investigation continued till near night. Bro. E. Snow & I dined with Bro. Theodore Turley[.] the [*sic*] Brethren of the 12 heard the complaints of the brethren[,] reproved the authorities for unwise policy which they had adopted to govern the people & told them that they should never over rate their influence among the people & then told the people that they were at liberty to remove to any settlement where they thought that they could better their condition. In tern reproved all, gave good council, blessed & dismissed. I sent some 50$ Deseret currency by the Brethren. Made a present of 15$ to Bro. E. Snow, took leve of them & returned home.[3]

Here is more than meets the eye. In less than a year after the massacre at Mountain Meadows, the feeling among the people was so strong against their local church leaders that they made a formal complaint against them, an action rare in Mormon society. Whether or not this grew directly out of the massacre is uncertain. It could have been resentment against the rigid military rules that had been put in force, under which people could not move from one place to another without permission of the military officers.[4] At any rate, the officers were reproved for their

[3] Original diary of John D. Lee, owned by the Henry E. Huntington Library.

[4] Many legends come down as to this period in southern Utah. During the time of military rule, people dared not move from one place to another without a permit from their leaders; particularly they dared not leave the territory.

It was not safe to discuss the Mountain Meadows Massacre, as the following story told by the writer's grandfather shows:

unwise policy, and the common man was sustained in his rights. There is evidence here also of dissension among the local leaders, for Lee says he was accused of using an influence against Haight. Though at the time there was a reconciliation, the difference later grew into an open rift.

It seems significant that on the very day this private investigation was completed, George A. Smith wrote the first official report of the Mountain Meadows Massacre to Brigham Young. Assisted by James McKnight, who had gone with him to the site, he wrote from what he called "the most authentic sources [see Appendix V]."

His report is the story of an Indian massacre, of a few white

"I was riding along the road to Cedar City when three horsemen jumped out of the bushes and stopped me. For a second I thought it was a hold-up; then I saw that they were men from Cedar City. Someone had been talking, they said. Stories were being whispered about. Men's names were being used.

"I looked them straight in the eyes. 'I don't know what you are talking about,' I said. 'You are the first to ever mention any massacre to me. This is the first time I ever heard tell of such a thing.'

"They dropped their heads and whipped up their horses and dashed across the country through the brush."

Olive Branch Millburn of Salt Lake City tells how her grandmother, Olive Coombs, was shot and killed because of her interest in the massacre. She had come to Cedar City, a widow with two small daughters, and set up a school there. She acted too interested in this incident, asked too many questions about it. Word went out that she was collecting evidence and planned to publish her findings.

At a small hotel next door, men gathered to visit and drink. One morning she was being discussed there as a wolf in sheep's clothing, pretending to teach their children while she tried to fasten crimes on their parents. In the crowd was George Wood. He had been drinking, and became much excited by the talk. When someone suggested that his son was interested in her thirteen-year-old daughter, he stalked out, went to the door of the house adjoining, opened it, and shot the mother twice before the crowd realized what had happened.

George Wood was brought into the probate court at Parowan, was tried and found guilty. He was sentenced "to imprisonment at hard labor in the Territorial Penitentiary, for and during the term of his natural life." On March 8, 1865, he was granted a full and complete pardon by Governor James Duane Doty. (See Executive Book B, 171, in the Utah State Historical Society files.)

Mrs. Millburn herself is a loyal member of the church, a guide on Temple Square. She does not blame the church for this, but tells it as illustrative of the spirit which would call for such an investigation as Lee here records.

interpreters, among them Nephi Johnson, who were threatened with instant death if they did not help the Indians, and who returned to Cedar City and left the natives to carry out their plans alone. He reported that when the Mormon officials arrived early Saturday morning, all the emigrants were slain. No mention is made here of any offenses of the emigrants, and no reason given for the bitterness and hostility of the Indians. Though Smith had earlier noted that the women were all in one place and the men in another, he made no attempt to explain the reason. The value of this report lies in the fact that it embodies the first admissions that any participants would make:

1. The siege began on Monday; the massacre took place on Friday.

2. A group of white men, accompanying Nephi Johnson, arrived on the ground on Wednesday morning.

3. The emigrants left their camp and started back to Cedar City. The men and women traveled separately.

4. Isaac C. Haight and William H. Dame arrived on the scene Saturday morning.

5. The Mormons buried the bodies in admittedly shallow graves, from which the wild animals had pulled and scattered them.

6. About two hundred Indians were present.

7. The original date, given as September 21-25, was changed in a footnote: "The massacre must have occurred earlier in the month, say about 15 days."

Haight might have insisted that he acted only upon orders of his military superior, or he might have tried not to bring in the militia at all, but the fact that a second private investigation was held at Parowan seems to indicate that George A. Smith knew substantially what had happened. Since John D. Lee had returned to Harmony on August 6, he was not present at this later meeting. Perhaps it would have been better for him if he had been present. Information now comes from the diary of Isaac C. Haight:

Tuesday [August] 10th Received a note from John M. Higby, by the request of Elders Smith and Lyman, to go to Parowan. Arrived about nine o'clock A.M. Was surprised to find that several charges had been preferred against Bro. Dame, President of Parowan, by the High Council, together with his council.

Thursday 12th. After a patient but painful investigation for three and a half days, most of the charges proved not true. Much good counsel and instructions were given, and some severe chastisement by Elders Smith and Lyman. Arrived home late in the evening.[5]

The subject for discussion must have been important to take three and a half days, and since it was "painful," and the local leaders were given "some severe chastisement," we may conclude that the responsibility for the massacre was a part of it. Otherwise, why would George A. Smith have written a second report, based upon details learned at Parowan, to his chief?

By this time, other facts were admitted. While the second report includes whole paragraphs verbatim from the first, the point of view has shifted. Now the offenses of the emigrants are listed in great detail; their connection with the murders and outrages inflicted upon the Mormons in Missouri and Illinois, and their generally hostile attitude are enlarged upon. The participants had evidently decided upon their story and stayed with it: interpreters had been sent out to try to conciliate the Indians, and having failed, had returned to Cedar City and had no part in the killing. In an attempt to justify their failure to actively defend the besieged emigrants, they said, "For the citizens to have attacked and killed the Indians in defense of the emigrants would have been little else than suicide, as you are well aware of the exposed condition of the Southern settlers." This would confirm the feeling of some that the massacre appeased the Indians and saved their own homes, and would support the story of an Indian massacre.

[5] Diary of Isaac C. Haight. Photostat in Henry E. Huntington Library; typewritten copies in Washington County library, St. George, Utah, and Utah State Historical Society files.

Dame was cleared of immediate responsibility. If the orders quoted by Higbee are authentic, Dame could well have argued that he had ordered no killing and that he had on the other hand been explicit in saying to save the women and children at all hazards. His quick action in sending out orders immediately for all men in authority to conciliate the Indians and take them off the road, and his promptness in hurrying men to the defense of the emigrant train at Beaver would all be in his favor. If he had a copy of his orders, he would have substantial grounds for denying any responsibility.

Among the papers of William H. Dame is one that gives official sanction to his acts. Dated August 12, 1858, it reads: "We have carefully and patiently investigated the complaints made against President William H. Dame, for four successive days, and are fully satisfied that his actions as a Saint, and administration as a President, have been characterized by the right spirit, and are highly creditable to his position in the priesthood and that the complaints presented before us are without foundation in truth." This is signed by twenty-three men, only three of whom—Nephi Johnson, Samuel O. White, and John M. Higbee—had been on the ground during that fateful day. The two apostles, George A. Smith and Amasa Lyman, had been far away; Isaac C. Haight, next in command, whose name appears midway down the list, had remained in Cedar City as had the adjutant, James H. Martineau. John M. Higbee commanded the Iron County militia, and Nephi Johnson was Indian interpreter, while the other members were from the Parowan group which was not ordered out.

If Dame were cleared, the responsibility must rest next upon Haight, Higbee, and Philip Klingonsmith, who was not present at this meeting. But Klingonsmith had assumed responsibility for the care of the children. Not present here to speak for himself, Lee had the finger of accusation pointed squarely at him:

It is reported that John D. Lee and a few other white men were on the ground during a portion of the combat, but for what pur-

Parowan August 12. 1858.

We have carefully and patiently investigated the complaints made against President William H. Dame, for four successive days, and are fully satisfied that his actions as a saint, and administration as a President, have been characterized by the right spirit, and are highly creditable to his position in the priesthood; and that the complaints presented before us are without foundation in truth.

Jes. I. Smith
Amasa Lyman
James H. Martineau
James Lewis
C. C. Pendleton
Charles Hall
Wm. A. Grandar
Job T. Hall
John Steele
J. C. Haight
Nephi Johnson
J. White
F. T. Whitney
H. Eyring
J. J. Smith
John M. Higbee
Samuel West
Tarlton Lewis
Elijah Elmer
Wm. Barton
P. Meeks
Orson B. Adams
J. N. Smith

pose or how they conducted or whether indeed they were there at all, I have not learned [see Appendix VI].

So the official story of the massacre was written. While the visiting authorities might reprove the leaders of the south, while they might administer severe chastisement in private, they would not turn the offenders over to the enemies of the church for judgment. Neither would they disgrace the local authorities before their followers. The group loyalty which through all the years before had meant their very existence would demand that, while they might make a report of the massacre for the church as a whole and the world at large, they should not bring into the public eye any of the participants if it could be avoided. In these circumstances, but one man, John D. Lee, was named.

There are a number of reasons which would explain why Lee was singled out, whether he was most aggressive or whether he carried out his orders under protest. Well might he have argued that he was not present at the first meeting where the fate of the emigrants was discussed; well might he have pointed out that, as a subordinate in the military organization, he only carried out orders. But he was not present to defend himself when the final responsibilities were placed. Those who accused him, his superiors, might argue that it was he who persuaded the emigrants to leave their camp, that he went with the Indians back to Harmony, that as farmer to the Indians, he had distributed much of the booty. Klingonsmith later swore that Lee accepted this responsibility at the order of Brigham Young, but such a thing would never have been suggested at Parowan in the absence of Lee.

Concerning the distribution of the booty, it would seem from Lee's report and expense account that they were all involved (see note 9, chapter eight). Lee named Dame as receiving $415; Klingonsmith, $315; Hamblin, $370; and Henry Barney, $520; each for teams, wagons, and cows given to the Indians of his district, evidently the loot from the murdered emigrants.

The entries made by Lee in his diaries of 1858 are especially enlightening. Made before the investigation at Parowan which named him alone as having been present at the massacre, these notations may indicate his activities with regard to the booty as well as his relationship to the Indians on the one hand and his superior officers on the other.

Monday, Jan 4 [1858. Lee was in Great Salt Lake City attending the legislature]. . . . this evening I had an interview with the gov; . . . I also signed quite a no. of vouchers, as claims against the government for servises among the Indians. [Might not these have been the ones which he had sent in on November 20 preceding? Brigham Young's report to Commissioner Denver was made January 6.]

Friday 5, Feb. 1858 [Lee had now returned to Harmony with his new wife, Emma, and had found that a number of local men had helped themselves to his property while he was away]. . . . J. M. Higbee sold a yoke of oxen and put the money in his pocket, that had been turned over to me by Prest. Young for the benefit of the Indians. . . .

Wed 10th [Feb. 1858]. . . . this morning I made a [word illegible] with Bro J Hamblin and am to receive 10 head of year old steers at the junction of the Santa Clara & Rio Virgin river or near by. . . . [On the nineteenth following, Hamblin wrote to Brigham Young asking about some cattle, and was advised to control them and use them for the best interest of both the missionaries and the Indians. While it might not have referred to this transaction, the date is interesting.]

Monday 12 April 1858. . . . The co consists of 14 waggons from 2 to 4 yoke of cattle to a waggon & 4 horses or mules to a waggon & some 15 yoke of extra oxen Of that no. I furnished 2 waggons & 18 yoke of oxen. I also sent up 75 head of beef cattle, cows & calves to meet my obligation with L. Stewart & W. H. Hooper G.S.L.C. I accompanied them to Fort Sidon where we corrald our stock & staid over night.[6]

These cattle and wagons, sent in answer to Brigham Young's letter of March 24, might well have been a part of the herd of the murdered emigrants. In his testimony in court, Nephi John-

[6] Original diary of John D. Lee. See note 3 above.

son said there were thirteen wagons in the emigrant train; Lee said there were eighteen in all, with but one of these having a light iron axle. It was reported early that some of the outfits which were sent to haul the Mormons out of the city were loot from the massacre, but whether or not Brigham Young guessed this can only be conjectured.

On May 4, Lee recorded that the Indians had abandoned farming "with a view of living on the spoil of their stolen booty taken from us." On May 6, Amasa Lyman and a large party were entertained at the Lee home, where they enjoyed themselves so well that they all voted to stay an extra day or two. In the midst of their hilarity, "Bro Lyman said that we only were here on a Philabustering mission by our father in Heaven &c," indicating that Lyman knew of the activities that had been carried on. Other entries tell that Lee furnished beef for the exploring parties that were sent out from Cedar City, for the cotton missionaries on the Virgin River, and for the Indians. All these activities were known, and most of them ordered, by his superiors in the church. Yet, for the time being, the closed church investigation was finished, the report written, and the whole affair closed.

In the meantime, government officials were making ready to investigate the massacre in their own way. While the investigation at Cedar City was under way, Jacob Forney, the new superintendent of Indian affairs, wrote to Jacob Hamblin, his newly appointed sub-agent on the Santa Clara. His first order was to "endeavor with all diligence to discover the remainder of the children supposed to be liveing. All such must be recovered whether among white or Indians at any sacrifice."[7] Hamblin had been recommended to this position with the government soon after he made his report of the massacre to George A. Smith.

Upon receipt of these orders, Jacob Hamblin collected the children at his home, or made arrangements with various families to continue caring for the ones they already had at government

---

[7] A copy of Forney's letter to Jacob Hamblin at Fort Clara, U.T., dated August 4, 1858, is found in the National Archives, Indian Affairs—Utah Superintendency, under that date.

expense. From the night of the massacre, the three little Dunlap sisters had lived with the Hamblin family; Mrs. Hamblin had nursed the youngest through a severe wound in the arm. It was not until the spring of 1859 that the children were officially turned over to the government officials, and bills for their care were made.

Under date of Wednesday, March 2, 1859, John D. Lee wrote:

> Jacob Hamblin by order of Forney Superintendent of Indian Affairs took from my house Chas Fancher, one of the children of the unfortunate company that was massacred by the Indians near the Mountain Meadows about Sept 25, 1857. Government having ordered it to be done I made out the following charge 1 horse saddle & bridle & blanket 150$ paid for said boy to the Indians for boarding clothing & schooling 48 weeks at 2$ per week 96$oo 5 months not reconed which he agreed to pay under another head.[8]

This policy of letting the government pay seems to have been general and probably was all included in the total paid to Hamblin.[9]

Forney visited among the people of the south, gathered what information he could, looked over the scene of the disaster, and had a long conversation with John D. Lee. From his findings, he was convinced that the Mormons were involved in the massacre, if not entirely responsible for it (see Appendix IX).

In April, 1859, Judge Cradlebaugh and his military escort started south, bent upon capturing and bringing to justice those responsible for the massacre. Though peace had been declared, the feeling between the citizenry and the soldiers amounted to one of mutual hate and suspicion. An eloquent expression of this is found in a letter written by William H. Dame to George A. Smith dated May 4, 1859, which says, in part:

> I hasten to give you a few hints of matters occuring at present in the south.

[8] See note 3 above.
[9] See note 8, chapter six.

173

About 200 U.S. troops and attaches, are now here. Cradlebaugh and Paul are with them. While at Beaver, they nearly cleared the town of chickens and in wantonness beheaded pigs, leaving in the stys such as they did not take away. Stole skillets, shovels, etc. drove off a fat ox belonging to one of the brethren when they left, and killed it at the springs in the valley, leaving the head and hide on the ground. Was followed to this place by the owner, who recovered an ox of the officers in payment, worth 15 dollars less in value than the one taken.

They camped night before last at the spring, a little west of our town. We put out a strong guard during the night, armed them with small canes about the size of a wagon rack stake, which no doubt appeared somewhat weightly, and the stragglers about town went to their quarters at a reasonable hour, and left us tolerably quiet for the night. Last night they camped about 1½ miles from Cedar City, by the big field. They are of the wormwood order.

The night they camped here, some 3 or 4 went to the Indian chief's house asked for his squaws, showing plenty of money, at which the Indians with their squaws fled, the visitors then fired several rounds into their wickaup.

We learn that Cat Fish Cook and another Cedar man is along with them, and ride in a covered wagon.[10]

This letter carries some inferences besides the animosity felt by the writer. That Cat Fish Cook[11] and another Cedar man were traveling with the company at all implies that they were traitors going along to identify Mormons or to give evidence; that they rode in a covered wagon hints that they would not have been safe in the open. The court and its bodyguard had everything against them from the beginning, for word had traveled ahead and all the suspected had gone into hiding.

That both John D. Lee and Isaac C. Haight were warned in

[10] "Journal History of the Church," May 4, 1859.

[11] It would seem that the man referred to here was Richard Cook, who joined the church in early days in Liverpool. He came to southern Utah in the 1850's, but became dissatisfied and apostatized soon after the massacre. He moved to California, where he lived for the rest of his life.

advance is shown clearly in their diaries. On March 7, Lee wrote:

> . . . about 2 P.M. an express came to me by H. & T. Woolsey from a friend in the north stating that all hell was about to brake loose, a detatchment of Johnsons troops were expected within a few days & to take care of myself, the bearer of the express was instructed not to sleep night nor day until the letter reached me.

Nearly a month later, on April 4, he wrote again that he:

> . . . met Bro Jo Horn & co returning to Heberville to farm cotton & sugar cane. He gave me confidentially a letter from a Friend appraising me of the prejudice that exists toward me in the District courts all founded on rumor. However, I felt to put my trust in the Lord, knowing that it was for the Gospel's sake that I was persecuted & hunted.

Again, on April 9, he recorded another express, this one carried by George Woolsey, to the effect that ". . . the road was waylaid by Enos, Tom Whitney, & a Pahvant Indian whose name I did not learn; the 3 Indians aluded to told some friendly Indians that they had been hired to take my scalp (reward 500$)."[12]

Haight made no mention of any warnings until April 29, when he wrote:

> A messenger came to us and informed us that Judge Cradelbaugh with 200 U.S. Troops were at Beaver, coming south, with sworn intention of taking me and some other of the Brethren and hang us without trial for supposed crime, taking the law into their own hands, in violation of the constitution of the United States.[13]

[12] See note 3 above. It is possible that this man was the Thomas Woolsey to whom Lee referred in his diary of February 16, 1847, when he registered delight to meet again "Thomas Woolsey, my first adopted son." Under the rites of the church, this man owed to him the same fealty which he in turn gave to Brigham Young, a relationship which they regarded as sacred.

[13] See note 5 above. The entries concerning his hiding from the officers, continuing from the one quoted, are:

"May 1st (1859) Not wishing to fall into their hands, as I considered them nothing better than a mob, I left home in company with J. M Higby, M. D.

He gives details of their route and hiding place, naming his companions as J. M. Higby [*sic*], M. D. Hambleton, and others. At Beaver they were joined by William C. Stewart. Skirting the town, they eluded the officers, proceeded north to Salt Creek [Nephi], and turned east to the mountains, where a hideout was prepared. They called it Balleguard, an inaccessible spot to which special messengers brought mail and supplies. Three weeks they remained here. Finally, having been notified that the troops were on their way back to the north, they came down and started home. By a twist of luck, they ran directly into the camp of the enemy and were held for questioning with regard to some stolen horses. The fact that they were not recognized, but were set free at daybreak, was considered by Haight as divine intervention in their behalf.

Lee and Klingonsmith had a private hiding place of their own

Hambleton, and others for the north, passing through lower Beaver, where we were joined by Wm. C. Stewart.

"Saturday 7th. Arrived at Salt Creek late in the evening and slept in the tithing office.

"Sunday 8th We went in the evening up in the mountains to a camp called Balleguard, where quite a number of Brethren who were prescribed by our enemies had fled for safety. We remained with them until the last of the month.

"Sunday 29th, We were informed that Judge Cradelbaugh and the troops were on their return, and had left the road at the Sevier Bridge and had gone up into Sanpete Valley, and the road being considered clear we thought best to return home. We started home in the evening, and came as far as Chicken Creek, where to our surprise we were hailed by a sentinel and taken into a camp of the troops, and compelled to remain until daylight, it being about two o'clock, they wanted to examine our horses to see if we had any U. S. Horses, as many of their horses had been stolen. After daylight they examined our horses and found them all right, and let us go on our way, and right glad we were to get away from them, as some of our bitterest enemies were in camp, among which was Judge Cradelbaugh. Their eyes were blinded so they did not know us, although some of them had seen us at Cedar City. We felt that the Lord had delivered us from their grasp. . . .

"August 7th. I again left home with several of the Brethren [–] went into the mountains, as we hear that our enemies were coming after us. We remained in the mountains until the 4th of September, then we returned home to attend to our affairs, as our enemies had given up their efforts to take us for the present, yet continually threatening the destruction of all the faithful Elders of the Church. . . .

on top of the high mountains near Harmony. Here, with his field glasses, Lee could watch many of the activities on his own farm. His daily record of this period is an illuminating commentary upon his character.

With the men they sought all in hiding, the officers naturally could make no arrests. In general, the attitude of the citizenry, however much they regretted the massacre, was not to betray their neighbors to the "enemy," but there were those who found the secret too heavy to bear. William H. Rogers told how, as soon as it became known in the vicinity of Cedar City that Judge Cradlebaugh:

> ... intended holding a court and investigating the circumstances of the massacre, and that he would have troops to insure protection, and to serve writs if necessary, several persons visited him at his room, at late hours of the night and informed him of different facts connected with the massacre. All those that called thus, stated that it would be at the risk of their lives if it became known that they had communicated anything to him; and they requested Judge Cradelbaugh, if he met them in public in the day time, not to recognize them as persons that he had before seen.[14]

With this kind of help, the Judge made out writs for some thirty-six men, only half of whom were the same as those listed by Lee in his *Confessions* as having been implicated. Of all these thirty-six writs, not one was served, and the marshal, unable to make a single arrest, wrote a formal statement to justify his failure. Even Jacob Hamblin, now an officer of the government, would not co-operate to take Lee into custody, though he confessed that he knew the hiding place.[15] Although he had talked

[14] Statement of William H. Rogers regarding the Mountain Meadows Massacre published in *The Valley Tan*, February 29, 1860. See Appendix IX.

[15] Jacob Hamblin's attitude is shown in the following affidavit, found in the "History of Brigham Young," 1859, pp. 471f.

"TERRITORY OF UTAH)
GREAT SALT LAKE COUNTY)

"Be it remembered that on this third day of June, 1859, A.D., before me, Elias Smith, Judge of the Probate Court, for said County and Territory, personally ap-

freely about the massacre to his church leaders the year before, and was to have another long conference on the subject in June following, he would give no names to the officers. Forced at last to admit that they could do nothing, the Judge and his escort started back to Salt Lake City, and the local leaders came out of hiding. Haight reports that he arrived home on June 3, while Lee wrote on May 28 that he had eaten his first meal at home in four weeks. Here the Indians visited him and "greeted me with a cordial welcome. Related the bribes that had been offered them by Cradelbaugh for my head. $5,000.00 reward, a considerable reward for a man that is endeavoring to obey the gospel requirements."

---

peared Jacob Hamblin of Washington County in said Territory, who upon being duly sworn in due course of law, deposeth and saith, that on or about the 1st day of May A.D., 1859, Judge Cradlebaugh of the 2nd Judicial District of Utah Territory, and William Rogers, Deputy United States Marshal of Utah, requested me to employ the Piute Indians to go into the mountains and hunt up John D. Lee, and assist said Deputy Marshal to arrest him, and bring him into camp, dead or alive.

"I told them according to the Marshals previous request I had made some inquiry of the Indians of the whereabouts of said Lee, and ascertained where he camped two nights before, but on going to the place I found that he had left. The Judge remarked that he had employed an Indian to testify in relation to the massacre at the Mountain Meadows and that he had paid him in blankets, etc., and that he had more blankets and required me to employ a large number of Indians to go out and rake the county and bring in said Lee—Deputy Marshal Rogers asked me if I thought I could get the Indians to turn out and assist him to take Lee. I told him I thought the Indians would assist if they were well paid for it. I also told them that Lee was armed with three revolvers and a six shooter rifle and it would cost life to take him. They replied they did not care what it cost, if the Indians would hunt him up. I then told them that it was contrary to my instructions as interpreter, from Dr. Forney, Superintendent of Indian Affairs for Utah to encourage the Indians in any way to interfere with the Whites.

"The above conversation took place in the tent at the encampment of Judge Cradlebaugh, and his escort, comprising two companies of Infantry, one hundred discharged Teamsters, amounting to 200 men, at the foot of Santa Clara, Washington Co., U.T.

"And further this deponent saith not.

"JACOB HAMBLIN

"Sworn to and subscribed the day and year first above written.

"E. SMITH"

John D. Lee (center), with his attorney William W. Bishop and
(left to right) Judge Jacob S. Boreman, attorney Enos D. Hoge,
attorney Wells Spicer, and an unidentified man.

Lee's willow shanty at The Pools, where his wife Rachel and her children lived for two years. Lee later constructed a stone house here. It is some twenty miles from "Lonely Dell."

Already Lee was made conscious of the disapproval of his neighbors and friends and of the fact that he was often the subject of critical discussion. When, on June 5, one of his daughters gave birth to a child after a long and agonizing delivery, the midwife in attendance, appreciating his help and support, apologized for the things she had said about him in his absence. "She said she repented from the bottom of her heart, and prayed God to forgive her," he wrote.

On June 12, Lee told of a visit from Haight, Hopkins, Klingonsmith, and four others whom he did not name. They had come, it would seem, to settle difficulties and misunderstanding among themselves with regard to the massacre. These could have arisen over the division of the booty or over the attempts to shift the responsibility. Clearly, for their mutual safety, they must stand by each other.

> Elder Hopkins said there were feelings now between me and Elder Haight that ought to be settled. I replied that if Elder Haight wished to be friendly and drop the past, he must not turn a cold shoulder to me nor wear an air of scorn thinking that I would bow to him for I never would with my present feelings. I am the injured person. If I had injured him I would readily make restitution. I have been seriously wronged. . . .

Could this refer to the fact that only Lee had been named as being involved in the massacre, when the report for public consumption was made? Whatever the grievance, it would seem that some kind of reconciliation was effected.

With Judge Cradlebaugh safely back in the north, George A. Smith set out on another of his annual trips south. On the night of July 17, 1859, he stayed at the home of John D. Lee, along with Amasa M. Lyman, Jesse N. Smith, R. Brown, James H. Martineau, C. B. Adams, and their wives, and when they set out to visit the settlements to the south, they invited Lee to accompany them. This may be made significant in view of the fact that neither Dame nor Haight nor others who often went with the visiting brethren from the north were included this year. If, at this time, they had held Lee as the only one responsible for the massacre, or even the most responsible, is it likely that they would have accepted his hospitality, traveled with him, had him sit beside them in public meetings, and invited him to speak?

Upon their return to Cedar City, the leaders took action to reorganize the church there, releasing both Haight and Klingonsmith from their positions. Reporting it, Lee wrote:

> Sunday, July 31, 1859. . . . Elder G. A. Smith returned to Cedar called a conference, disorganized the stake droped the present Bishop P. K. Smith, Pres. I. C. Haight, Higbee and Morris. Appointed Henry Lunt presiding Bishop Richard Morris first coun. & 2 Bishop & clerk to keep the tithing books   Thos Jones 2 con & bishop the 3 was there ordained to the office of Bishop. The present change was satisfactory I believe to the entire settlement. This evening returned, first gave me a receipt in full for all accts settled satisfactorily.

Of the same incident, and under the same date, Isaac C. Haight's diary records:

> Sunday 31st [July, 1859].   Elder G. A. Smith paid us a visit and appointed a new Bishop, Bro. Henry Lunt.
> In consequence of the persecutions of our enemies, I solicited to be released from the presidency of this Stake, as my enemies swore that they would destroy me if they could get me, and there was little prospect of my being at home much of the time to come to attend to the duties of my office, accordingly the organization of the Stake was suspended for the present.

The reasons for these actions were no doubt the complaints and investigations of the year before, along with the growing stigma which was attached to all who were connected with the massacre. Since William H. Dame continued in his office as bishop, it would seem that he had, to some degree, cleared himself.

Lee was not a bishop or even a presiding elder in Harmony at the time, but the attitude of the visitors toward him was one of friendly intimacy.

By this time the policy of the church was well crystallized: the leaders and the people as a whole did not approve of murder; if any had been committed it was against the teachings of the church and out of harmony with its doctrines. A group of people had been massacred upon Utah soil by Indians, but they had provoked violence by their own acts and were thus responsible for their own fate. Although a few white men might have been on the scene at the time, it was not known why they were there or what part they had in it all, or indeed, whether they were actually there or not. If they were, and *if* they had any part, it was entirely upon their own responsibility as individuals, without the knowledge or consent of the church as a whole, or the leaders of it. With the fervor and excitement of the war gone, in the light of cool, calm reasoning, this seemed the logical explanation.

A letter from George A. Smith to T. B. H. Stenhouse, dated April 13, 1859, shows that no admissions were to be made. Although writing to a trusted associate, Smith does not tell what he could not help knowing just from his visit to the scene, without his private investigations. Instead, there seems to be a deliberate attempt to befog the affair and direct attention away from any possibility of Mormon implication (see Appendix VII). As a matter of policy, at a time when the leaders of the church, and the people of Utah generally, were in disrepute, that must have seemed the best front to assume. In view of the hostile attitude of the court, and the indirect responsibility which must have fallen back upon both Brigham Young and himself, he could have done nothing else.

With the election of Abraham Lincoln and the change of national administration in 1860, Governor Cumming and all the federal officers were withdrawn and a new set appointed. Now, for the duration of the Civil War, the attention of the nation was turned from the Mormons to the rebellion in the south. The new officers in Utah made little or no attempt to probe into the Mountain Meadows Massacre, and, except for the whisperings which went on assiduously among the Mormons themselves, the matter was quiet. Repeated counsel of the authorities was to keep it quiet; there was nothing to be gained by constant agitation of it. "The more you stir a manure pile, the worse it stinks," Brigham Young is often unofficially quoted as saying.

In May, 1861, the Mormon leader came into southern Utah to see for himself the possibilities for establishing the cotton industry in the warm valleys below the rim of the basin. He took time to visit every tiny village en route; if we are to trust the legends, he took time also to inquire into the Mountain Meadows Massacre. A daughter of Isaac C. Haight told how he had had a private conversation with her father, sitting in a carriage in the street away from eager listeners. After a long and earnest talk, the president had held out his hand and had seemed to give approval and blessing to what had been said.

Whatever legends may be told, the fact that Brigham Young did visit the scene of the massacre is established by the following entry in the diary of Wilford Woodruff:

> May 25 [1861]. A very cold morning much ice on the creek. I wore my great coat & mittens. We visited the Mt. Meadows Monument not up at the burial place of 120 persons killed by Indians in 1857. The pile of stone was about twelve feet high but beginning to tumble down. A wooden cross is placed on top with the following words, Vengeance is mine and I will repay saith the Lord. Pres. Young said it should be Vengeance is mine and I have taken a little. A stone at the bottom bore the following description 120 men women & children murdered in cold blood early Sept 1857 From Arkansas. And on the side of the slab Erected by Company K 1st Dragoons May, 1859. Most of those killed were buried some distance north in a hollow and not at that monument. We left and drove down the canyon and in a few hours ride we passed over the rim of the basin. . . .

The account copied for posterity into the official "Journal History of the Church" is taken almost verbatim from the above, except that President Young's remark is omitted.[16] On the return trip, President Young and his party were entertained by John D. Lee at Fort Harmony, where they partook of

[16] The quotation copied direct from the Journal of Wilford Woodruff in the archives of the Latter-day Saints historian is without doubt the basis for the entry in the "Journal History of the Church" for the same date, since the wording is identical, except that the remark of President Young has been omitted.

Regarding this monument, Roberts, in his *A Comprehensive History of the Church*, Vol. IV, in a footnote on p. 176, gives a description of the monument and adds that it "later was destroyed either by some vandal's hand or the ruthless ravages of time. . . . The destruction of this inscription is unjustly connected by the judge with President Young's first visit to southern Utah after it was erected (1861). It is also said that when Brigham Young read the inscription he changed the purport of its language, and said to those around him that it should read thus: 'Vengeance is mine saith the Lord, and I have repaid.' "

See also Thomas B. H. Stenhouse, *Rocky Mountain Saints*, 453, and Catherine V. Waite, *The Mormon Prophet and his Harem*, 71.

By a strange coincidence, the story is verified by a legend in the writer's own family. My grandfather, Dudley Leavitt, was present, and he told the incident repeatedly, so that it has been verified by three of his sons. One preserved it in these words, quoting his father:

"I was with the group of elders that went out with President Young to visit the spot in the spring of '61. The soldiers had put up a monument, and on top of that a wooden cross with words burned into it, 'Vengeance is mine, saith the Lord, I will repay.' Brother Brigham read that to himself and studied it for a while and then he read it out loud, 'Vengeance is mine saith the Lord; I *have* repaid.' He didn't say another word. He didn't give an order. He just lifted his right arm to the square, and in five minutes there wasn't one stone left upon another. He didn't have to tell us what he wanted done. We understood."

The story of the destruction of the monument has been occasion for discussion among scholars because some later travelers refer to it as standing. On July 1, 1864, Lorenzo Brown wrote: ". . . went past the monument that was erected in commemoration of the Massacre that was committed at that place by officers & men of Company M Calafornia volunteers May 27th & 28th 1864 It is built of cobble stone at the bottom and about 3 feet high then rounded up with earth & surmounted by a rough wooden cross the whole 6 or 7 feet high & perhaps 10 feet square On one side of the cross is inscribed Mountain Meadow Massacre and over that in smaller letters is vengeance is mine & I will repay saith the Lord. On the other side Done by officers & men of Co. M Cal. Vol. May 27th & 28th 1864 Some one has written below this in pencil. Remember Hauns mill and Carthage Jail. . . ." Typescript of the Lorenzo Brown Journals is at Brigham Young University.

This entry p. 492 of typescript.

a "sumptuous dinner," with fifty people at the table. It would seem that cordial relations still existed between Lee and the president up to this time, although the former had lost prestige among his neighbors. In March, 1859, when the county court had been moved to Washington, Lee was relieved of his position as judge, and some of the vouchers which he presented for work on the roads were not allowed.

Following the activities of Lee as recorded in official writings of James G. Bleak is interesting. Under date of December 22, 1861, he says, "The Saints met in John D. Lee's family hall at Harmony, and organized a branch of the Church with John D. Lee as presiding Elder; Wm Pace, Branch Clerk. . . .

"25 Dec. 1861   John D. Lee gave a public dinner and social party in his family hall, in which the whole branch participated."

It was not until the fifth of March, 1864, that "John D. Lee, on suggestion that he do so, resigned his position as presiding Elder of Harmony Branch, and Elder James H. Imlay was appointed in his stead."

As time went on, the massacre remained a subject of perennial interest. Bit by bit, more damning evidence came out and the weight of public disapproval drove one after another of the participants to move away, some to Idaho on the north, others to Arizona or Mexico on the south. Finally, sentiment from within the church became so strong that by 1870 the leaders were forced to formally excommunicate Isaac C. Haight and John D. Lee for their part in it.

Although the *Deseret News* was silent on the subject, the *Daily Union Vidette* and later non-Mormon papers in the territory would not let the matter rest. Finally, there appeared in the Corinne *Utah Reporter* a series of articles in the form of an open letter to Brigham Young, demanding that the guilty be brought to justice and that the shame of this deed be lifted from the shoulders of innocent members of the church. This was signed "Argus," and seems to have been written by one C. W. Wandell, who had been a member of the church during the Nauvoo era and had worked in the church historian's office for a time with

Franklin D. Richards. The *Salt Lake Tribune* for January 31, 1873, reported that the massacre was the work of white men. In court later, when asked whether or not he had discussed the massacre with anyone before he made his formal affidavit, Philip Klingonsmith testified that he had told the facts to Charley Wandell. Whoever the author, the open letter drew an instant reaction wherever it was read.

Excommunicated at the same time as Lee, Isaac C. Haight was readmitted to the church less than four years later, having evidently been able to shift full responsibility to Lee and the men on the ground. The Mormon historian, B. H. Roberts, says Haight was cut off for failure to *restrain* Lee; Roberts makes no mention of the troops or the military aspect of the massacre. A son-in-law of Haight, Christopher J. Arthur, writing in his diary, says:

[March 3, 1874]. I telegraphed to my father-in-law, Isaac C. Haight, the death of his beautiful daughter. He received the telegram a few moments after entering his house from returning thither from the waters of baptism whither he had gone by instruction of Brigham Young to renew his covenant. He had been cut off the church on account of a misunderstanding of the President about his course in the Mountain Meadow Massacre after which all his former blessings, priesthood, washings, annointings, and endowments were restored fully by the instructions of Pres. Young. It is generally thought that about the time Caroline died her father was being immersed.[17]

Lee says, concerning his own excommunication, that he protested at once, that he went immediately to Brigham Young and demanded a hearing, insisting that:

I did nothing designedly wrong on that occasion. I tried to save that company from destruction after they were attacked, but I was

[17] Christopher J. Arthur was a prolific writer, copying or rewriting some of his earlier experiences a number of times. Parts of his diaries are in the Washington County library at St. George, Utah; these and at least one additional are at the Utah State Historical Society. The Henry E. Huntington Library has photostats of some of them.

overruled and forced to do all that I did do. . . . I have suffered in silence, and have done so to protect the brethren who committed the deed. I have borne the imputation of this crime long enough, and demand a rehearing. I demand that all the parties concerned be brought forward and forced by you to shoulder their own sins. I am willing to bear mine, but I will not submit to carry all the blame for those who committed the massacre.[18]

Lee goes on to say that Brigham Young told him to arrange for a rehearing with Erastus Snow:

I did so. We arranged the time of the meeting. It was agreed that if the telegraph wires were working, all parties interested were to be notified of the meeting, and required to be present at St. George, Utah, on the following Wednesday at 2 P.M. . . .

Soon after I left Washington, Erastus Snow, one of the twelve apostles, arrived at my house and asked for me. My family told him that I had gone to Harmony to arrange for the new hearing and trial before the Church authorities. He appeared to be much disappointed at not meeting me, and told my family that Brigham Young had reconsidered the matter, and there would be no rehearing or investigation; that the order cutting me off from the Church would stand; that he would send a letter to me which would explain all the matter, and that the letter would reach Harmony about as soon as I did.

On the next Tuesday night an anonymous letter was left at my house by one of the sons of Erastus Snow, with orders to hand it to me. The letter read as follows:

"John D. Lee, of Washington:

"Dear Sir: If you will consult your own interest, and that of those that would be your friends, you will not press an investigation at this time, as it will only serve to implicate those that would be your friends, and cause them to suffer with, or inform upon you. Our advice is to make yourself scarce, and keep out of the way."

There was no signature to the letter, but I know it came from apostle Snow, and was written by orders of Brigham Young.

[18] Lee, *Confessions*, 265ff.

Thus it was that, so far as the official church records were concerned, the entire blame of the massacre was shifted to the shoulders of John D. Lee. Ostracized by his former friends, early in 1872 he moved, at the order of Brigham Young, to the ferry on the Colorado River at the mouth of the Paria. Here he built a small house, cleared a garden spot, and appropriately named his place "Lonely Dell." Hunted by the law and shunned by his own people, cut off from the church he loved, he prepared to spend his remaining days in seclusion.[19]

[19] It is interesting to know that during the years 1948–49 descendants of John D. Lee asked repeatedly at the office of the historian of the Latter-day Saints church for specific evidence of his excommunication in the form of a minute of the meeting, the exact date, etc., and as yet have not been able to secure it, although the employees there have always promised that they would try to find it.

The exact date has been recorded in only one place that has yet been located, and that was by Lee himself. Under date of November 22, 1870, after receiving mail at Pipe Springs, Arizona, he returned to the sawmill at Skutumpah and showed his letter signed by Albert Carrington, notifying him of the action of the Twelve Apostles, to his wife Rachel, who "received the inteligence of my expulsion from the church with firmness & reminded Me of a Dream or Night vision that I had related to her about the time, about the 8th of Oct., 1870, which was the date of my being droped from the Church." *A Mormon Chronicle*, II, 146.

10

An Official Sacrifice

With his excommunication from his church, John D. Lee's whole life-pattern changed. Before, he had owned land, cattle and sheep, houses at Harmony, and an impressive stone "mansion" at Washington, whose spacious rooms were ample to entertain the best of Mormon gentry; now, he had a tiny cottage in one of the loneliest spots on earth. Here, with the Colorado River before him, with towering red walls of stone behind him, and utter silence and desolation stretching in all directions around him, life must have been monotonous indeed. Here Nature's work is designed on such a colossal scale as to dwarf man, if not to crush him. Now this man, whose dinner bell had been the signal for all within range of its call to come and eat, whose cordial greeting did not wait for famous guests to arrive at the gate but went out on horseback to meet and escort them in—now this same man must slink into hiding at the sight of approaching dust and remain until the signal was given to come out. For one of the temperament of John D. Lee, this was bitter medicine.

Many legends remain of the years at the ferry, from boys stranded there and from passing parties whom he seemed eager to help. At least two visitors wrote for publication of their contact with him. J. H. Beadle, traveling newspaper correspondent, was there on June 28, 1872, and had a long conversation in which Lee gave his own version of the massacre, insisting that he had had to carry "the most infamous charges ever cooked up on a man," because he could not clear himself without incriminating others. Beadle made extensive notes, which he transcribed the next day, and later incorporated into his book, *Western Wilds*. With regard to the emigrants, he quotes Lee as saying:

They was the worst set that ever crossed the plains, and they made it so as to get here just when we was at war. . . . Their conduct was scandalous. They swore and boasted openly that they helped shoot the guts out of Joe Smith and Hyrum Smith at Carthage, and that Buchanan's whole army was coming right behind them, and would kill every G——d d——n Mormon in Utah, and make the women and children slaves and . . . . They had two bulls, which they called one "Heber" and the other "Brigham" and whipped 'em through every town, yelling and singing, blackguarding and blaspheming oaths that would have made your hair stand on end. . . .

It is told around for a fact that I could tell great confessions, and bring in Brigham Young and the Heads of the Church. But if I was to make forty confessions, I could not bring in Brigham Young. His counsel was: "Spare them, by all means." But I am made to bear the blame. . . . Bad as that thing was, I will not be the means of bringing troubles on my people; for, you know yourself, that this people is a misrepresented and cried down community. Yes, a people scattered and peeled, whose blood was shed in great streams in Missouri, only for worshiping God as he was revealed to them; and if at last they did rise up and shed blood of their enemies, I won't consent to give 'em up.

A few weeks after this visit, Frederick S. Dellenbaugh, of the Powell exploring expedition, called upon Lee. In the course of their conversation, the ever current subject of the massacre came up. Mr. Dellenbaugh reproduced the discussion in a letter to a newspaper, with the notation that Lee's own words were reported, not verbatim, but without exaggeration. Lee gave the killing of the emigrant man, Aiden, as the immediate cause of the massacre, and insisted that he had wept like a child at the plan, at which the Indians had named him "Crybaby." "Although Mr.

Lee has been cut off the Mormon Church, he says he is still a staunch Mormon. He believes that if a man has been guilty of nothing which would separate him from the Church he cannot be cut off," Dellenbaugh concluded.[1]

[1] Frederick S. Dellenbaugh, manuscript "Diaries" at The New York Public Library. Entries relating to the author's stay at Lonely Dell occupy pages 149–54. More significant than these is a letter of July 11, 1872, to the *Buffalo Express*, a clipping pasted in the diary on pages 227 and 229.

In this letter, Dellenbaugh begins by saying that Lee "had one house at Lonely Dell and one at Jacob's Pools, 30 miles towards Kanab. At each place he has one of his wives. . . . Although John D. Lee has the reputation of a notorious villain, yet I saw nothing dangerous about him, and in fact, he treated us handsomely. . . .

"Lee spoke of the various accusations and publications which were in circulation against him; the persecutors driving him from place to place, and causing him to abandon home after home, until at last he had brought up in Lonely Dell. . . ."

Lee is then quoted as saying: "I will not be taken; as I would then be obliged to betray men who did the act through their great zeal in serving our church, and thought they were doing right. . . .

Dellenbaugh continues:

"The party of emigrants who met with the disaster swore and cursed through the streets of the settlements, saying, 'Where's your d——d Mormon biship,' etc., and it was with the greatest difficulty that the authorities of Spanish Fork withheld the people from killing them there; but they went on and arrived at Cedar City, cursing and swearing the same way which so roused the citizens that they held a council, and of this council Mr. Lee was a member. Meanwhile the emigrants poisoned the water of several springs, causing the death of two or three Indians. This enraged the other Indians, so that they began to attack the train.

"The council proceeded. Most of the councilors were in favor of putting the emigrants out of the road, by setting on the Indians, but, said Mr. Lee, 'I told them that instead of resulting in good it would result just as it has done, and had I at that time known the President's feelings upon the subject I should have opposed it even more strongly than I did. However I think they would have escaped unharmed could we have drawn the Indians off, but for the fact that two or three of them, I forget which, mounted their horses and attempted to escape one night; these were met by three of the opposite party, one of them killed and the two others driven back. Then the council resolved upon the plan they carried out. I wept like a child and would not consent to have anything to do with it, but pleaded for the women and children's lives. The Indians, although I offered to pay them for every life saved, would not promise to spare any but the children, and they called me Nah-gaats (cry-baby), a name by which I am known all through Utah tribe to the present day. . . .'

"The messenger rode from Beaver to Salt Lake in three days and a half. When Brigham Young heard the news he said: 'For God's sake stop it; take fresh horses and return immediately and do all in your power to prevent them from carrying

During the first years of his exile, Lee occasionally left his retreat to visit one or another of the wives who remained true to
him through all his trouble. He felt quite secure, except that he
felt keenly the changed attitude of his former associates. But with
the passage of the Poland Bill in 1874, withdrawing criminal jurisdiction from the probate courts and arming the federal courts in
Utah, his whole status changed. Now he was definitely hunted,
a man with a price upon his head.

During a visit to his family in Panguitch, Utah, on November
7, 1874, he was taken into custody by William Stokes, deputy
United States marshal. The trial was to be held at Beaver, but
with the law's delay and the difficulty in securing witnesses, the
case did not come into court until the following summer.

The court was presided over by Judge Jacob S. Boreman; the
jury which was finally selected consisted of eight Mormons, three
Gentiles, and one Jack Mormon. From the first it seemed that
there was a difference in attitude among the attorneys for the
defense, for while Spicer and Bishop seemed seriously trying for
the acquittal of Lee and were willing that the Mormon leaders
should be shown as issuing the orders which he obeyed as a man
in the ranks, Sutherland's and Bates's chief concern seemed to be
to have the inquiry stop with Lee and not involve anyone else,
especially the church leaders. Thus they were often at cross-
purposes with each other. The prosecution, while intent upon
convicting Lee, was also eager to extend the guilt to others and
to show that the whole thing was church inspired, with the guilt
going all the way back to Brigham Young and his immediate
subordinates. Trial began on Friday, July 23, 1875, with no Mormon in good standing present to give evidence.

The first witness was Robert Keyes, who testified that he had
passed over the ground on October 2, 1857, some three weeks

out their mistaken ideas.' But by the time the messenger returned the deed had
been done.

"That is the story as Mr. Lee told it—a horrible affair, at the very best.
Although Mr. Lee has been cut off from the Mormon Church, he says he is
still a staunch Mormon. He believes that if a man has been guilty of nothing
which would separate him from the Church he cannot be cut off."

after the massacre, and had seen the nude bodies—one pile of women and some children, the other of men—pulled about by wild beasts. Asahel Bennett, of the same party, verified the story. The chief witness, however, was Philip Klingonsmith, participant in the massacre, former bishop of Cedar City, and first to break the blood pact and turn state's evidence. Four years before, he had made out an affidavit of what happened; now he swore to substantially the same facts. A large, heavy man, he told his story slowly and simply, but showing emotion as it progressed. He related how the militia had been mustered and had gone to the scene in wagons and on horseback; how they had marched to the spot in full view of the emigrant's camp where they had stood in formation a long time while Lee had negotiated with the people within the enclosure. Higbee, on horseback, had ordered the proceedings and had taken charge on the field; Lee had gone ahead with the wagons. From where he had been in the ranks, Klingonsmith said that he had seen only the killing of the men, about fifty of whom had been shot down with the first volley with the few remaining being shot as they ran.[2] When questioned by the attorneys, he admitted that Lee was not present at the meeting where the fate of the company had been discussed and the messenger sent to Brigham Young; Klingonsmith insisted that Higbee had carried orders from Haight, and he thought they had come in turn from William H. Dame at Parowan. When first asked about the Indians, he said that he did not know the number, but "the hills were pretty full of them." Later he estimated them to have been between one hundred and one hundred fifty in number.[3]

[2] Beadle, in his *Western Wilds*, pp. 506–507, describes Klingonsmith thus: "He was a heavy, rather stolid looking Dutchman, six feet high, well muscled, slow, heavy, phlegmatic. He had been indicted along with the others and a *nolle* entered. He began with extreme slowness, amounting almost to stupidity, but as he went along gradually grew more animated; his dull eye lit up, the blue veins stood out on his forehead, and his every feature and muscle seemed to work in sympathy with the horrors he was reciting."

[3] A transcript of the full text of the testimony at the trials of John D. Lee is now owned by the Henry E. Huntington Library. It is far too voluminous to be reproduced in this study.

He told of his trip to Salt Lake City to attend conference on October 6, and said that he had called upon Brigham Young in company with Charles Hopkins and John D. Lee. They had discussed the massacre and the disposal of the property. The president had cautioned them about discussing the matter, even among themselves, and had advised them to let John D. Lee manage the cattle, since he was the Indian farmer. He testified further that Haight had traded forty or fifty head of the emigrants' cattle to Hooper, Utah delegate to Congress, for boots and shoes.[4]

During the five days before the defense began, a great deal of evidence was presented, much of it very shocking to the members of the Mormon church who had moved into the area after the massacre took place and did not understand the passions of 1857. One witness after another testified to the orders not to sell grain or provisions to the company and to the strictness of the military discipline everywhere enforced. One person had been cut off the church for trading a cheese for a bed quilt; another had been struck over the head with a paling from a fence for giving some onions to one of the emigrants with whom he had become acquainted years before, and from whom he accepted hospitality while on a mission. A number of witnesses testified to the inflammatory nature of the sermons of George A. Smith just preceding the arrival of this company.

When finally the case was closed and given to the jury, they could not agree upon a verdict, the eight Mormons all being for acquittal and the other four, all for conviction. The court was obliged to begin all over again and try the case before another jury.

---

[4] Lee's diary of 1858, under date of January 23, while he was yet in Great Salt Lake City attending the legislature, says: ". . . bought a cook stove of Sanford Porter for 8 head of sheep. . . . Closed my accts with Stewart & William Hooper by note to the amount of $1500."

The next spring, under date of April 12, he records that ". . . I also sent up 75 head of beef cattle, cows & calves to meet my obligation with L. Stewart & W. H. Hooper G.S.L.C. . . ."

Haight sent cattle north in the same herd to pay for purchases he had made at the same time.

The trial closed on August 5, 1875. On August 9, late in the evening, the officers set out to take John D. Lee to the state penitentiary in Salt Lake City. On that date Lee started a new diary, one of the most remarkable of all his records. In it he gives details of the journey by carriage, describes clearly the prison and its environs, and chronicles each day's events. The reader becomes acquainted with the inmates, the regulations, the difficulties, the penalties, even the violence of a prison break. More important still, he reads the mind and hopes of John D. Lee and senses the stamina Lee must have had to resist all attempts to persuade him to place the blame upon Brigham Young.

The book was filled on April 18, 1876. On May 11 following, Lee was released on bail of $15,000, to appear in court in three months. He was there according to his promise for the second trial.

Even the most cursory examination of the court records will show that between the first and second trials of Lee, something happened.[5] When court opened again on September 14, 1876, the

[5] One would have to go through the records of the court proceedings to see what a complete about-face was made by the prosecution between the two sessions. What went on behind the scenes, by what means the very obvious agreement was made, is not known. An interesting bit of evidence that there was an attempt to tamper with the processes of the law is found in a letter in the collection of manuscripts left by Judge Boreman, now in custody of the Henry E. Huntington Library. Although the letter is unfinished, and there is no evidence that it was ever mailed, it does speak eloquently, as the following excerpt will show:

"BEAVER CITY, UTAH TERRITORY

FEB. 13, 1875

"MESSRS SUTHERLAND & BATES
 ATTYS AT LAW
 SALT LAKE CITY, UTAH
"SIRS:

"Your letter of the 5th inst has been received, inclosing the petition of J. H. Higbee, I. C. Haight, William Stewart, Edward Wilden, Samuel Bates, and George W. Adair, the petition having been prepared by you and sworn to by one of you. You also advise your motion on the petition asking that these parties be allowed to give bail 'for their free and voluntary surrender at the next term of court,' etc.

"Your letter and the petition and motion referred to are very remarkable

The arrival of John D. Lee at Mountain Meadows on the day of
his execution.

John D. Lee seated on his coffin, awaiting execution.

whole tone was changed, the whole approach of the prosecution different. R. N. Baskin and other non-Mormons insisted that the leaders of the Mormon church had entered into an agreement with District Attorney Howard whereby Lee might be convicted and pay the death penalty if the charges against all other suspected persons would be withdrawn. This was to be done by a jury composed only of Mormons, who would bring in a verdict of "guilty" if names of other participants were left out of the discussions.

Now, there was no lack of Mormon witnesses; memories, in general, were much sharpened since the first trial, at which no member in good standing had been willing to testify at all. Attorney Howard now proposed to prove that John D. Lee, without any authority from any officer or council, but in direct opposition to the feelings and wishes of the authorities of the Mormon church, had gone to the Meadows, accompanied only by one little

documents, to eminate from men claiming to be lawyers. One of you most solemnly swears that the constitution of the United States guarantees a speedy trial by jury and that the accused be confronted with the witnesses against them & &c These are most astonishing discoveries, and it is gratifying to know that their truthfulness is substantiated by the solemn oath of the attorney. . . .

"Stripped of all verbage, your petition, motion and letter, are substantially as follows: You say these men are alleged murderes, indicted for participation in the Mountain Meadows Massacre; that you are in communication with them and that they are your clients and of course acting under your advice; that they have run off and are now outside of the Territory and have concealed themselves from the officers of the law; that they will not come in and go to prison for months and months, waiting trial; that they will come in and surrender themselves if I will decide before hand whether I will allow them to give bail and decide beforehand, and when the parties are not before me—what the amount of bail shall be and will order that all warrants be revoked and recalled; and then *if I consent to do as you ask*, that you will come to Beaver and attend to the giving of the bail.

"For downright effrontery and cool impudence, your proposition is unsurpassed even in Utah. You well know I have no right to accede to your request. You well know that the law does not allow such a thing; you well know that no court holds intercourse with alleged criminals, not under arrest, but being at large and boasting that they are 'concealed from the officers' and 'out of the jurisdiction of the court.' You well know that no court makes terms with alleged criminals under such circumstances, and you well know that law refuses alleged criminals to be before the judge or court unless in charge of the officer. . . ."

Indian boy, and had assumed command of the Indians, whom he had induced, by promises of great booty, to attack this company of emigrants. He went on to show that Lee had sent word to the various settlements for men to be sent to him under false pretenses, either to help draw off the Indians or to bury the dead, and that these men had gone in response to his call, thinking they were going to perform a humane act; that he had then persuaded the emigrants to leave their enclosure. As to how all these people had been killed, or by whom, Attorney Howard did not pretend to know; his only object in this trial was to show that Lee had murdered some of them.

From the beginning it was clear that no other names would be mentioned, in so far as it was possible to omit them; the attorneys throughout insisted that Lee alone was on trial. Furthermore, Howard said, he would present evidence that Brigham Young had known nothing of the matter until after it was over, and that Lee then had misrepresented the facts, so that the Mormon leader had not learned the truth until 1870, at which time he took immediate action to cut Lee off the church. Most reassuring was the attorney's promise that he would not prosecute any who had been lured to the Meadows at the time, many of whom were young boys, ignorant of the vile plan which Lee had formulated.

This time the trial proceeded with dispatch. Depositions from Brigham Young and George A. Smith, refused at the first trial, were now read and placed in evidence (see Appendix XIII). Men who had participated, and for almost twenty years had sealed their lips, now came forward to testify. If one is to trust verbal reports, these men were ordered to appear by Brigham Young. The following story, told by a daughter of Nephi Johnson, bears this out:

Her father, she said, received a letter from Brigham Young instructing him to appear in court and testify. Just before the second session opened, the sheriff and the bishop of Beaver were talking outside the courthouse.

"I expect Nephi Johnson to come in today and testify," the Bishop said.

"Oh, no," answered the officer. "He'll never come in. He has been hiding too long himself. He would be afraid to come in."

While they were talking, Nephi Johnson rode up on a mule. He dismounted and came over to greet the bishop, who in turn introduced him to the officer.

"I don't believe I ever saw you before," the sheriff said, looking at Johnson keenly.

"No," Johnson answered, smiling, "you've never seen me, but I've seen you many, many times."

The point the narrator wished to make was that her father had for years been evading the law and dodging the officers, and now, openly and fearlessly, he came in to the court. Although she had seen the letter advising him, she did not have it in her possession nor did she know where it could be found. The family of Jacob Hamblin said that he received a similar letter from Brigham Young, but again the actual letter is not available.

Whatever the motive that prompted their appearance, they were there to testify; Laban Morrill, who had opposed the plan in the council meeting, told of the decision to await orders from Brigham Young and made clear that the orders had been definite that "those men must be protected and allowed to go in peace." He could remember only Haight and Klingonsmith as favoring the massacre. Joel White, who had been a messenger to Pinto to stop hostilities, testified that he had passed Lee en route and that Lee had said something to the effect that "I don't know about that," or "I have something to say about that," as though he meant to carry on the massacre in opposition to orders. Samuel Knight, who had driven the wagon which carried the wounded, told how he had brought his wagon to the scene, thinking that he was coming on an errand of mercy to help the emigrants back to Cedar City. He told of the general arrangements for the killing, but could remember none who had been present except Klingonsmith and Lee; many Indians had been there, but he had seen Lee kill one woman, he said. He also admitted that all the wagons and cattle had been taken away at once. Samuel McMurdy, who had driven the other wagon, testified that he had been on the scene by orders of Higbee, but that Lee had directed him after he arrived. He, too, could remember the names of no others who had been present, and when asked if he had helped with the killing, he answered, "I believe I am not on trial, sir." He had seen Lee kill some, but he did not know how many.

Nephi Johnson, the Indian interpreter who later admitted that he had helped Lee make the arrangements with the Indians, was kept on the witness stand longer than the others. He had seen the massacre from the top of a nearby hill whence he had gone to catch his horse. Like the others, he could remember no names of living men except Klingonsmith and Lee, although he did insist that his orders to go to the Meadows had come from Haight and not from Higbee; he pictured Lee as the dominating figure on the ground. His whole story was clearly an effort to center all the responsibility upon these two: Klingonsmith, the apostate; and Lee, whose conviction would clear all others.

Although absent at the time of the massacre, Jacob Hamblin gave the evidence which seemed most unquestioningly accepted. He testified that Lee himself had told him of the massacre and of the killing of the two girls, that his Indian boy, Albert, had taken him to the place and shown him the bodies, and that local Indian chiefs had told him of the circumstances. Like the others, he could not remember what he did not want to tell; like the others, his whole purpose was to convict Lee without involving anyone else.

Because of such evident co-operation in the types of questions asked and patience displayed with short memories of the witnesses, the trial was soon over. On September 20, the case was given to the all-Mormon jury, who deliberated three and one-half hours and brought in a verdict of "guilty." Convicted of murder in the first degree, Lee was asked if he had anything to say before sentence was passed, but he declined to speak. When the judge gave him the choice of the method of his execution, he replied simply, "I prefer to be shot."

At this point it seems appropriate to pause for a brief consideration of the condemned man. If the many writings of John D. Lee

—the diaries now in the archives of the Latter-day Saints church and those owned by the Henry E. Huntington Library, as well as the scattered papers in private hands—should ever be collected and printed, this man would stand prominently before the world in another character than that of a murderer alone. Even with the relatively limited amount of material in print, he may be one of the better-known Mormons. There are frequent references to his activities through the bitter years before the Mormons reached Utah, and many of his letters are on file in the "Journal History of the Church." Few men were more unselfishly devoted to the Mormon cause or contributed more to it than John D. Lee.

Why, then, were his own people so willing to sacrifice him, to let him take the punishment for both himself and his immediate superiors? The answer seems to be that, as time passed, the people became more and more conscious of the enormity of the crime that had been committed; as tempers cooled and heads cleared, it took on an aspect different from that it had had during the fervid days of 1857. Lee had never denied participation, but he always insisted that he had acted as a subordinate in the military organization. Now that he was caught and the evidence against him unmistakably presented, many felt that he should die for his part in it, especially if his execution would settle once and for all any implication of guilt against the authorities of the church as a whole. Their reputation was so closely tied up with that of the organization, both in the minds of the membership and the world at large, that it must be closely guarded. Any arrangement which would settle this matter finally would be a welcome one; too much discussion could not help matters any. The fact that Lee had been most generous in distributing the loot from the massacre to help move either the Saints from Salt Lake City or those from San Bernardino, that he had given beeves to church groups and had furnished horses and supplies to those called on missions for the church need not be mentioned, nor need his years of subservient devotion to Brigham Young. To brand him as an "apostate" was much simpler and easier.

As a man, John D. Lee presents two different pictures. Dr. Herbert E. Gregory of the United States Geological Survey, an avid student of the history of southern Utah, says that as an explorer and frontiersman Lee towers above all his companions and that, regardless of religion or morals or any connection with the massacre, he should hold a prominent place in the history of the area for his explorations. Andrew Jenson, for many years assistant historian of the Latter-day Saints church, stated many times, that in all his experiences he never saw more accurate or better kept records than those of John D. Lee.

On the other hand, he has come to represent to many in the church the arch villain, a fiend in human form, the man solely responsible for the murder of more than a hundred people, a man who could violate two girls in their early teens and then cut their throats, a man whose very name should be blotted entirely from history. His descendants should not admit their lineage or tell their children that they descended from this man.

Through the years following the massacre, rumors grew and stories multiplied, until people unacquainted with Lee came to regard him as evil incarnate, with strange and mystic powers. A story told by Eliza Kelsey of New Harmony, in 1936, illustrates the length to which such beliefs went. She said:

> I remember that once, when I was about thirteen years old, John D. Lee came up from Washington with a load of fruit, with a lot of apples loose in the back of the wagon bed. We did not have any fruit ripe at New Harmony, and those apples smelled so good. The children all gathered around, he lifted the cover and told them all to help themselves. I was with another girl about my own age, and when we saw the other youngsters biting into those juicy apples, our mouths fairly watered. "Come on," he would say. "Take some. Not just one. Take two or three. Help yourselves."
>
> When we stood back a little and hesitated, he picked out two extra nice ones and handed them to us. We took them and started out, and as we were about to eat them, we remembered the terrible things we had heard about this man. It was whispered that he had

some magic power, and that if we ate anything that he had touched, he would have power over us. It was all rather tied up in stories of love powders or potions and fairy tales that would make a girl submissive to a man. Anyway, hungry as we were for fruit, and good as the apples looked and smelled, we would not taste them, but handed them to some little boys who did not share our fears, and hurried to the ditch to wash our hands for having even touched anything that John D. Lee had handled.

One who reads from his writings, or the writings of his contemporaries, might conclude that Lee was a gifted and intelligent man, generous and kindly, but egotistical and apt to be dictatorial. It seems that he expected the same unquestioning obedience from those over whom he presided that he gave freely to Brigham Young. He was a man who was either ardently loved or heartily disliked.

Thomas D. Brown, recorder for the southern Indian mission, was one of those who did not admire Lee, as he plainly shows in his writings. Soon after the first Indian missionaries had arrived, when they met to organize, some one had proposed the name of Lee as president. After the motion had been put and carried, Brown arose to protest, saying, "If it is not out of place, I would state the opinion of the missionaries and my own feelings, we would prefer another president to Bro. Lee. I would say Patriarch E. H. Groves." Brigham Young, who was presiding, acceded to the suggestion.[6]

Later, in giving the minutes of a meeting, Brown writes:

Sunday 3 December 1854. . . . in the evening went to meeting, sat in much pain hearing J. D. Lee hammering, whaling or lampooning some unknown person, telling a dream about some one cutting his hair short and what woes would befall him, who should interfere with the head. . . .

At the close of the same account he remarks:

[6] Thomas D. Brown, "Journal of the Southern Indian Mission," under date of Friday, May 19, 1854.

Such a meeting! Government so absolute, power so despotic, I have not witnessed in the Kingdom of God! How long will this people endure or be suffered to be humbugged?[7]

As has been mentioned by many who knew him, there is abundant proof that John D. Lee was absolutely loyal to the Mormon church all his life. He regarded Joseph Smith to the last as a prophet of God, and until he knew that he had been betrayed, he loved Brigham Young with all the fealty of an adopted son, as indeed he was. His frequent letters to his president are warm with devotion and trust; he left no question but that Brigham Young's will was his law. Legends among his descendants are to the effect that he told them all that, regardless of what happened to him, they should remain loyal to the church.

Some interesting pictures of the man come to us from the writings of contemporaries. The following, by William Ashworth, would indicate that Lee had reason to think that the church would not desert him:

During the time that Mr. Lee was under guard at the military post, Fort Cameron in Beaver, I accompanied President George A. Smith and two or three of his associates who were passing through Beaver, up to the post to see the prisoner. The officers permitted Lee to come out of the guard house and sit on a bench in front. The guard would pass back and forth with a carbine on his shoulder, but would pay no attention to what was said. President Smith and his companions shook hands with the prisoner. Pres. Smith began by referring to Lee's early life in the church, and to his activities in many ways in protecting the life of the Prophet and otherwise aiding the people in their troubles. Then he said, "John, you never turned a hungry person from your door, did you?" Lee nodded, and I noticed tears as big as peas running down his cheeks.[8]

The hospitality of Lee was proverbial in the south, and has been

[7] *Ibid.*, Sunday, December 3, 1854.
[8] William B. Ashworth, "Autobiography," I, 107. Typewritten copy in Brigham Young University library.

spoken of by many. Benjamin Platte and his wife, who had lived for a number of years in the Lee household, often told how kind and affectionate he was to his wives and children, how considerate even of his animals, how generous to any who called at his home.

In an interview in 1936, Independence (Penn) Taylor, then an old man, told the writer that he had known John D. Lee well, and spoke of him as a helpful neighbor, an eloquent speaker, and a graceful dancer. He told in detail an incident where a little girl had been healed by the prayers of Lee. On April 27, 1947, James E. Taylor, a cousin of Penn, told the same story, which was taken down in his own words:

> I knew John D. Lee well; he was often in our home, and I have been in his. He was a man who had the Spirit of the Lord and lived his religion.
>
> Once when my sister Adelia was very sick, he came to our place about sundown. Mother was walking up and down in the dooryard, crying because it looked as if the child was about to breathe her last. John D. Lee came up to the gate and said, "How are you Sister Taylor?"
>
> "Oh, Brother Lee, they tell me that my little girl is dying," Mother told him, starting to cry again.
>
> "Now I know why I was prompted to come down into town," he said, coming into the yard. "I felt impressed to come." He was in hiding at the time.
>
> He washed his hands at the wash basin outside the door, went into the room, kneeled by her bed and prayed for her. He promised her that she should live and become a mother in Israel. She was instantly healed. She grew up and married John Homer and had a large family.

Mr. Taylor went on to give the conventional explanation of the massacre, making the Indians responsible for it all. "I knew the old Indian Poinkum very well," he concluded. "I asked him why he called John D. 'Yauguts' and he said it was because he sat down and cried like a baby, and the Indians were mad at him and called him crybaby. They called him that all the rest of his life."

The incident of healing told above seems to be a pattern for others which are very similar. Nathan Tenney told one wherein the girl was his niece, Rowena McFate, who had inflammatory rheumatism. The parents, Joseph McFate and Olive Tenney Mc-Fate, lived in Kanarra, Utah. In this case, Lee prayed for her and promised her parents that she should live to be a mother in Israel. She grew up to womanhood, married Edward Whipple, and had sixteen children, fifteen of whom were still living in May, 1938. At that time the family lived in Sholow, Arizona.

Such stories are typical of many that are told within the family of John D. Lee, and of statements that have been collected by some of his descendants, who feel that he was a great and good man—a martyr whose life was given to save the good name of his church. They insist that, placed in a most difficult situation and under strong pressure, he did what he was ordered to do, but under protest, and with the belief that it was necessary to save the lives of his people in the southern settlements. While they admit his part in the affair, they resent the fact that he bears alone the shame that should be shared by others, and that Mormon history names him as the only one responsible for the darkest blot in its pages.[9]

Dellenbaugh, Beadle, and others who became acquainted with him during the years of his exile were favorably impressed with him. Wells Spicer wrote a detailed description of him during the last trial, which concludes:

> ... His appearance is that of a good-natured, agreeable old gentleman. He said he was sad today, yet when cheered up by a pleasant remark, his eyes shone with a laughing twinkle and his mouth evidenced an amiable smile. His teeth are full and perfect, above and below; he talks with ease and smoothness; his voice is mild and even musical; he is an amiable conversationalist,—nothing of the stern, fierce, selfish and cruel look about him that I expected from a man of his reputed character, but on the contrary he seems like a good

[9] Mrs. Edna Lee Brimhall, Ashhurst, Arizona, a granddaughter of John D. Lee, has collected many statements and affidavits that tend to strengthen this stand.

natured, kind hearted, easy going, pleasant spoken old Pennsylvania farmer.[10]

Between the dates of his conviction and execution, two identical petitions addressed to Governor G. W. Emery and asking that the death sentence be stayed were circulated in southern Utah, one in the Beaver area and one in Panguitch. The originals, recently found among the papers of the governors of Utah, are in the state archives, and on microfilm at the Utah State Historical Society. The petitions were supported by the following arguments:

". . . the crime for which he has been convicted was committed nearly Twenty years ago. . . .

". . . Lee is now an old man past sixty-four years of age & . . . his health is very poor. . . .

". . . he is but one of many who are equally guilty. . . . Lee is made to suffer death upon the testimony, connivance & procuration of those equally or more guilty than himself. . . .

". . . the whole proceedings were more properly Military acts, than personal deeds—that they were committed under such circumstances of excitement and consternation as to arouse and nerve the parties to phrenzy & madness so that they lost their judgement and discretion. . . . They were . . . seeking homes for themselves in lieu of those they had recently been driven from . . . among savage, treacherous & relentless Indians . . . with whom they held but short and precarious terms of peace, their wives and children liable at any moment to be massacred by an outbreak of these treacherous foes. Exciting rumors of an army of the U S under Gen. Johnston being then on its march to Utah to Subjugate them & drive them from their new found homes, added to their consternation & aroused the spirit of resistance. Martial Law was declared by the then Governor of Utah & . . . the militia force of the territory (of which Lee was a member) were enrolled and

[10] *Salt Lake Herald*, November 22, 1874, "A Pencil Picture of this Now Noted Man."

205

called out: the people were preparing to abandon their homes again and flee to the mountain fastnesses to find safety for themselves, their wives and children. . . . in prospect of misery & starvation for themselves & families, with bitter memories of past wrongs, that they were precipitated into the commission of the crime, under the firm belief that they were engaged in a war, acting under military orders, and struggling to protect & defend their homes . . . & families

"And that this crime has been condoned & pardoned . . . terms of peace & friendly relations were established between the authorities of the U S and the people of the Territory . . . granting full pardon and Amnesty to all persons for all crimes and offenses committed against either the Laws of the United States or the Laws of the Territory of Utah. . . ."

These petitions bore the signatures of more than five hundred people.

During his imprisonment, Lee had been writing his autobiography; after his conviction, while he waited for an appeal to the Supreme Court, which was denied, and waited again for the day of his execution, he continued to write. He gave the manuscript into the hands of W. W. Bishop, who had defended him, with the understanding that it should be published and Bishop would have first of the proceeds in payment for his work. If the avails were more than that, they should be used for the benefit of his family. His closing remarks read:

CAMP CAMERON
13 MARCH 1877

Morning clear, still and pleasant. The guard, George Tracy, informs me that Col. Nelson and Judge Howard have gone. Since my confinement here, I have reflected much over my sentence, and as the time of my execution is drawing near, I feel composed and as calm as the summer morning. I hope to meet my fate with manly courage. I declare my innocence. I have done nothing designedly wrong in that unfortunate and lamentable affair with which I have been implicated. I used by utmost endeavors to save them from their sad fate. I freely would have given worlds, were they at my command, to have averted that evil. I wept and mourned over them before and after, but words will not help them, now it is done. Death to me has no terror. It is but a struggle, and all is over. I much regret to part with my loved ones here, especially under that odium of disgrace that will follow my name. That I cannot help.

I know that I have a reward in Heaven, and my conscience does not accuse me. This to me is a great consolation. I place more value upon it than I would upon an eulogy without merit. If my work is done here upon the earth, I ask God in Heaven in the name of His son Jesus Christ, to receive my spirit, and allow me to meet my loved ones who have gone behind the veil. The bride of my youth and her faithful mother, my devoted friend and companion, N.A., also my dearly beloved children, all of whom I parted from with sorrow, but shall meet them with joy. I bid you all an affectionate farewell. I have been treacherously betrayed and sacrificed in the most cowardly manner by those who should have been my friends, and whose will I have diligently striven to make my pleasure for the last thirty years at least. In return for my faithfulness and fidelity to him and his cause, he has sacrificed me in a most shameful and cruel way. I leave them in the hands of the Lord to deal with them according to the merits of their crimes, in the final restitution of all things.

TO THE MOTHERS OF MY CHILDREN

I beg of you to teach them better things than to ever allow themselves to be let down so low as to be steeped in the vice, corruption and villany that would allow them to sacrifice the meanest wretch on earth, much less a neighbor and a friend, as their father has been. Be kind and true to each other. Do not contend about my property. You know my mind concerning it. Live faithful and humble before God, that we may meet again in the mansions of bliss that God has prepared for His faithful servants. Remember the *last words* of your most true and devoted friend on earth, and let them sink deep into your tender aching hearts; many of you I may never see in this world again, but I leave my blessing with you. Farewell.[11]

On the date set for the execution, March 23, 1877, Lee was

[11] Lee, *Confessions*, 291.

taken to Mountain Meadows to the scene of the massacre almost twenty years before. The arrangements were made, the witnesses and spectators placed, the photographer instructed to give each of Lee's wives who had remained true to him a copy of the picture that was taken as he sat upon the edge of his coffin. Then he was given a chance to speak. He arose from the coffin, looked calmly around, and delivered his last message in a clear, strong voice, which showed emotion only when he referred to his wives and children. He said:

I have but little to say this morning. Of course I feel that I am upon the brink of eternity; and the solemnities of eternity should rest upon my mind at the present. I have made out—or have endeavored to do so—a manuscript, abridging the history of my life. This is to be published. In it I have given my views and feelings with regard to these things.

I feel resigned to my fate. I feel as calm as a summer morn, and I have done nothing intentionally wrong. My conscience is clear before God and man. I am ready to meet my Redeemer and those that have gone before me, behind the vail.

I am not an infidel. I have not denied God and his mercies.

I am a strong believer in these things. Most I regret is parting with my family; many of them are unprotected and will be left fatherless. When I speak of these things they touch a tender chord within me. I declare my innocence of ever doing anything designedly wrong in all this affair. I used my utmost endeavors to save those people.

I would have given worlds, were they at my command, if I could have averted that calamity, but I could not do it. It went on.

It seems I have to be made a victim—a victim must be had, and I am the victim. I am sacrificed to satisfy the feelings—the vindictive feelings, or in other words, am used to gratify parties.

I am ready to die. I trust in God. I have no fear. Death has no terror.

Not a particle of mercy have I asked of the court, the world, or officials to spare my life.

I do not fear death, I shall never go to a worse place than I am now in.

I have said to to my family, and I will say it today, that the Government of the United States sacrifices their best friend. That is saying a great deal, but it is true—it is so.

I am a true believer in the gospel of Jesus Christ. I do not believe everything that is now being taught and practiced by Brigham Young. I do not care who hears it. It is my last word—it is so. I believe he is leading the people astray, downward to destruction. But I believe in the gospel that was taught in its purity by Joseph Smith, in former days. I have my reasons for it.

I studied to make this man's will my pleasure for thirty years. See, now, what I have come to this day!

I have been sacrificed in a cowardly, dastardly manner. I cannot help it. It is my last word—it is so.

Evidence has been brought against me which is as false as the hinges of hell, and this evidence was wanted to sacrifice me. Sacrifice a man that has waited upon them, that has wandered and endured with them in the days of adversity, true from the beginnings of the Church! And I am now singled out and am sacrificed in this manner! What confidence can I have in such a man! I have none, and I don't think my Father in heaven has any.

Still, there are thousands of people in this Church that are honorable and good-hearted friends, and some of whom are near to my heart. There is a kind of living, magnetic influence which has come over the people, and I cannot compare it to anything else than the reptile that enamors its prey, till it captivates it, paralyzes it, and rushes it into the jaws of death. I cannot compare it to anything else. It is so, I know it, I am satisfied of it.

I regret leaving my family; they are near and dear to me. These are things which touch my sympathy, even when I think of those poor orphaned children.

I declare I did nothing designedly wrong in this unfortunate affair. I did everything in my power to save that people, but I am the one that must suffer.

Having said this, I feel resigned. I ask the Lord, my God, if my labors are done, to receive my spirit.[12]

When he had finished speaking, Lee was told that his hour had

12 *Ibid.*, 387–89.

come, and that he must prepare for the execution. Throughout it all, he was calm and resigned, asking only one favor, that the executioners spare his limbs and shoot through his heart. He shook hands with all those around him, bidding each farewell, took off his overcoat, muffler, and hat to give to his friends. His eyes were bound, but at his request, his hands remained free. The minister who had accompanied him knelt on the ground and uttered a short, earnest prayer, to which Lee listened attentively.

As he sat posed on the coffin, waiting for the order, the condemned man said again, "Center my heart, boys. Don't mangle my body!" When the shot was fired, he fell back without a cry or groan or any visible twitching of the limbs.

The body was arranged in the casket, hauled back by wagon to Parowan, and given to members of his family, who took it to Panguitch, Utah, for burial.

For some eighty years, his grave was marked by a simple stone monument. On August 11, 1960, his descendants held a family reunion at Panguitch, and the activities included the dedication of a stone blanket on top of the grave, upon which is engraved the following inscription: "Know the Truth, and the Truth shall make you free."

11

Causes and Effects

WITH THE EXECUTION of John D. Lee as a sop to justice, the affair of Mountain Meadows was considered closed. People in southern Utah could resume the tenor of their lives, free at last from this disturbing prick of the social conscience. For had not Lee been punished, and their leaders vindicated? The other men who had participated, scattered in other parts of the territory or in other states, passed the years in security and honor, among neighbors who would never guess that there could be any connection between these men and the bloody murder at Mountain Meadows.

Of those listed as being most responsible, William H. Dame was as little affected, evidently, as any upon whom the shadow had fallen. He had joined the church in 1841 and had gone through all the persecutions of the expulsion from Nauvoo. Among the first to be called to settle in Parowan, he had been made the second stake president in the south. When the massacre took place, he was thirty-eight years old. Because of his immediate action to help protect later companies on the road, and because he stoutly denied responsibility and evidently had some proof, he was not released from his position in the church, as were Haight and Klingonsmith. In 1860, he was called on a mission to England, but returned a little short of his two years because of poor health. On his return, he lived again at Parowan, where, from 1866 until his death in 1884, he acted as agent for the presiding bishop of the Mormon church.[1]

[1] *The L. D. S. Biographical Encyclopedia*, I, 532, gives a brief sketch of the

Like Dame, Isaac C. Haight had served long in the church. He had been in Nauvoo at the death of the Mormon Prophet; for the year 1853, he had directed the church emigration, buying the outfits, cattle, and supplies—from Dutch ovens and log chains to such wholesale purchases as 326 ox yokes, 105 sets of tent poles, 6,000 pounds of clean bacon sides, and other items in proportion. From this, it is clear that he had been accustomed to taking responsibility. In 1854, he had been sent to take charge of the ironworks at Cedar City. At the time of the massacre, he was forty-four years old, a tall, well-built man such as would be picked out in a crowd, and an eloquent speaker. Released from his church position in 1859, he established a home in Toquerville for a part of his family, while he himself spent much of his time in hiding. He lived at Manassa, Colorado, and at Thatcher, Arizona, where he assumed his mother's maiden name of Horton. He died there, away from all his family, at the age of seventy-four.[2]

John M. Higbee remained in exile most of the time until after the death of Lee, when he returned to Utah to stay. The affidavits and petitions in the temple at St. George show that it was the opinion of many Mormons that he should be absolved of all responsibility and restored to full fellowship in the church.

Philip Klingonsmith was born in Pennsylvania and had joined the church early. He had been a pioneer of Manti, where the census of 1850 lists him as a blacksmith, thirty-four years old, with a wife, Hannah, and four children. In the first election in Cedar City in 1853, he had been named as an alderman, and, in 1854,

---

life of William H. Dame, an honor which is not accorded any other man whose name has been in any way connected with the Mountain Meadows Massacre. From this sketch, it is evident that he remained all his life in active service in the church.

[2] Christopher J. Arthur, "Autobiography and Diary," under date of September 9, 1886, records the death of Haight: "Recd a telegram from Hyrum Brinkerhoff living near the Gila River, Arizona, that my father in law, Isaac Chauncey Haight, my wife Caroline's father, died on the morning of September 8, 1866, affection of the lungs being the cause. He is 74 years of age. None of his family were present. He was born May 27, 1813, in Wyndam Green Co N. Y. and died in Thatcher, Graham Co, Arizona Sep/8/86."

George A. Smith reported that Klingonsmith had come to conference with about thirty wagons and had succeeded in procuring about one hundred and fifty persons, who were brought over by the Perpetual Emigration Fund, to return them to Iron County.[3] Scarcely six months before the massacre, on March 21, 1857, he had married Margaret Alicer as a plural wife. At that time, he was forty-two years old.

Immediately after the massacre, he was sent to Las Vegas, Nevada, to help mine lead for bullets in the expected war, and by the time he returned, the booty from the massacre had all been disposed of. After he was released from his office as bishop, he spent most of his time in hiding, moving finally to the mining camps of Nevada. In Pioche, Nevada, in April, 1871, he made his affidavit regarding the massacre, the first of all who had participated to break openly the pact of silence. After acting as a witness in the first trial of Lee, he returned to Nevada. The *Salt Lake Tribune* for August 4, 1881, quotes the Pioche *Record*'s report that he was found dead in a prospector's hole in the state of Sonora, Mexico, apparently murdered, the inference being that he had been pursued by avenging members of the Mormon group and had been killed for being a traitor to them.

At the time of the Lee trials, the *Salt Lake Tribune* made a complete coverage, and, in 1875, published a pamphlet summary of the evidence presented at the first trial, along with samples of press comments throughout the nation. The *Deseret News*, on the other hand, was strangely silent on the whole affair, giving only short, inconspicuous items. The attitude up to the time of the arrest of Lee was expressed in an editorial by George Q. Cannon in the issue of November 26, 1869. He began by saying, "our silence upon this subject is frequently construed as an evidence of the inability of the people of this Territory to defend themselves against the vile charges," and then went on to state that Brigham Young had *urged* Governor Cumming to investigate, that the jury at Provo *wanted* to go into the case when Cradle-

3 *Millennial Star*, XVII, 61.

baugh dismissed them. He told of the poisoned springs and meat, which had aroused the Indians; he said that a company from Cedar City had gone out to help, but had been too late. His conclusion was that the Gentiles did not want the truth, for "rumors serve their purpose better than investigation because it gives an excuse for keeping troops in Utah."

By March 24, 1877, after Lee's execution, the *Deseret News* changed its tone somewhat. After denying the intimation of Lee's last words that the massacre had been the result of the teachings of Brigham Young, it admitted that Lee might have planned it "because of erroneous and distorted views of true principles."

Lee's *Confessions* ran through many editions, but was disparaged until members of the church were reluctant to admit that they owned a copy. The massacre was still discussed only in private and in whispers.

Legends and folklore have grown up which persist to this day.[4] The most prevalent is that the spot was haunted; travelers over the ground saw strange forms rise out of the earth and heard moans and shrieks. The same woman's specter moved among the scrub brush night after night, as though forever searching for something—her baby, perhaps, or a missing, unburied bone that had been dragged away by the wolves. Within a few months of the massacre, the story was current of one beautiful young woman whose body the wild animals left entirely untouched. So many were the tales, so vivid the imaginations, and so revolting the reality, that local people shrank from traveling over the place, even in the daytime.

A general belief was that because of the blood that had been shed there, God had cursed the land, so that nothing could grow. What had been a meadow of deep, luxuriant grass, became desolate, a dry, gravelly waste, barren of any vegetation. Students of soil erosion point to this as a classic example. Here, they say, the land was overgrazed, the protective covering removed so that

[4] Austin E. Fife, "Popular Legends of the Mormons," *California Folklore Quarterly*, Vol. I (April, 1942), discussed legends connected with the massacre.

rain which should have quietly soaked into the grass formed little rivulets; these began washing gullies, joining forces to make deep arroyos down which all the precious top soil drained. But old-timers knew better. They understood the deeper, more fundamental reasons which were tied up with man's evil deeds and God's stamp of disapproval.

At least one song was composed about the massacre, a ballad which, sung in a slow chant to the strum of a guitar, is in itself a haunting thing.

> *Come all good men of freedom, and to my song give ear*
> *And of the dreadful massacre you presently shall hear. . . .*

In true ballad style, it proceeds to tell the story. While the entire song has not been made available for this study,[5] enough has been obtained to give its general tenor. It seems that variants were known in different sections of the state.

> *In Indian garb and colors those bloody hounds were seen*
> *To attack the little train all on the meadow green*
> *They were attacked in the morning, and as they got under way*
> *Forthwith corralled their wagons and fought in blood all day.*
>
> *When Lee, the leader of the band, his word to them did give*
> *That if their arms they would give up, he'd surely let them live*
> *And as their arms they did give up and started for Cedar City*
> *He rushed on them in Indian style, Oh what a human pity!*
>
> *They melted down with one accord like wax before the flame*
> *Men and women, old and young, O Utah, blush for shame!*
> *To see mothers and their children lie bleeding in their gore*
> *Oh, such an awful sight I think was never seen before.*

[5] Excerpts of this ballad have been found in various parts of Utah. Mrs. Mae Hammond of the Brigham Young University Training School, Provo, Utah, has a complete recording with words and music.

Austin E. Fife has found some seven variants of this ballad. He has put in pamphlet form *A Ballad of the Mountain Meadows Massacre*, reprinted from *Western Folklore*, Vol. XII (October, 1953), in which he discusses these.

Verses following tell that the participants had decided "to flock together for their wealth, these robbers were inclined," but suggest that:

This life will soon be over and another coming on
And the perpetrators of the deed must suffer for the wrong
'Tis true they do deny it, and the crime they will disclaim
To get out of it the best they can, the Indians bear the blame.

In one version, the closing verses promise that the government will ferret this thing out and bring the guilty to justice. This indicates that the song was written before the execution of Lee, perhaps even before his arrest. One singer thinks it was written by the soldiers who erected the monument in 1859.

Some seven years after the execution of Lee, while the press was still busy with the subject, Charles W. Penrose wrote the account which came to be the accepted story of the church, his whole purpose being to clear the name of Brigham Young from any implications of guilt.[6] Since that time a number of reputable Mormon scholars have begun research on the subject, only to be turned away from it for one reason or another. Two of these men have said that they discontinued because they were "counseled" with such vigor to leave it alone that they felt sure that to continue would cost them not only their positions in church schools, but their membership in the church itself.

As late as 1929, in a study of the relations between Utah and the federal government during the period 1846–61, another Utah writer introduced the subject of the massacre by paraphrasing the comment of B. H. Roberts that members of the church "have been slow to admit all the facts of the case and unwilling to fix the responsibility for the crime upon those individuals of their

[6] In a speech delivered in Salt Lake City, October 26, 1884, Charles W. Penrose set forth the arguments that the massacre was not in harmony with the teachings of the church, and that Brigham Young did not order it or know of it until too late to prevent it. This speech was later printed in pamphlet form and widely distributed throughout Utah. It represents the stand of the church.

own faith who shared in the participation of the tragedy," and then, after all his research, concluded lamely that "from the nature of the evidence available, the writer feels that it is unsafe to make any positive conclusion relative to the responsibility for the massacre,"[7] as though he, too, might be slow to admit all he knew.

An even better illustration, perhaps, is *Essentials in Church History*, by Joseph Fielding Smith. In the 1945 edition, Smith devotes one chapter to the massacre, in which, without mentioning names, he can hardly find language strong enough or words vigorous enough to condemn the participants. He quotes one footnote, and one only—Bancroft's statement that it "was the crime of an individual, the crime of a fanatic of the worst stamp."[8] Yet in the collections of the historian's office of the Latter-day Saints church, records of which he is the custodian, there is ample evidence that this was definitely *not* the crime of a single individual, nor the responsibility of only one man. Even the most superficial research would show the utter ridiculousness of such a statement.

It seems that, once having taken a stand and put forth a story, the leaders of the Mormon church have felt that they should maintain it, regardless of all the evidence to the contrary. In their concern to let the matter die, they do not see that it can never be finally settled until it is accepted as any other historical incident, with a view only to finding the facts. To shrink from it, to discredit any who try to inquire into it, to refuse to discuss it,[9] or to

[7] Leland H. Creer, *Utah and the Nations*, 216.

[8] Herbert H. Bancroft, *History of Utah*, 547, says: "Indeed it may as well be understood at the outset that this horrible crime, so often and so persistently charged upon the Mormon Church and its leaders, was the crime of an individual, the crime of a fanatic of the worst stamp, one who was a member of the Mormon Church, but of whose intentions the church knew nothing, and whose bloody acts the members of the church, high and low, regard with as much abhorrence as any out of the church."

[9] Some time before his death, the late Judge David H. Morris, of St. George, Utah, told the writer of affidavits which he had taken at the order of the First Presidency of the Church from the participants in the massacre who still lived in southern Utah. He suggested that "sometime when it is convenient" he would show these to her.

hesitate to accept all the evidence fearlessly is not only to keep it a matter of controversy, but to make the most loyal followers doubt the veracity of their leaders in presenting other matters of history. This is especially true in dealing with college students and people trained in research.

Perhaps, when all is finally known, the Mountain Meadows Massacre will be a classic study in mob psychology or the effects of war hysteria. It seems to be a clear case of how a group, stirred and angered by reports perhaps only half true, frenzied by mistaken zeal to protect their homes and families and to defend their church, were led to do what none singly would have done under normal conditions, and for which none singly can be held responsible. A careful study of the lives of the participants will show that they were normally not highwaymen or murderers; they were sober and industrious folk, deeply religious, superstitious, perhaps, but unquestioningly loyal to their church. To understand how such men as these could bring themselves to take part in such an atrocity may be to understand also war crimes of more recent occurrence.

After his death, the writer asked his daughter, Mrs. Paul Hafen, about them and learned that in compliance with the advice of her attorney, Orval Hafen, she had taken the affidavits to Salt Lake City and given them to David O. McKay of the first presidency of the Latter-day Saints church.

After two unsuccesful attempts to get an interview with President McKay, the writer made an appointment by long distance telephone. After traveling more than three hundred miles to keep that appointment, she was refused audience as soon as the office girl learned "specifically, what is it you wish to speak to him about?"

The writer then asked for another appointment, offering to stay in the city indefinitely, if necessary. This was refused. She was, however, permitted to talk to Mr. Joseph Anderson, private secretary to the first presidency, who listened to her request and promised to do what he could for her. He asked her to return the next morning.

At that time, Mr. Anderson said that he and President J. Reuben Clark had read the affidavits and President Clark had decided that they should not be made available. The large, worn envelope which contained them and the telegram authorizing them lay on the table during this conversation. The most difficult thing to understand about all this is not so much the refusal to show the affidavits as the consistent and repeated refusal to discuss the question.

In summary, it seems that these are reasonable conclusions to be arrived at from the evidence at hand:

1. While Brigham Young and George A. Smith, the church authorities chiefly responsible, did not specifically order the massacre, they did preach sermons and set up social conditions which made it possible.

2. That this particular company met disaster was due to a most unhappy combination of circumstances: they were the first to pass when the war frenzy was at its height; their own attitude was such as to fan that frenzy and provoke added violence. Had they been of the temperament of the group immediately following, they would likely have escaped unharmed, although short of provisions and robbed of their cattle. But the reckless boasts and acts on the part of those who called themselves "Missouri Wildcats" culminated in disaster for the whole train.

3. While he did not order the massacre, and would have prevented it if he could, Brigham Young was accessory after the fact, in that he knew what had happened, and how and why it happened. Evidence of this is abundant and unmistakable, and from the most impeccable Mormon sources.

Knowing then, why did not President Young take action against these men? At the time, he was involved in a war and was too occupied and too far away to do anything about it. After he was relieved of his position as governor, he felt no responsibility, he claimed. He did have the men chiefly responsible released from their offices in the church following a private church investigation, but since he understood well that their acts had grown out of loyalty to him and his cause, he would not betray them into the hands of their common "enemy." Perhaps the nameless "friend" who kept John D. Lee posted as to the movements of the government officials was not Brigham Young, but it could well have been. Someone assuredly warned all the participants, so that for many years they were all able to evade arrest.

4. The church leaders decided to sacrifice Lee only when they could see that it would be impossible to acquit him without assum-

ing a part of the responsibility themselves. It was a case where the duties of a statesman were weighed against the loyalties of a personal friend, and the duties of the statesman, of necessity, were given precedence. To air the whole story would have done injury to the church, both among its own membership and in the eyes of the world, and this token sacrifice had to be made. Hence the farce which was the second trial of Lee. The leaders evidently felt that by placing all the responsibility squarely upon him, already doomed, they could lift the stigma from the church as a whole.

It was pressure from within the church, perhaps, as much as that from without, which demanded that Lee be convicted. He had never denied being present; he was known to have made the arrangements with the emigrants which decoyed them from their camp; and he had handled much of the booty. If by sacrificing one man the incident could be closed, why not co-operate to that end? "Better that one man should perish than a whole nation dwindle in unbelief," was a quotation often applied to this case.

So, for more than fifty years, the story stood, except that in the family of John D. Lee and among the people of southern Utah the essential facts were known and discussed. By early 1930, William R. Palmer of Cedar City began to urge that a suitable monument should be erected here to mark the burial place of the emigrants. Through his persistent efforts, the Pioneer Trails and Landmarks Association became interested, the Mormon Church officials gave their approval, and local people built an enclosing rock wall around the grave where most of the emigrants were finally buried. This wall is of stone set in cement; it is four feet high and approximately thirty feet wide by thirty-four feet long. Stone steps with an iron-pipe rail lead over the wall to the west; to the south of the steps is a bronze tablet which bears the following inscription:

Causes and Effects

Erected   No. 17   1932

MOUNTAIN MEADOWS

A FAVORITE RECRUITING PLACE ON THE

OLD SPANISH TRAIL

IN THIS VICINITY SEPTEMBER 7TH, 1857, OCCURRED
ONE OF THE MOST LAMENTABLE TRAGEDIES IN THE
HISTORY ANNALS OF THE WEST. A COMPANY OF
ABOUT 140 EMIGRANTS FROM ARKANSAS AND MIS-
SOURI LED BY CAPTAIN CHARLES FANCHER, ENROUTE
TO CALIFORNIA, WAS ATTACKED BY WHITE MEN AND
INDIANS. ALL BUT 17 SMALL CHILDREN WERE KILLED.
JOHN D. LEE, WHO CONFESSED PARTICIPATION AS
LEADER, WAS LEGALLY EXECUTED HERE MARCH 23RD,
1877. MOST OF THE EMIGRANTS WERE BURIED IN
THEIR OWN DEFENSE PIT. THIS MONUMENT WAS
REVERENTLY DEDICATED SEPTEMBER 10TH, 1932, BY
THE UTAH PIONEER TRAILS AND LANDMARKS ASSOCI-
ATION AND THE PEOPLE OF SOUTHERN UTAH.

On the day of dedication, some four hundred people gathered for the services. The music was appropriate for a funeral; the speeches gave no word of justification or condemnation either of the emigrants or the participants. Everywhere was the feeling of regret that such a thing had happened, a sense of awe in the presence of the dire results of such violent passion, a hope that in man's effort to achieve the Christian life such a catastrophe might never happen again. The service was one in which the emigrants, themselves, or their families and friends could have joined wholeheartedly.

Today, the rock wall stands in the sunshine and silence of Mountain Meadows, off the beaten path, but attracting more and more visitors each year. A permanent United States Forest Service sign points out its location clearly, so that there is no need for the searching of the past. The two-mile road is steep and narrow, but passable in dry weather, and the traveler must descend into and climb out of a deep gully to reach the monument.

Although there have been efforts to have the two-acre plot

221

named a national historic site, or a national burial spot, or to secure it as a part of either the National Forest or the National Parks system, it still remains in private hands and so sterile and barren that it would actually seem to bear the curse of God upon it.

Local groups—Chamber of Commerce, Sons of Utah Pioneers, the Washington County Road Commission, to mention a few—could easily do what needs to be done: grade and widen the road, erect a foot bridge across the gully, plant trees and grass, put in benches and comfort facilities. Respect for the bodies of those buried there would seem to demand that much. But whether they will or not, the place is more and more a point of interest for such groups as boy scouts, history classes, and convention visitors. Here local historians tell the story as a tragedy in which white men, not Indians, were chiefly responsible.

Addendum

IT IS CLEAR that the tragedy at the Mountain Meadows grew out of a complex chain of circumstances and that it involved many people. The secrecy which surrounded it, the mystery, the horror of it created stories and myths, folklore and songs, all dealing with one facet or another.

The complete—the absolute—truth of the affair can probably never be evaluated by any human being; attempts to understand the forces which culminated in it and those which were set into motion by it are all very inadequate at best. Yet bringing it into light in its proper setting has had some rewards.

For more than a hundred years, the families of John D. Lee have borne the opprobrium of the massacre alone. For that reason, they have welcomed every effort to probe the question; certainly no truth could be worse than the stories to which they were subjected. Now they have special cause to rejoice, for on April 20, 1961, the First Presidency and the Council of Twelve Apostles of the Church of Jesus Christ of Latter-day Saints met in joint council, and: "It was the action of the Council after considering all the facts available that authorization be given for the reinstatement to membership and former blessings to John D. Lee." Word of this was sent out to members of the family, and on May 8 and 9, the necessary ordinances were performed in the Salt Lake Temple. A complete record is in the files of the Latter-day Saints Genealogical Society.

APPENDIX I

STATE OF UTAH)
) ss
COUNTY OF WASHINGTON)

Nephi Johnson, being first duly sworn, says that I am 75 years of age, a resident of Mesquite, Clark County, Nevada, that during the year 1857 I was living at Johnson's Springs, now called Enoch, Iron County, then Territory of Utah; that during the month of September I was working in the harvest field when two men came to my place and stated that Isaac C. Haight had sent them to request me to come to Cedar City immediately. I went to Cedar City and there Isaac C. Haight told me he wanted me to go to the Mountains and settle a difficulty between John D. Lee and the Indians, as the latter had threatened to kill Lee. Haight also said that Lee and the Indians had went to the Meadows to kill the emigrants, and had made three attacks upon them, but had found the emigrants better fighters than they had expected and as some of the Indians had been killed and quite a number had been wounded they were getting tired of it and Lee had suggested to withdraw and let the emigrants go, and that Haight had sent word to Lee to clean up the dirty job he had started, and that he had sent out a company of men with shovels to bury the dead, but they would find something else to do when they got there.

In company with John M. Higbee and others I went to the Mountain Meadows. We arrived at the springs where the Meadows or Hamblin is situated about 10 o'clock at night where we found John D. Lee and the principal Indian chiefs were gathered. After discussing the trouble between Lee and the Indians, Lee stated that they would try and get the emigrants to leave their camp and give up their arms after which they would kill them. This satisfied the Indians. I acted as interpreter between Lee and the Indians when the above arrangements were made. Lee and John M. Higbee with some of the Indians then went to their camp on the east of the emigrant camp.

The next morning I went over to the camp, having been sick during the night; when I reached the camp they were discussing the best way to get them out of their camp. They decided to take the white men and go toward the emigrant camp from the north along the road and to send a man with a flag of truce, and was met by a man from the camp. No Indians were in sight.

The message sent to them was for some of the principal men to come out and arrange for leaving their camp, which they did. Three men came out from the camp and John D. Lee, John M. Higbee, and another man went and met them. Upon the return, Lee stated they had agreed to come out under a promise to take them to Cedar City pending a settlement with the Indians.

The arrangements were that the wounded emigrants and the little children should be put into wagons, the women followed on foot behind the wagons, and the men were drawn out single file behind the women, each man of the emigrants walked by the side of a white man, the white man walking on the right side of the emigrant along the road. After marching along for some time, the signal Halt was given, at which each white man was to kill the emigrant man at his side. The Indians were in ambush at the place where the signal was given, and at that signal quite a number of the posse failed to kill his man, for the reason that they did not approve of the killing.

The plan was for the Indians to kill the women and children and wounded and the white men of the posse to kill the men of the emigrants, but owing to some of the white men of the posse failing to kill their men, the Indians assisted in finishing the work. There were about 150 Indians present.

I don't think the killing required more than five minutes. I was within 25 yards of the head of the column of men as they marched up the road and saw it all. Immediately after the killing I was sent with a posse to prevent the Indians from looting the wagons of the emigrants; when I arrived the Indians were looting the wagons and I let them take what they had and stopped them from doing any more. I remained there until Isaac C. Haight arrived from Cedar City about half hour after the killing.

Haight asked me what I would do with this property. I asked him if he wanted to know my real feelings about it and he said yes. Then I said you have made a sacrifice of the people, and I would burn the property, and let the cattle roam over the country for the Indians to kill, and go home like men.

There were some fifteen or sixteen children saved and taken to Cedar.

After burying the bodies, they gathered up the cattle, hitched them to the wagons, and drove to Cedar City where John D. Lee sold them at auction for anything the people had to give for it, and the Indians got most of the proceeds.

NEPHI JOHNSON

APPENDIX II

Preface[1]

In the interest of humanity I have taken great pains and trouble to inquire into the tragedy that hapened at M. M. in 1857. How & by whom it hapened and the causes that brought it about and who was responsible for the same. I propose proving by as honerable men as there is west of the Misouri river when truth and justice takes the place of prejudice.

All the Mormons, especially their leaders, were accused of the great crime or being accessory before or after the fact.

Were the Mormons guilty or accessory and responsible for that matter? Let us look the ground over.

I will review the matter as a whole and the exciting times it hapened under to the end that truth and justice may some day be vindicated.

SNORT.

In 1857 the Buchannen army were marching against Mormons. Martial law was proclaimed and the people all mustered into service. Drilling and standing guard was the order of the day. Scouting parties were organized and marched hundreds of miles

---

[1] In presenting the account of John M. Higbee, the original wording and spelling has been adhered to strictly. For the sake of ease in reading, periods have been inserted, and the habit of the author in capitalizing some letters has been corrected. Although this is signed "Bull Valley Snort," there is no question of its authorship.

226

each way to prevent any portion of the army from approaching the Territory at any point. The further from Salt Lake the greater the excitement. The Indians all through the country partook of the *same spirit* in a twofold degree. As a people we had to be good friends with the Indians at all hazards. Their talk was generally about helping the Mormons when the army came.

About this time the doomed company came traveling through the country and the Indians began gathering in a threatening manner and after some of their number had eaten the animals poisoned by company and had died, the Indians began swearing vengeance and by the time said company got to the rim of the basin with their threats & hostile attitude to reds, the savages were angry and thirsting for blood & the further they followed company the more their numbers increased and the more saucey they got till people of the settlements began to fear for their own safety. Excitement was at fever heat.

About this time Indian Farmer Lee was heard of as being with Savages who reported to him that they had killed all the emigrant company and if Mormons wanted to bury them they could. Accordingly Lee sent an express to Cedar City asking for help to come and bury the dead. The bell was rung. The people came together; the express was read from Lee in regard to emigrant company. After which a dozen or more of as honorable good citizens as lived in the country volunteered and started at once to go and bury the dead.

After we got out there we came to the conclusion that sending the express to us was only a ruse to get more whites out there because Lee was afraid of Indians. At any rate when we got out there we found we were in bedlam or hell. Lee's camp with two or three painted like Indians were camped a little way from savages who were camped one mile east over hill from the doomed company who had fortified themselves close by a spring of water & were protecting themselves as best they could.

Upon our arrival a terrible picture met our gaze. The valley was strewn with carkuses of cattle and horses which the Indians had shot down through revenge. Indians were painted like devils, as though they had just arrived from the infernal regions & howling with rage over some of their braves being wounded, all tending to make everything as hideous and demon like as could be imagined. Lee was trying to pacify them and have them scatter and go away and let the emigrants go. So he said to us.

The savages then came to Lee and said if he and the Mormons did not help them to kill the Merrycats they would join the soldiers and fight the Mormons. The number of Indians there were variously estimated at anywhere from three to six hundred, all determined it seemed to accomplish the destruction of the company if they had to fight all the Mormons in the southern country. J. D. Lee being a Major in the Nauvoo Legion and commander over Kane County where we were then said we dare not make war with Indians. He then ordered all men present to join his command for self preservation.

Lee being Indian Farmer and Clingensmith being bishop where some of Indians often went to get something to eat when hungry, it seemed that these two *men* would have more influence with Indians than anybody in the southern country, but even these seemed to have lost their influence at this particular time when it was so much *needed*.

The men that had just came from Cedar held a council and decided after a good deal of deliberation what should be done.

It was agreed to send Higbee to inform Col. Wm. H. Dame, Commander of Iron Military District, the condition of things at M. M. [Mountain Meadows] Higbee proceeded at once to Cedar about thirty-five miles and reported to Major Haight that emigrant company were not killed as Lee express had stated the day before, but were fortified and were under a state of siege surrounded night and day by savages who were blood thirsty and crazy because some of their number had been wounded. To all appearances and attitude of Indians there were not men enough in Southern Utah to protect the company with force against the savages.

Under these circumstances Co. W. H. Dame was asked to say what should be done. I. C. Haight went to Parowan in the night

and made the report to Col. Dame and returned next morning
with orders which Higbee caried same day to Lee. Those from
Cedar stopped there till he returned thinking to hold some restraint on Indians. When Mesenger returned he said Col. Dames
orders given to Haight for Higbee to carry to Major J. D. Lee
were:

> Compromise with Indians if possible by letting them take all the
> stock and go to their homes and let the company alone, but on no
> conditions you are not to precipitate a war with Indians while there
> is an army marching against our people.
>
> As Indian Farmer and a Major in the Legion, I trust you will have
> influence enough to restrain Indians and save the company. If not
> possible, save women and children at all hazards, Hoping you will
> be able to carry out the above orders in helping to make peace be-
> tween the two parties
>
> by WM. H. DAME *Col. Commanding Iron Military District*

About this time a council was called of the leading men in
Cedar, the nearest point of any importance to the excitement. The
council decided to send an express to the commander of the district, Col. Wm. H. Dame, which he forwarded to Governor
Young stateing the excitement that was going on and the attitude
and number of Indians and general outlook. Lee was notified to
do all that was possible to persuade Indians to let company alone
till express returned from Governor Young.

The next morning after Lee told this to Indian several of the
Chiefs came to Lee and he came over to where whites were
camped and said the chiefs had come over very much excited
over one of their big chiefs being wounded and they wanted to
talk with him and Clingensmith. They said if we offered to be-
friend the Merry Cats they would fight us right away and if we
did not help them to get the emigrants out of their fort today
they would burn them out and kill men, women, and children
and then fight the Mormons.

After a great deal of big talk and threatening about a half day
with savages howling with rage and geting more excited all the

time, Lee said he and Clingensmith had desided there was onley one way to stop having an Indian war and save wimen and children. After all this talk we have agreed with Indians Chiefs that we would get the men of the company out where they could get at them without loosing any more of their men on the following conditions that they would let the women and children go to Cedar City unmolested and they take all the stock and other property. Indians agreeing to perform there part of compact. Lee said then to whites, "As Major in command of this county, I call on all of you in the interest of humanity and the liberty of the scattering and helpless condition of our settlements to help me to carry out our part of this agreement. Major Higbee, you will assist, I trust."

Higbee said, "I have no command and am not an officer in this county. You older men know what is best to do. Is there no other way?"

Clingensmith said, "No, we are almost in an Indian war now. In our helpless condition we must obey Major Lee."

I think most of the whites from Cedar were where they heard what Lee said, though the savages were yelling like demons.

The whites I think generally felt quite timed [timid] and enough to make them or the heart of a stone cry out against what seemed to be inevetable according to all appearances. Major Lee ordered all whites to get into line singel file about six or eight feet apart and march down on plain in sight of the doomed and he and another would go down to emigrant camp and disarm them and load arms and helpless into waggons and send them up the road towards Cedar. When they pased by Clingensmith's Co. one fourth of a mile, women & children were sent up the same road. After they had past same point about a half mile, men from emigrant camp came marching up the same road and when oposite to Clingensmith's company both the companies marched along on each side of the road as they were then about twenty feet apart, the doomed company on west and Clingensmiths on east till they came to a smooth open space on the west side of the road and a patch of oak brush clost by on east side of road. Then the word halt was given. It is not known positiveley who by. Some say White. Others says him & two others were back at camp over the hill. Some say Clingensmith gave order who was at head of Company. One thing is known by all persons out there: it was Major Lee's orders whoever gave them. That was the signal for guns to fire. Lee said, "those that are to big cowards to help the Indians can shoot in the air then squat down so Indians can rush past them and finish up their savage work begun many days since."

It was said most of our company were nervious and afraid of Indian treachery and kept their guns loaded for their own protection. No doubt each individual knows more about that than any other person living and how they felt at that particular moment when some guns were fired and the men squatted down and the Indians seemed to be there the same moment as they jumped out of the brush and rushed like a howling tornado apast us. And the hideous, demon-like yells of the savages as they thirsting for blood rushed past to slay their helpless victims. It seemed to chill the blood in our veins.

A part of the doomed men fleeing from the yelling demons ran up amongst the women and children. The Indians say that was the reason they could not keep their young wariors from killing all but a few little children that some of the old Indians saved and they wanted pay for saving them.

It did not seem five minutes from the time the Indians rushed past us until all was still in death. Before it had been known that there had been any treachery, the woemen and children were all killed but the few small ones.

Soon after this had all hapened Col. Wm. H. Dame came with a squad of men, having received an express from Governor Young to help the company get out of the power of savages and let them go. Haslem's ride 6 hundred miles in 6 days. You can judge his consternation when he arrived and found all still in death. Then all they could do was to give them burial and make the best of a terrible calamity. As Indian Farmer the Indians allowed Lee to take charge of all property for their use. Report says Lee went and reported all this matter to Governor Young and the Governor took steps to have this matter investigated and before it could be accomplished he was superceeded as governor of Utah. That ended his responsibility.

For the next eighteen years there was a great many blood kirdling stories told about some of those that had been out to help burry those that had been killed. These men generally, seeing the growing prejudice and feeling bad and ashamed of the cowardly part they were compelled to take in that tragedy realizing they could not prove a negative, they kept very still over the matter. Their reticence was taken for guilt by their neighbors. The presure brought against them & their fameleys was hard to bear. Many on this account moved to other parts of the territory & some to other territories and states. Hunt them up then or now and you will find them generally law loving and law abiding, leading, honerable citizens, farmers, stock raisers, merchants, miller, and lawyers.

The prejudice was so great and a fresh invoice of U. S. Officials it is not to be wondered at that several inditements were found. Almost invariable through prejudice, heresay, common gossip & it was generally understood the men indited dare not stand trial, for prejudice ran so high and the jury law was so elastice that men could be convited easy if caught by packed juries and a prejudiced court.

The Mormon Church with its leaders were accused of this offense & declared guilty and they new nothing of it till twas all over. At this critical moment it took all the efforts that the Mormon people could put forth in the Lee trial to vindicate the leaders of the church by helping the court all that was posible to convict Lee, who tried to purger his soul by laying it to Brigham and leaders of Mormon Church.

Question: Were Mormons responsible for that tragedy? According to the best information to be obtained, laying prejudice aside is: The trouble grew out of the news of Buchannen's army marching against Mormons, which was the cause of martial law being proclaimed through the territory of Utah by Govenor

Brigham Young. This seemed to be the cause of all the trouble and excitement in the country. If so, the marching of Buchannen's army against Utah was the cause of the excitement and this was the soul cause of all this trouble and the cause of this tragedy.

This being conceeded then, President Buchannen's General Amnesty issued in 1857 covered the whole ground.

The strained relations and vindictive feeling through prejudice caused by this tragedy being wickedly laid to and makeing the Mormons responsible for made it possible for and gave political birth to the Liberal Party and their untiring zeal and persiverence against Mormons has been proverbialey vindictive and worthey of a better cause.

It is a well known fact that in the days of Judge McKean and other Federal officials with x-Bishop Warren of Parowan for a tool, Clingensmith was scared so near to death that he purgered his soul to try to save his own neck. As though that matter was not wicked and bad enough without so much determined zeal to make a whole people responsible for it, that knew nothing about the matter till it was all over, nor then either, for whenever the truth has been told it has been exagerated it was worse than a lie. Them that knew the truth did not dare tell it for fear of being brought in as accesories. So it has been left for gosip to tell what it pleased or imagined.

Why has this tragedy never been ventilated and shown up in its true light? The same reason that the men indicted has not stood trial—too much prejudice everywhere. Mostley in U.S. officials who come here full of zeal, anxious to make a record. The first people they get acquainted with generaley are the exciting, disafected ones, always having fault to find with something or somebody. A great and powerful nation could afford to be just and be as zealous to show up the plain truth as to convict someone, if it did happen to be a *Mormon.*

What I have written here can be verified by men that today are living in two nations and three territories who will tell the truth that it may be vindicated and justice satisfied and the blame rest where it belongs. If the publick ever get a true historical account of that tragedy it will read almost as I have written it here. [NOTE: The word "almost" in the last sentence was marked through with pencil several times as if the author did not intend for it to be read.] And the men that voluntered from Cedar to go and bury the dead are the men that will verify this statement, whenever they can speak without being held as accesory to the tragedy. If the time ever comes when officers of the law are as anxious to free the innosent as to condemn the guilty.

A good many of them Cedar volenteers are still living and can tell how unjustly Federal officers have with prejudice tried to rule and ruin Utah and how they have succeeded as far as some men are concerned is well known.

Who is responsible for driving into exile as a fellon a man like Higbee onley about thirty years old at the time that matter happened? You would say, "If he is not guilty, let him stand his trial." Perhaps not. Let us weigh the matter and see. Because he went out there in the interest of Humanity, his friends are satisfied that with an elastick court and jury they would convict him as an axcessory upon the same principle as he was indited by, and through prejudice it shows on the face of the indictment and also on its back the grand jury, only eleven of them concurring and yet it is said they were got for the occasion. Then the witnesses against him must of been on the elastick principle also.

The jury knew as well as the witnesses themselves or me that not one of them were within thirty miles of that tragedy when it hapened, and two of them was in California. This all proves that these ten witnesses were willing tools to swear away a man's life to please and incur favor with federal authority. History says an imported jury is about the same as an exported fellon, not emblems of justice or peace.

It is high time that State Hood came and corected the elastic part of our jury law so the acused can be tried by their peers instead of trancient, iresponsible hobos that can be bought and sold all along the line wherever and when ever wanted to create and manufacture newspaper excitement.

Here is a man spoken of above has been driven from the face

of man and called a fellon for a third of a sentuary, financialey, socialey, and politicaley damned, his family scattered, some dead, others grown up and strangers to him. The heritage left them & their children is Grandfather & Father was a fellon and a fugitive from justice.

It seems Somebody has contracted a *Great* debt.

The man is either guilty or innocent. Our great and magnanamous government ought to be generous enough to inshure him a speedy and fair trial by his peers. Will they? Echo says, we will see.

Yours truly

BULL VALLEY SNORT

SALT LAKE, FEBRUARY 1894

APPENDIX III

To Whom It May Concern

I, Daniel S. Macfarlane, deeming it my duty to correct some of the errors, which are circulated and being enlarged upon by evil designing men, regarding the unfortunate circumstance which happened in the year 1857. So I now take this opportunity of making a statement from my own observation concerning that sad affair, which for the sake of the living as well as the dead should be corrected and if possible forgotten. There are some merciful men that volunteered to go out there and bury the dead; for John D. Lee had sent an express from the Mt. Meadows to Cedar City, stating that the Indians had killed all the Immigrants Co. and asking for volunteers to come out and help bury the dead. I was one of the Co. of volunteers, who went on the humane errand. When we reached "the meadows" the Indians were still fighting the Imigrants.

About this time Lee got an express from Col. Wm. H. Dame telling him to treat the Indians in some way and let the Immigrants go and the natives take part of their stock and go to their homes. When we came to where Lee was, he and Klingon Smith were talking to some of the chiefs who seemed very much excited.

235

Quite a number were present and heard what I did, but I have forgotten who they were, only they were those that voluntered to bury the dead.

Higbee asked Lee what the Indians were saying. He answered, "They say—I Lee told them we were at war with the Mericats, and you sent for all of us to come and bring our warriors and help you fight them, and now you want us to take part of their stock and go home and let them go and you know some of our men have been shot and my warriors are mad and their blood is up."

"Some of you want to take their part. We will fight you as well as them if you don't help us to get them out of their Fort."

Lee said further that himself and Klingon Smith had talked the matter over and come to the conclusion, under the circumstances that we had to make our appearance of helping them or we must fight them and the latter we cannot think of doing.

John M. Higbee, said "Is there no way that the women and children can be saved?" Lee said, "The Indians agreed not to molest the women and children if he (Lee) would get the men out so they could get at them." Then Higbee said, "Is there no way to satisfy the Indians and save the Immigrants." Klingon Smith said, "No we have got to do as Lee says." Then Lee spoke up in an important slurring manner and said, "If any of you are too big cowards to appear to help the Indians you need not shoot nor anything else. Only form a line, single file and march down to where I will call a truce and get the men out of their Fort and I will send the women and children ahead. The Indians will let them past half a mile or more, then the Indians will rush past you when the signal is given and take the men." Lee then said to Higbee and Klingon Smith "You will see that my orders are strictly obeyed." So the line was formed and marched down to the road and up as directed. After women and children had passed a half mile or more. Then Klingon Smith gave the word, "Halt" signal agreed upon by Lee and Smith. When Klingon Smith fired his gun, our men dropped to the ground. Then Indians rushed past them yelling and like a tornado, they pounced upon their helpless victors [sic] and all was over in a few minutes, and still as death,

236

and not till then did we realize that treachery had been practiced when only a few small children had been saved.

No one knew of the treachery before hand unless Lee and Smith. Perhaps they did not as Lee said it was the young bucks and the old ones could not stop them.

I always felt it was a base insult thrown at Higbee and volunteers by Lee and uncalled for at the time.

When Higbee asked Lee if there was no other way to dodge the issue and he (Lee) said or used the word "Cowards" as thru brute force he would brow beat us all. For we all felt as Higbee had expressed himself to avoid such a result and being also deceived in the object for which we consented to go to the "meadows."

I am willing and I think it is my duty to swear to the facts mentioned above when and where I can do any good for humanity's sake. I know there are others who heard and felt as I did, but I cannot remember their names, all of which I do solemnly declare to be the truth. "So help me God."

DANIEL S. MACFARLANE.

Signed in presence of C. C. Bladen and S. T. Leigh.

STATE OF UTAH
             S.S.
COUNTY OF IRON

Be it remembered that on this 29 day of June 1896, before me Mayhew H. Dalley a notary republic, within and for said county, Daniel S. Macfarlane well known to me to be a person described and who executed the within and forgoing instrument, and duly acknowledged to me that he executed the same freely and voluntarily and wished not to retract such execution.

In witness there of I have here unto set my hand and affixed my official seal at my office in Cedar City, Iron Co. State of Utah.

MAYHEW H. DALLEY

Notary republic Iron Co., Utah. (My commission expires Dec. 12, 1897 State of Utah, County of Iron) S.S.

On this 29th day of June 1896, before Mayhew H. Dalley, a Notary Republic within and for said Co. personally appeared before me, Cornelius C. Bladen and Samuel T. Leigh personally known to me to be the same persons whose names are subscribed to the within and foregoing instruments as witnesses hereunto, who being by me duly sworn each for himself and not for the other deposed and said that he resides in Cedar City, Iron County, Utah, that he was present and saw Daniel S. Macfarlane, (personally known to them, to be the same person described in and who executed the said instrument as party thereto) Sign the same and that the said Daniel S. Macfarlane duly acknowledged in the presence of said affiants, that he executed same of his free and voluntary act and deed, and that they each of said affiants, thereupon, and at the request of the said Daniel S. Macfarlane subscribed his name as a witness thereto. In witness thereof I have thereunto set my hand and affixed my official seal at my office in Cedar City, Iron Co., State of Utah, the day and year in this Certificate first above written.

MAYHEW H. DALLEY *Notary Republic* Iron Co. Utah. My commission expires Dec. 12, 1897.

Copied from a paper held by Emma Adair, daughter of said Daniel S. Macfarlane and copied by Mrs. Keith Macfarlane from the original instrument written by the above people and placed in the St. George Temple by D. S. Macfarlane.

This copied by Charlotte H. Esplin.

APPENDIX IV

STATE OF NEVADA, COUNTY OF LINCOLN, SS:—

Personally appeared before me, Peter B. Miller, Clerk of Court of the Seventh Judicial District of the State of Nevada, Philip Klingon Smith, who being duly sworn, on his oath, says: My name is Philip Klingon Smith; I reside in the county of Lincoln, in the State of Nevada; I resided at Cedar City, in the County of Iron, in the Territory of Utah, from A.D. 1852 to A.D. 1859; I was residing at said Cedar City at the time of the massacre at Mountain Meadows, in said Territory of Utah; I had heard that a company of emigrants was on its way from Salt Lake City, bound for

238

California; after said company had left Cedar City, the militia was called out for the purpose of committing acts of hostility against them; said call was a regular military call from the superior officers to the subordinate officers and privates of the regiment at Cedar City and vicinity, composing a part of the militia of the Territory of Utah; I do not recollect the number of the regiment. I was at that time the Bishop of the Church of Jesus Christ of Latter-day Saints at Cedar City; Isaac C. Haight was President over said church at Cedar City and the southern settlements in said Territory; my position as Bishop was subordinate to that of said President; W. H. Dame was the President of said Church at Parowan in said Iron County; said W. H. Dame was also colonel of said regiment; said Isaac C. Haight was lieutenant-colonel of said regiment, and said John D. Lee, of Harmony in said Iron County, was major of said regiment; said regiment was duly ordered to muster, armed and equipped as the law directs, and prepared for field operations; I had no command nor office in said regiment at the time, neither did I march with said regiment on the expedition which resulted in said company's being massacred in the Mountain Meadows, in said County of Iron; about four days after said company of emigrants had left Cedar City, that portion of said regiment then mustered at Cedar City took up its line of march in pursuit of them; about two days after said company had left said Cedar City, Lieutenant-Colonel I. C. Haight expressed in my presence, a desire that said company might be permitted to pass on their way in peace; but afterward he told me that he had orders from headquarters to kill all of said company of emigrants except the little children; I do not know whether said headquarters meant the Regimental Headquarters at Parowan, or the Headquarters of the Commander-in-chief at Salt Lake City; when the said company had got to Iron Creek about twenty (20) miles from Cedar City, Captain Joel White started for Pinto Creek settlement, through which said company would pass, for the purpose of influencing the people to permit said company to pass on their way in peace; I asked and obtained permission of said White to go with him and aid him in his endeavours to save life; when said White and myself got about three miles from Cedar City we met Major John D. Lee, who asked us where we were going; I replied that we were going to try to prevent the killing of the emigrants, Lee replied, 'I have something to say about that;' Lee was at that time on his way to Parowan, the Headquarters of Colonel Dame; said White and I went to Pinto Creek; remained there one night, and the next day returned to Cedar City, meeting said company of emigrants at Iron Creek; before reaching Cedar City we met one Ira Allen, who told us 'that the decree had passed, devoting said company to destruction;' after the fight had been going on for three or four days, a messenger from Major Lee reached Cedar City, who stated that the fight had not been altogether successful, upon which Lieutenant-Colonel Haight ordered out a reenforcement; at this time I was ordered out by Captain John M. Higbee, who ordered me to muster, 'armed and equipped as the law directs;' it was a matter of life or death to me to muster or not, and I mustered with the reenforcing troops; it was at this time that Lieutenant-Colonel Haight said to me that it was the orders from headquarters that all but the little children of said company were to be killed; said Haight had at that time just returned from headquarters at Parowan, where a military council had been held; there had been a like council held at Parowan previous to that, at which were present Colonel Dame, Lieutenant-Colonel I. C. Haight, and Major John D. Lee; the result of this first council was the calling out of said regiment for the purpose already stated; the reenforcement aforesaid was marched to the Mountain Meadows, and there formed a junction with the main body; Major Lee massed all the troops at a spring, and made a speech to them, saying that his orders from headquarters were to kill the entire company except the small children; I was not in the ranks at that time, but on the side talking to a man named Slade, and could not have seen a paper in Major Lee's hands; said Lee then sent a flag of truce into the emigrant camp, offering said emigrants that 'if they lay down their arms, he would protect them'; they accordingly laid down their arms, came out from their camp, and delivered themselves to said Lee; the women and children were then, by the order of said Lee, separated from the men, and were marched ahead of the men; after said emigrants had marched about a half mile toward Cedar City, the order was given to shoot them down; at that time said Lee was at the head of the column; I was in the rear. I did not hear Lee give the order to fire, but heard it from the under officers as it was passed down the column; the emigrants were then and there shot down except seventeen little children, which I immediately took into my charge; I do not know that total number of said company as I did not stop to count the dead; I immediately put the little children in baggage-wagons belonging to the regiment, and took them to Hamlin's ranche, and from there to Cedar City, and procured them homes among the people; John Willis and Samuel Murdy assisted me in taking charge of said children; on the evening of the massacre, Colonel W. H. Dame and Lieutenant I. C. Haight came to Hamblin's, where I had said children, and fell into a dispute, in the course of which said Haight told Colonel Dame, that, if he was going to report of the killing of said emigrants, he should not have ordered it done; I do not know when or where said troops were disbanded; about two weeks after said massacre occurred, said Major Lee (who was also an Indian Agent), went to Salt Lake City. and, as I believe, reported said fight and its results to the commander-in-chief; I was not present at either of the before-mentioned councils, nor at any council connected with the aforesaid military operations, or with said company; I gave no orders except those connected with the saving of the children, and those, after the massacre had occurred, and said orders were given as bishop and not in a military sense; at the time of the firing of the first volley I discharged my piece; I did not fire afterward, though several subsequent volleys were fired; after the first fire we delivered I at once set about saving the children; I commenced to gather the children before the firing had ceased. I have made the foregoing statement before the above-entitled court for the reason that I believe that I would be assassinated should I attempt to make the same before any court in the Territory of Utah. After said Lee returned from Salt Lake City, as aforesaid, said Lee told me that he had reported fully to the President, meaning the commander-in-chief, the fight at Mountain Meadows, and the killing of said emigrants. Brigham Young was at that time the commander-in-chief of the militia of the Territory of Utah; and further deponent saith not.

(*Signed*) PHILIP KLINGON SMITH

Subscribed and sworn to before me this 10th day of April A.D. 1871.

District Court, seventh Judicial District, Lincoln County, Nevada.

(Copy of seal.)

Utah Territory, County of Salt Lake, ss: I, O. F. Strickland, Associate Justice of the Supreme Court of Utah Territory, hereby certify that I have carefully compared the foregoing copy is a true literal copy of said original, and such comparison was made this 4th day of September, 1872.

(*Signed*) O. F. STRICKLAND

Territory of Utah, Salt Lake County ss.:—I, James B. McKean, Chief Justice of the Supreme Court of said Territory, do certify that I have carefully compared the above copy of an affidavit with the original of the same, and know the same to be in all particulars a true copy thereof.

(*Signed*) JAMES B. MCKEAN,
Chief Justice of the Supreme Court, Utah Territory

APPENDIX V

"Journal History of the Church," September 11, 1857:

The following account of the Mountain Meadows affair was written by Geo. A. Smith and James McKnight at Cedar City, Aug. 6, 1858, from what they considered the most authentic sources:

The Emigrant and Indian War at Mountain Meadows, Sept. 21, 22, 23, 24 and 25, 1857.

On Tuesday, Sept. 22nd, rumor reached Cedar by Indians that

an emigrant train had been attacked in camp by the Indians on Monday, 21, at day break, at Mountain Meadows, some 45 miles from Cedar; that several of the emigrants had been killed and that some of the Indians had been killed and wounded, and that the Indians were gathering in from various parts, in considerable numbers, with a determination to exterminate the emigrants, being exasperated in consequence of the poisoning of springs by those emigrants, thus causing the death of several Indians.

Immediately upon the arrival of much intelligence, efforts were made to raise men to go and, if possible, conciliate the Indians; which party, with interpreters, left Cedar on Tuesday night about 9 o'clock. When they arrived, the next morning, they found the Indians in a great state of excitement, in consequence of the killing and wounding of some of their men, and, when Nephi Johnson, an interpreter, sought to conciliate them, they threatened him and his party with instant death if they did not either leave immediately or turn in and help them, accusing them of being friendly to the emigrants or "Mericats" as they called them. The Indians said that, if they attempted to go to the emigrants' camp, they would kill every one of them. Finding that their services could avail the emigrants nothing, they returned to Cedar and reported the condition of the camp.

On Friday evening, Wm. H. Dame, Isaac C. Haight and a party of men started out for the scene of hostilities to endeavor to put a stop to the fight, arriving there about day light on Saturday morning. The Indians had killed the entire company, with the exception of a few small children, which were, with difficulty, obtained from them. The Indians were pillaging and destroying the property and driving off the cattle in every direction, without respect to each others rights, each one endeavoring to get to himself the most plunder. When they had secreted one pack load in the hills they would return and get another, thus continuing, with the most unremitting energy, till everything was cached.

They found the bodies of the slain stripped of their clothing, scattered along the road about half a mile. They obtained a few spades from Hamblin's Ranch and buried the dead as well as they could under the circumstances. The ground was hard and, being destitute of picks, and having a limited number of spades, the pits could not be dug to very great depth.

From the appearance of the camp ground, the wagons were scattered promiscuously, but upon being attacked, they had gathered most of them into a close circle and dug inside two rifle pits.

It appears that, on the fifth day, the Indians withdrew from the siege, and that, towards evening, the emigrants left their camp and started back towards Hamblin's Ranch, and after proceeding about a mile and a half, were again attacked and all slain except the children above mentioned.

It was supposed that there must have been some 200 Indians engaged in this fight.

A large number of the dead were killed with arrows; the residue with bullets, the Indians being armed with guns and bows.

The Indians had also killed a large number of horses, mules, and cattle, which were lying scattered over the plain, which was done in accordance with their tradition, requiring a sacrifice to be sent along with their departed warriors.

(The above statement is doubtless incorrect as to the dates, as the massacre must have occurred earlier in the month, say about 15 days. Geo. A. Smith.)

APPENDIX VI

"Journal History of the Church," September 11, 1857:
This is the day on which it is reported that the horrible Mountain Meadow Massacre occurred, an account of which was written in a letter from Geo. A. Smith, to Pres. Brigham Young, dated nearly a year after the terrible transaction.

PAROWAN, AUG. 17, 1858.

PRES. YOUNG

DEAR SIR: I have recently canvassed the precincts in my council district, I have been enthusiastically received and listened to by the people with seeming pleasure. I have gathered some information in relation to the difficulties between the emigrants and Indians which terminated in the horrible massacre at the Mountain Meadows.

It appears that the emigrants, who passed over this route last fall, conducted themselves in a hostile manner towards the Indians, as well as the citizens. While at Fillmore they threatened the destruction of the town, and boasted of their participation in the murders and other outrages that were inflicted upon the Mormons in Missouri and Illinois.

While camping at the sink of Corn Creek, 15 miles beyond Fillmore, they poisoned the springs and the body of an ox which had died. The carcass was eaten by a band of Piedes from the desert, who were on a visit to the Pahyants. I was informed by the people living at Meadow Creek, the nearest settlers to Corn Creek, that ten Indians died from the poisoned meat and that a considerable number of cattle also died from the poisoned water. Some of these cattle were fat and the owners "tried them up" to save the tallow. A son of Mr. Robinson of Fillmore, was poisoned from the handling of the meat, and died. Among the cattle that died of poison were several belonging to the Hon. John A. Ray. He being at the time in Europe. Mrs. Ray attended to saving the tallow, and was so poisoned as to endanger her life and permanently injure her hand.

This party of emigrants consisted of some 50 or 60 men. They were attacked about 45 miles beyond Cedar City, which was the most southern settlement of any importance on the road to California.

While passing through the lower settlements the emigrants boasted of their participation in the expulsion of the Mormons from Missouri and threatened to stop at some convenient point, and fatten their stock, that when the U.S. troops should arrive, the emigrants would have plenty of beef to feed them with, and would then help to kill every "God damned Mormon" that there was in the mountains.

This course of conduct on their part, coupled with the rumor which they spread, that some four or five hundred dragoons were expected through on the Fremont trail, whom they would join, caused them to be regarded by the settlers with a feeling of distrust.

When the attack was made upon the emigrant party, the Indians sent out runners to the various bands in every direction, to gather additional help. The news reached the settlements at Cedar through that means. Ahwonup, the Piede Chief at Parowan, received an invitation to join the foray against the emigrants. He went to Col. Dame to tell him what he was going to do, upon which the Colonel succeeded in inducing him and most of his warriors to abandon the project.

At this time another company of emigrants fired upon a party of Pahvants in the neighborhood of Beaver, some 35 miles north of Parowan, and wounded one of them. This occurrence created so much excitement among the Pahvants of that region, that they were determined to exterminate those emigrants which was only prevented by a detachment of militia sent from Parowan by Col. Dame, who effected a compromise with the Indians, and guarded that company safely from that place to the Vegas, some three hundred miles.

No news of the attack at the Mountain Meadows had reached Parowan, except the Indian rumor, until it was too late for Col. Dame to take any measures to relieve the company, which was some 60 miles distant.

On the 6th of September I understand that rumor reached Cedar City that the emigrant train had been attacked in camp by the Indians at Mountain Meadows, that several of the emigrants and Indians had been killed and others wounded, and that more Indians were gathering from various parts in considerable numbers, being very much exasperated.

Immediately upon the arrival of this intelligence, Major Haight dispatched some interpreters to conciliate the Indians, The interpreters left Cedar the same evening, and when they arrived the next day at the scene of the difficulty, they found the Indians in a state of intense excitement, in consequence of killing and wounding of some of their men.

The interpreters sought to conciliate them, but they threatened them with death if they did not either leave immediately, or turn in and help them, accusing them of being friendly to the emigrants or maricats, as they called them. The Indians said that if the interpreters attempted to go to the emigrants camps they would kill every one of them. Finding that their services could avail the emigrants nothing, the interpreters returned to Cedar, after a ride of some 80 miles on the same animals and dallying most of the day with the Indians and reported the condition of the camp.

On the 9th Major Haight, with a party of about 50 men started from Cedar City to endeavor to relieve the emigrants and arriving at Mountain Meadows the next morning, found the Indians had killed the entire company with the exception of a few small children, who were with difficulty obtained from them, The Indians

246

were pillaging and destroying the property and driving off the cattle in every respect to the others. When they had secreted one pack load in the hills, they returned and got another, thus continuing with the most unremitting energy, till everything was cached.

Major Haight and party found the bodies of the slain stripped of their clothing and scattered along the road for half a mile. The party obtained a few spades from a ranch about 5 miles distant, buried the dead as well as they could, under the circumstances. The ground was hard and the party being destitute of picks, and having had a limited number of spades, the pits could not be dug to a very great depth.

From the appearance of the camp ground, the wagons, previous to the attack, were scattered promiscuously, but the emigrants, upon being attacked, gathered most of them into a close circle, inside of which they dug two rifle pits.

It appears that on the 9th the Indians withdrew from the siege; that, towards evening, the emigrants left their camp and started back toward Hamblin's ranch, and that after proceeding about a mile and a half they were again attacked, and slain, except the children above mentioned.

It is reported that John D. Lee and a few other white men were on the ground during a portion of the combat, but for what purpose or how they conducted or whether indeed they were there at all, I have not learned.

It is supposed that there were upwards of 200 Indian warriors engaged in this massacre. A large number of the emigrants were killed with arrows, the residue with bullets, the Indians being armed with guns, as well as bows and arrows. The Indians also killed some horses and a large number of cattle, which lay scattered over the plain. This was probably done in accordance with their custom required a sacrifice to be sent along with their departed warriors.

Some 16 or 18 children were preserved from death and placed in charge of families, where they were well cared for.

The prejudice that these emigrants had themselves excited during their passage through the territory, contributed not a little to inspire in the minds of the people an indifference as to what the Indians might do, but nobody dreamed of nor anticipated so dreadful a result. There were not a dozen white men living within 30 miles of the spot where the transaction occurred, and they were scattered two or three in a place, herding cattle. Mr. Hamblin, the nearest settler, was in G.S.L. City at the time, and the stock at his ranch were in the custody of his children and two or three Indian boys.

It was the impression of Mr. Haight that the interpreters would succeed in bringing about a compromise, to enable the emigrants to buy the Indians off. For the citizens to have attacked and killed Indians in defense of the emigrants would have been little else than suicide, as you are well aware of the exposed condition of the Southern settlers, and the annoyance to which the Indians had been subjected for many years by emigrants killing them, as they passed through the Indian Country.

I have been told that, since this transaction, many of the Indians who had previously learned to labor have evinced a determination not to work and that the moral influence of the event upon the civilization of the Indians has been very prejudicial.

Considerable improvements have been made in every settlement, except Cedar, during my absence from this district. The failure of the Iron Company to make iron satisfactorily, has caused a large number of the operatives in that department to seek employment elsewhere, thereby much reducing the population of that city.

I have given you the substance of the information I have received from various individuals during my canvass, and I regret exceedingly that such a lamentable occurrence should have taken place within the limits of this territory.

Your friend and well wisher,

GEOR. A. SMITH

[From "History of Brigham Young," 1857, pp. 481ff.]

APPENDIX VII

This letter is inserted, without explanation or comment, in the "Journal History of the Church," under date of April 13, 1859:

G.S.L. CITY, APRIL 13, 1859

DEAR STENHOUSE: —

During the fall of 1857 a party of emigrants were inhumanly massacred at or near the southern boundary of this Territory.

248

Whether the transaction occured within the jurisdiction of the Utah or New Mexico authorities, has been a matter of dispute among lawyers, as no observation of latitude to determine whether it was north or south of 37 Degrees, has ever been made in the vicinity. The Prosecutors of the Mormons have attributed this massacre to these, and a great deal of ink has been shed to give universal currency to this charge.

Being intimate to some extent with the south part of the country of this Territory, as well as the south western part of New Mexico, and somewhat acquainted with the different Indian tribes who inhabit that desert and mountainous region, and having taken some pains to collect facts in relation to the above named transaction, I submit for your consideration the following statement: —

It has been customary for many years for emigrants in passing through these southern deserts to shoot these Indians, whenever they approached their camps.

By reference to Col. J. C. Fremont's tour through this country as early as 1845, it will be seen that his party killed several of these Indians and that he was surrounded by about a thousand of them and closely besieged for several days until the Indians succeeded in killing one of the number of his party, which it would seem according to the Indians account, settled for the four that had been killed by them. The man killed for one, his gun for another, his mule for the third, and his clothes and tobacco for the fourth.

The tribes of which I speak which were concerned, have been denominated "Pah Utahs," they reside on Coal Creek, Ash Creek, Santa Clara, the Rio Virgin, the Muddy and about other small streams and springs in that vicinity. They are most adroit thieves and exceedingly fleet on foot, making little use of horses, except to eat and steal them from the Emigrants for that purpose.

These are a part of the Indians whose extermination was recommended by Gov. Calhoon [Calhoun] of New Mexico some years since.

From the commencement of the settlement of Southern Utah, the settlers have endeavored to conciliate the feelings of these Indians, and made efforts to induce them to work, and in some few instances proceeded so far as to induce them to cultivate some patches of grain. Their benevolent and peaceful efforts are constantly frustrated by emigrants passing to California, and continuing the old policy of shooting these Indians whenever they approached their camps, without even ascertaining whether their intentions were friendly or otherwise. This mode of treatment grew into an intolerable enmity, which caused them to distinguish between Mormons and "Americats." The settlers invariably treated them with the utmost kindness, and in all their dealings endeavored to preserve the most exact justice, teaching them to understand at the same time the value of property, and making them return labor or something else, for provisions and other necessaries with which they were furnished.

In fact this was the only one policy for these pioneers of civilization, who were few in number, hundreds of miles from settlements; their families exposed and unprotected, a peaceful policy was the only one that could preserve them and their families from the poisoned arrows and tomahawk of these savages, whose mode of warfare was extermination of adults and slavery of children.

Many of the Indians gradually became provided with rifles and other arms in addition to their bows and arrows which with their poisoned points are dangerous weapons.

The party of Emigrants who were destroyed had about twenty wagons and a considerable amount of stock and had manifested a very singular hostility to the natives. When encamped at the sinks of Corn Creek they gave an ox which died to a party of Indians, they ate of it and ten of them died immediately.

Some of the survivors said they saw the Captain of the Company go to the carcass with a bottle after the main body of the camp had left the ground, the water was also poisoned so that several Indians died from drinking of it.

The Indians poisoned were members of different bands of the Pah Utahs and Pah Edes, who were up from the South on a visit to their friends, the Pahvantes.

The news of this tragedy spread through the different bands of Indians for hundreds of miles and caused the concentration of reckless warriors who consummated the massacre.

News of the attack of the Indians upon the emigrants reaching the settlements, some interpreters repaired to the spot to effect a compromise. Some of the Indians had been wounded and others killed and the whole emigrant party were closely invested and all communication with them, cut off.

The interpreters were prohibited from having any intercourse with them.

The Indians manifested considerable hostility towards them because they (the interpreters) were unwilling to assist them.

Finding that they were unable to render the emigrants any assistance, they returned to Cedar City, about 50 miles.

A party of about 50 volunteers was raised and repaired as speedily as possible to the spot, but alas, too late to afford any other assistance than to rescue a few children that had been preserved by the Indians in accordance with their usual custom for the purpose of trade or slavery.

Whenever a fair and impartial investigation of this bloody massacre is had, the establishment of the above facts will doubtless be the result.

—GEORGE A. SMITH

[From the "History of Brigham Young," 1859, pp. 348ff.]

APPENDIX VIII

Extract from Garland Hurt's "Report" taken from *Senate Executive Document 42*, 36 Cong., 1 sess., 94–95:

On the tenth day of September last, George W. Hancock, a merchant in the town of Payson, came to the Indian settlements to look at some fat cattle that I proposed selling, and in the course of conversation, said that he had learned that the California emigrants on the southern route had got themselves into a very serious difficulty with the Piedes, who had given them to understand that they could not pass through their country, and on attempting to disregard this injunction, found themselves surrounded by the Indians, and compelled to seek shelter behind their wagons. He said he had learned these facts from an express man, who passed his house that morning with a message from the Indians to *President Young*, inquiring of him what they must do with the Americans. The express man had been allowed one hundred consecutive hours in which to perform the trip of nearly three hundred miles and return, which Mr. Hancock felt confident he would do. On the day following, one of the Utah Indians, who had been absent for some days gathering pine nuts, west of the Sevier Lake, returned, and said that the Mormons had killed all the emigrants. He said he learned this news from a band of the Piedes, but could not tell when the fight occurred, or how many had been killed. One of the Utahs, named Spoods, came to the farm on the morning of the 14th, having traveled all night, and also confirmed the report of the difficulty between the emigrants and the Piedes, but stated that when his brother Ammon (chief who lives in the Piede country,) went to Iron county to persuade the Piedes to leave the road, the bishop told him he had no business with the Piedes, and had better leave, where upon an altercation arose between the bishop and the chief.

Spoods thought that the Piedes had been set upon the emigrants by the Mormons.

It soon began to be talked among the employes at the farm that all the emigrants on the southern road had been killed by the Piede Indians, and the report was confirmed by several other persons who visited the farm; but Indians insisted that Mormons, and not Indians, had killed the Americans.

This affair had become so much the subject of conversation, that on the 17th, I started an Indian boy, named Pete, who speaks the English language quite fluently, with instructions to proceed to Iron county on a secret route, and to learn from the Piedes if possible, and also from the Utahs, what the nature of the difficulty was, and who were the instigators of it. He returned on the 23rd, and reported that he only went to Ammon's village, in Beaver county, where he met a large band of Piedes, who had just returned from Iron county.

They acknowledged having participated in the massacre of the emigrants, but said that the Mormons persuaded them into it. They said that about ten or eleven sleeps ago, John D. Lee came to this village, and told them Americans were very bad people, and always made a rule to kill Indians whenever they had a chance. He said, also, that they had often killed the Mormons, who were friends to the Indians. He then prevailed on them to attack the emigrants, who were then passing through the country, (about one hundred in number,) and promised them that if they were not strong enough to whip them, the Mormons would help them. The Piedes made the attack, but were repulsed on three different occasions, when Lee and the bishop of Cedar City, with a number of Mormons, approached the camp of the emigrants, under pretext of trying to settle the difficulty, and with lying, seductive overtures, succeeded in inducing the emigrants to lay down their weapons of defense and admit them and their savage allies inside of their breastworks, when the work of destruction began, and in the language of the unsophisticated boy, *"they cut all of their throats but a few that started to run off, and the Piedes shot them!"* He also stated that there were some fifteen or sixteen small children that were not killed, and were in charge of the bishop.

Lee and the bishop took all the stock (over a thousand head,) as also a large amount of money. The Mormon version of this affair is that the Piedes went to the emigrant camp and asked for meat, and they gave them beef with strychnine upon it, and that when Brigham learned this fact, he sent word back to them *"to do with the Americans as they thought proper."* But I have not yet been able to learn that the strynchaine [*sic*] had killed any of the Indians, or even made them sick.

APPENDIX IX

Senate Executive Document 42, "Forney's Report," 1859, 36 Cong., 1 sess., 74–80:

SUPERINTENDENT'S OFFICE, UTAH
GREAT SALT LAKE CITY
AUGUST, 1859.

SIR: it has been my intention, for some weeks past, to give you a more full statement than heretofore given of the Mountain Meadow tragedy, and of the children saved from it.

July, 1858, I received instructions from the Acting Commissioner, C. E. Mix, in relation to certain children. In pursuance to which, I commenced without delay to make inquiry after the children supposed to have been saved, and living among whites and Indians. I very soon obtained satisfactory information that thirteen to seventeen children were spared at the massacre of a certain emigrant company the 8th or 9th September, 1857, in Mountain Meadow valley, Utah Territory, whilst on their way to California. Sixteen of the children were very soon collected and subject to my directions, and for whom I commenced providing immediately. It was my earnest desire and purpose to visit the southern portion of the Territory early last fall, but the safety of the United States mail on the northern California road, and the public interest generally, required my immediate presence in and adjacent to the Humboldt valley, and I returned too late from the Humboldt to travel north with so many little children. I, however, suggested to the department to have the children taken to the States by way of California and the San Francisco and New York steamers. There is no impediment at any season of the year to travel to the Pacific by the southern route from where the children were then living.

A massacre of such unparalleled magnitude on American soil must necessarily excite much interest in the public mind. From information received from various sources during the last twelve months, I am enabled to give you a reliable account of the emigrant company in question, and the children remaining, and also some of the causes and circumstances of the inhuman massacre.

The company was composed of about thirty families, and one hundred and thirty to one hundred and forty persons, and, I think, principally from Johnston county, Arkansas.

I have deemed it a matter of material importance to make strict inquiry relative to the general behavior and conduct of the company towards the people of this Territory in their journey through it, and am justified in saying that they conducted themselves with propriety.

It is generally conceded that the said company was abundantly supplied with traveling and extra horses, cattle, &c. They had about thirty good wagons, and about thirty mules and horses, and six hundred head of cattle, when passing through Provo City, Utah Territory. At Corn Creek, fifteen miles from Fillmore City, and one hundred and sixty-five miles south of this city, the company camped several days. At this place, and within a few miles of the Indian farm, (commenced a few years ago for the Pah-vant tribe, and all living on it,) it is alleged that the said emigrant company treated the Indians most inhumanly; such as poisoning a spring with arsenic, and impregnating dead cattle with strichnine. John D. Lee, living one hundred and fifty miles south of Fillmore, informed me that about twenty Indians and some cattle died from drinking of the poisoned water, and Indians from eating the poisoned meat.

Dr. Ray, of Fillmore City, assured me that one of his oxen died while the company was encamped in the neighborhood, and that his wife, while engaged rendering the tallow of the dead ox, became suddenly ill, and that a boy who was assisting her died in a few days.

I have not been apprised of any investigation at the time by the Indian officials who were then in the Territory, or of an official investigation by the proper authorities of Fillmore. It seems obvious that Dr. Ray's ox died about the time these unfortunate people were camped in the neighborhood. I cannot learn, however, of any difficulty the company had with the Pah-vant Indians while camped near them. The ox died unquestionably from eating a poisonous weed that grows in most of the valleys in this Territory, and it is by no means uncommon for cattle to get poisoned and die from the effects of this weed. One or two Indians died from eating of the dead ox, but I have not been apprised that this excited any of them against the emigrants. After strict inquiry I cannot learn that even one Pah-vant Indian was present at the massacre. Those persons in Fillmore, and further south, who believe that a spring was poisoned with arsenic, and the meat of a dead ox with strichnine, by said company, may be honest in their belief, and attribute the cause of the massacre to the alleged poisoning. Why an emigrant company, and especially farmers, would carry with them so much deadly poison is incomprehensible. I regard the poisoning affair as entitled to no consideration. *In my opinion, bad men*, for a bad purpose, have magnified a natural circumstance for the perpetration of a crime that has no parallel in American history for atrocity.

I hear nothing more of the emigrant company until their arrival in Mountain Meadow valley, about the 2d or 3d of September, 1857. This valley is seven miles in length east and west, and one to three wide—a large spring at each end. In about the centre, and from north to south-east, is what is termed the "rim of the basin." East of this the waters go to the lakes of Utah Territory, and those west into the Pacific. The valley is well hemmed in by high hills or mountains; is almost a continuous meadow, affording an abundance of pasture.

At the spring in the east end is a house and corral, occupied in September, 1857, by Mr. Jacob Hamblin. It is due to Mr. Hamblin to say that he left home several weeks before the company arrived in the valley, and returned home several days after the massacre.

David Tulis (was living with Mr. Hamblin) says: "The company passed by the house on Friday, September 2d or 3d, towards evening; that it was a large and respectable-looking company. One of the men rode up to where I was working, and asked if there was water ahead. I said, yes. The person who rode up behaved civilly. The company camped at the spring in the west end of the valley. I heard firing on Monday morning, and for four or five mornings afterwards; if there had been firing during the day, I could not have heard it on account of the wind."

I then asked Mr. Tulis the following questions, and received answers, to wit:

1. When you heard the firing first what was your opinion of its cause?

ANSWER. I believed it was the Indians fighting the emigrant company camped at the spring at the other end of the valley.

2. Why did you not notify the nearest settlement?

ANSWER. I thought or expected that the people of the nearest settlement knew of the fight.

3. Why did you suppose so?

ANSWER. Because I saw Indians riding back and forwards on the road.

4. Was you afraid?

ANSWER. I was a little timid.

5. How soon did you see white men?

ANSWER. Two or three days afterwards, (that is, after the massacre;) these persons looked like travelers. I think they went to bury the dead.

6. Did you see many Indians during the fight?

ANSWER. During the fighting the Indians continued to run to and fro on the road.

7. How many were in the train?

ANSWER. I suppose 70 to 100; there seemed to be a good many women and children.

8. Did you hear any talk about the massacre?

ANSWER. Yes.

9. What did you hear was the cause of the massacre?

ANSWER. I heard afterwards; because the emigrant party poisoned the spring or some cattle at Corn creek.

10. What was your own opinion of the cause?

ANSWER. I thought there must have been some fuss with the Indians along the road somewhere. I heard that the emigrant party had poisoned a spring at Corn creek.

11. What became of the property?

ANSWER. The Indians drove all the cattle and horses away. I heard they burned the wagons where they were camped.

12. What was done with the children immediately after the massacre?

ANSWER. I heard the Indians took them to Cedar City. I also saw the Indians drive some cattle towards Cedar City.

13. Did you ever see any of the property in the possession of whites?

ANSWER. No.

14. Did you ever hear any one talk about the property?

ANSWER. No.

15. Did you ever hear of any one escaping from the fight or massacre?

ANSWER. I heard of one; and he was afterwards killed at the Muddy or Los Vagos river.

This is part of the statement of D. Tulis, made to me in presence of William H. Rodgers, April 13 last, while on my trip to Santa Clara. He was traveling with us from *Painter* Creek.

I will give you a few extracts from the statements by Alfred [*sic*], who is a civilized Shoshonee Indian, raised by Mr. Jacob Hamblin, and was then and is still living with him. Alfred says:

"I saw the company passing our house about sun down. It was a large company. They camped at the spring in the other end of the valley. A day or two after passing our house, I heard firing when in bed; it continued all day four days."

QUESTION. Why did you not go there?

ANSWER. I had not time; I was attending to the sheep. The time they were killed, I was about a mile from them. I saw some Indians killing them. They shot some with arrows and guns, and others were killed with clubs. I talked with some of the Indians (the day they were killed;) they were mad and I was afraid to talk much to them. Some of the Indians, during the four or five days firing, rode to and from towards *Painter* Creek settlement, about ten miles east of the Mountain Meadow valley; they were riding over the hills, and riding very fast.

QUESTION. Why did you not, during the four or five days firing, notify the people of *Painter* Creek and Cedar City of the fight?

ANSWER. I told Mr. Tulis and those at the house, when I came in from herding, about the Indians fighting the emigrants. Mr. Tulis told me to mind my business and attend to my herding. I saw the Indians killing the whites.

QUESTION. How did the emigrants get out of the corral?

ANSWER. They thought the Indians had all left, and then they started out and were coming to our house, and when they were about a mile from the wagons, the Indians who were hid behind oak brush and sage fell on them. I went to the place the same day and saw the dead lying about. Some were stript and some were dressed. The Indians were mad, scolding and quarreling. I saw the children going past our house. (Mr. Hamblin's). All the children stopped at our house.

QUESTION. Who brought the children to Mr. Hamblin's house?

ANSWER. Mr. David Tulis brought them all to our house in a wagon about dark, the same evening of the day of the massacre.

QUESTION. Was Mr. Jacob Hamblin at home when the company arrived in the valley and the day of the massacre?

ANSWER. He left home several weeks before the company arrived, and returned several days after the massacre.

These persons lived at Mr. Hamblin's, and within three and a half miles of the spot where the killing was done; yet neither were there, if one is to believe them.

I conclude from the most reliable information that the company promiscuously camped near the spring, intending to remain some days to recruit the stock, preparatory to crossing the several deserts before reaching California. They had no apprehension of serious danger when they first reached the valley, and for several days afterwards, or from Friday until Monday morning. The company then corraled the wagons and made a protective fort, by filling with earth the space under the wagons. I saw evidences of this last April.

The Indians got into a state of tremendous excitement, through misrepresentations of the foulest character, about the supposed poisoning at Corn Creek.

The Peyute Indians, inhabiting the southern portion of this Territory are divided into ten bands, roaming from Beaver valley to the California line, and have received and are receiving considerable assistance from the whites. Most of the Indians from the several bands, adjacent to the Mountain Meadow valley, were concentrated at or near the valley. These Indians received their instructions from white men. In pursuance to arrangements, the first attack was made on the unfortunate company by Indians on Monday morning, and continued daily until Friday morning, September 9. The camp was surrounded continually, preventing any one from leaving the corral without hazarding life, during five or six days.

It is impossible to comprehend the immense suffering. On the fatal morning two wagons approached the corral, and several whites effected a compromise, the emigrants giving up all their arms, with the assurance that the lives of all should be saved and conducted back to safety to Cedar City. The company started under the care and direction of white men; the wounded, old women, and children were taken in the two wagons. They proceeded about one and a half mile toward Cedar, when suddenly, and in obedience to a signal, the work of death commenced. The murderers were secreted in a few acres of oak brush and sage, the only thing of the kind I saw in the valley. My impression is that from one hundred and fifteen to one hundred and twenty were there murdered. Several escaped; only three got out of the valley; two of whom were overtaken and shot down. One adult got as far as the Muddy, and was returning with two persons from California; but he was also overtaken and shot by Indians.

From the evidence in my possession, I am justified in the declaration that this massacre was concocted by white men and consummated by whites and Indians. The names of many of the whites engaged in this terrible affair have already been given to the proper legal authorities.

I will in due time take the necessary steps for the recovery of the property, which was sold and divided among certain parties.

The seventeen little children, all that I can learn of, were taken after the massacre to Mr. Hamblin's house by John D. Lee, David Tulis, and others, in a wagon, either the same evening or the following morning. The children were sold out to different persons in Cedar City, Harmony, and Painter Creek. Bills are now in my possession from different individuals, asking payment from the government. I cannot condescend to become the medium of even transmitting such claims to the department.

I feel confident that the children were well cared for whilst in the hands of these people. I found them happy and contented, except those who were sick.

Below is a list of the children recovered by me and brought to this city, fifteen of whom are now *en route* to Arkansas, and two detained to give evidence:

John Calvin Sorel; Lewis and Mary Sorel; Ambrose Miram, and William Taggit; Francis Horn; Angeline, Annie, and Sophronia or Mary Huff; Ephraim and Sara Dunlap; William (Welch) Baker.

I remain, very respectfully, your obedient servant,

J. FORNEY
Supt. Indian Affairs Utah Territory

HON. A. B. GREENWOOD,
COM. OF INDIAN AFFAIRS,
WASHINGTON, D. C.

APPENDIX X

The Valley Tan, Vol. 1, No. 28 (May 10, 1859):

G.S.L. CITY,
MAY 5, 1859
KIRK ANDERSON, ESQ:

DEAR SIR:— I returned yesterday from a laborious trip, through the extreme southern portion of the Territory, at the same time interesting however.

The purpose of my visit was, to see and learn the condition, locality and character of the Pi-ute Indians, and to bring certain children to this city.

The Pi-ute Indians living in the southern part of the Territory, are divided into ten bands, each band numbering from 60 to 150, which live and roam on and adjacent to the Southern California road, from Beaver to the California line, and along the Santa Clara, Los Vegas, and Rio Virgin rivers. There is one principal chief, whom all the bands recognize as such: each band has one or more sub-chiefs.

Appendix X

I saw all the chiefs, and many of the Indians, during my recent visit. The Pi-ute Indians are not in exception to the other Indians in the Territory in regard to poverty; these are, if any thing, the most destitute. There is less game in the country claimed by the Pi-ute Indians than in any other part of the Territory; everything growing with a life sustaining principle; roots, seeds (grass, &c), and a peculiar plant called umea. All these are collected with great care.

A few bands cultivate small patches of land; already, however, most of the land, which is advantageously located for irrigation, is occupied. Begging among the whites, and all sorts of shiftings, these Indians merely sustain life; and I very much fear that necessity has compelled them heretofore to steal cattle, horses and mules, and to commit the crimes too fresh in our memory. I will render them such assistance in future as will be in my power.

There was during last winter, and is still, considerable travel on the Southern California road; most of the travel consisted in trains, with goods from California for Utah territory. This was during the season of the year when the Indians are most destitute; indeed many in a starving condition. I am informed that some of these trains were severely taxed by the Indians.

You are well aware that, owing to the entangled conditions of affairs here I could do but little officially until last June; since then I have been constantly engaged among the Indians, endeavoring to ameliorate their condition in different parts of the Territory. It was my desire to have visited the Pi-utes much sooner—this was impossible. The awful Mountain Meadow tragedy was perpetrated in the Pi-ute country. More of this by and by.

I found much of the road on my way south exceedingly bad, in consequence of snow, mud, tremendous hills, and innumerable rocks and stones. One wheel of each wagon and my carriage "smashed flat," besides minor accidents, and occasionally the mules straying away; and always at a place 10 or 20 miles from any place. Patience being the only help under such circumstances, never having had much to spare, necessity and circumstances, however, have furnished me with some.

After I got south of Fillmore I found it difficult on my way south to procure a sufficiency of grain for my stock; for what reason I cannot tell. We, however, got to Santa Clara finally.

I neglected mentioning that Mr. Rogers accompanied and rendered me valuable assistance. I reached the memorable Mountain Meadow valley 300 miles South of the City, Wednesday April 14th, and nooned at the Spring in the south end of the valley, and where the unfortunate emigrant party was camped from five to eight days.

The valley, usually called Mountain Meadows is about six miles long, south east and one to three wide, and almost a continuous meadow, and already excellent grass throughout the whole valley. The road leading into the valley from the east, goes through a narrow canyon, the road from the valley south, turns abruptly northeast, and passes over a considerable hill. There are two narrow outlets from the valley, besides those already mentioned, and through which the water runs. The entire valley excepting the roads, and out-lets above alluded to, are surrounded by high hills, with several small ravines or gullys between broken and abrupt hills. From several points within the valley proper, I could have a distinct view of anything that might be transpiring in the whole valley. There is one house with corrall &c., in this valley situated in the east end.

I have now traveled over much of this extensive Territory, and the Mountain Meadow valley is the most extraordinary formation west of the Rocky Mountains, probably in a higher altitude than any other valley small or large, on the continent; yet a continuous and handsome meadow furnishing grass for much stock, but in too high an altitude for agriculture of any kind, even if it would admit of agriculture, nature has not supplied it with sufficient water, there being but two springs in the whole valley.

In about the center of the valley is what is called the "Rim of the Basin," or point where the water, either finds its way to the Pacific or lakes of Utah territory, nature always profuse in making provision for the weary traveler and his stock, has, it would seem, designed this extraordinary and beautiful little valley, in so high an altitude that it can never be despoiled by the hands of the agriculturist, for a resting place, and resusitating the broken down stock of the anxious traveler before reaching the Deserts, that all travelers over the Southern California road must encounter, before reaching the healthful and rich California climate and soil and on which deserts are now bleaching the bones of thousands of human beings, and of tens of thousands of animals.

I fear I have taken up too much space in discribing the Mountain

Meadow valley. But the terrible "Drama" consumated in this little valley, hardly eighteen months ago, with the cries of women and children almost sounding in one's ears, must necessarily make this peculiar valley among the clouds a subject of concernment to the inquiring mind.

I informed my then guide and interpreter (Mr. Ira Hatch) that I was anxious to see the spot where the massacre took place, and also where the dead were buried. I saw the three places where the dead are buried.

From information received from persons in and out of the Mormon Church, and observations whilst at the place, enables me to say that the emigrant party in question, arrived and camped at the spring in the south end of the valley, Friday, Sept. 7th or 8th, 1857. The amount of property is variously (given or estimated) from 200 to 700 head, and ten to thirty wagons. My own impression is, that they had 600 head of cattle and about 40 wagons.

It is said the firing commenced Monday, Sept. 10, before daylight, and that the firing was by the Indians fighting the said emigrant party then in camp at the spring, as already stated. The firing was continued, some say five, others say seven days. During the five or seven days of firing and fighting by the Indians, the emigrant party was corralled, that is, they made a corral and temporary fort by their wagons, and filled under the wheels and to the bed of the wagons with sand and earth dug in the center of corrall. I saw the ditch and other evidences of there having been a corrall. Sept. 17th, 1857, morning, a friendly Indian, and who could talk English, came in the corrall, the inmates having then been without water from five to seven days; made arrangements or treaty with said Indian. The Indians to have the property, and to spare the lives of the whites, and permit them to return to Painter Creek and Cedar City. From the spring and corrall to the place where it is said they were murdered, and where I saw the graves (or imperfect holes) is at least one mile and a half.

I walked over the ground where it is supposed they were killed, the evidences of this being unmistakable from skulls, & other bones and hair lying scattered over the ground. There are there buried, as near as I can ascertain, 106 persons, men, women and children; and from one to two miles further down the valley, two or three who, in attempting to escape, were killed, partly up the hill, north side of the valley, and there buried and three who got away entirely, but overtaken and killed at or near the Vegas or Muddy; in all 115. I made strict and diligent inquiry of the number supposed to have been killed, and 115 is probably about the correct number.

April 15th, arrived at Santa Clara this afternoon, and camped in town. Here I met Mr. Jacob Hamblin, who has been in my employ since last fall, collecting certain children, and other business among the Indians. Here (Santa Clara) myself and party were kindly treated during our stay, two days.

I say in the beginning of my letter, that I purposed bringing to this city certain children remaining of the Mountain Meadow massacre. These children, sixteen in number, I have now in my possession. Thirteen I got in Santa Clara, at Mr. J. Hamblin's who collected them in pursuance to my directions, and three I got in Cedar City on our way home, left there by Mr. Hamblin. I am pleased to say that Mr. Hamblin has discharged his duty in relation to the collection and keeping of these children.

The following is all I have been able as yet to collect of the history of these unfortunate, fatherless, motherless and pennyless children.

John Calvin, now 7 or 8 years old, does not remember his name; says his family lived at Horse Head, Johnston co., Arkansas.

Ambrose Mironi, about 7 years, and William Taggit, 4½ years, brothers; these also lived in Johnston co.

Prudence Angeline, 6 years, and Annie, about 3 years; these two are said to be sisters.

Rebecca, 9 years; Louis, 5 years; and Sarah, 3 years, from Dunlap.

Betsy, 6 years, and Annie, 3 years, said to be sisters; these know nothing of their family or residence.

Charles Fancher, 7 or 8 years, and his sister Annie, 3½ years.

Sophronia or Mary Huff, 6 years, and Elisha W. Huff, 4 years.

A boy; no account of him. Those among whom he lived call him William.

Francis Hown or Korn, 4½ years old.

I have come to the conclusion, after different conversations with these children that most of them come from Johnston co., Arkansas. Most of them have told me that they have grandfathers and grandmothers in the States.

Mr. Hamblin has good reason for believing that a boy about 8 years, and belonging to the party in question, is among the Navajos Indians, at or near the Colorado river.

My communication is already too long, but I must ask your indulgence for a few lines more.

I will keep the children under my immediate supervision, until the person approved to take them to Fort Smith arrives.

The massacre of an entire train, not one remaining to speak of the "drama" but sixteen fatherless, motherless and pennyless children, supposed probably to be too young to give the affair tangibility, cannot remain long uninvestigated.

The cause or reason for the commission of a crime so terrible as that of killing 115 persons, must assuredly become a subject of enquiry with the proper legal authorities.

The Pi-ute tribe of Indians have been, and are charged with the above crime. Last August, my attention was called to the Mountain Meadows affair officially. Since then I have made diligent enquiry, got the written statements of persons living in the neighborhood, and finally visited the southern country; and now, after full enquiry and examination, I deem it to be my imperative duty to say that the Indians had material aid or assistance from whites; and in my opinion the Pi-ute Indians would not have perpetrated the terrible massacre without such aid and assistance.

Mr. Jacob Hamblin and others, of Santa Clara, expressed much anxiety to bring the guilty to justice.

I remain, very respectfully, yours,
J. FORNEY.

APPENDIX XI

From *The Valley Tan*, Vol. 2, No. 16 (February 29, 1860):

Statement of Mr. Wm. H. Rogers

To the Editor of the Valley Tan:—I have observed on the part of one or both the Mormon newspapers published in this city an evident purpose to treat with a light and cavalier manner the statement that has been many times made, that the Mormons were concerned in the Mountain Meadows Massacre. By their references to the matter, they would evidently produce the impression, that the whole story in regard to the Mormons being in any way concerned in the transaction, is one that has been framed for the purpose of increasing the prejudice and dislike with which they are already regarded by the great body of the people of the country. As I have never seen a published statement of the facts connected with that wholesale butchery, so far as the facts in regard to it have been brought to light, I have determined to supply this omission, by a statement of facts and circumstances in relation to it, gathered during a trip which I made with Dr. Forney, Superintendent of Indian affairs for Utah Territory, into the region where the massacre occurred, in the Spring of 1859.

Dr. Forney left Camp Floyd in the last of March, 1859, to go down to the Santa Clara settlement, 350 miles south of Salt Lake City, to obtain and bring back with him the children saved from the Mountain Meadows Massacre, who had been collected, and were then in charge of Mr. Jacob Hamblin, Dr. Forney, having some time previously employed him to collect the children and take care of them till he could take them away. On this trip Dr. Forney employed me to accompany him as an assistant, and I first joined him at the town of Nephi 80 or 90 miles south of Salt Lake City. From Nephi we proceeded through Fillmore to the Indian farm on Corn Creek, 15 miles south, where we distributed some goods to the Indians; from thence, accompanied by Kanosh, an Indian chief belonging to the Parvant tribe, we proceeded to Beaver, Parowan, Cedar City; and Painter Creek. This latter is a small place in the immediate vicinity of the Mountain Meadows, where the celebrated massacre occurred in September 1857. In passing through each of the towns named, the Doctor and myself made diligent inquiry concerning the massacre of this party of emigrants; the number of persons composing the emigrant party, and other matters deemed of interest in relation to them. We however, ascertained but little. The number of emigrants was generally estimated at from 120 to 140; but no one professed to have any knowledge of the massacre, except that they had heard it that was done by the Indians. At Painter creek, an Indian guide that had been sent to us by Jacob Hamblin, already referred to as the man that Dr. Forney had employed to collect and take charge of the children saved from the Mountain Meadows massacre, came up with us. This guide conducted us to the scene of the massacre.

The small valley known as the Mountain Meadows, in which it occurred and which will hereafter impart to its appropriate and once inviting name a sad and horrible history, is situated about 6 miles south of Painter Creek, a small Mormon settlement in Iron County. The valley is about 5 miles in length, and in the widest part does not exceed a mile in breadth. It is covered mostly during the summer with rich and luxuriant grass, and is nearly the last place where grass can be found on the southern road to California, before striking the desert. In the north end of the valley, near where the road enters it, a ranch has been constructed for the purpose of herding and taking care of the cattle brought there during the summer to graze. This ranch is owned by Jacob Hamblin. He lives there only during the summer months and spends the winter with his family at the Santa Clara settlement, some distance south of the Mountain Meadows. This ranch was unoccupied at the time that our Indian guide conducted us into the valley. The immediate locality of the massacre of the emigrant party is about four miles from the ranch on the road leading south. The valley at the place slopes gently toward the south a small ravine runs parallel with the road on the right hand side at the spot.

When we arrived here in April, 1859, more than a year and a half after the massacre occurred, the ground, for a distance of more than a hundred yards around a central point, was covered with the skeletons and bones of human beings interspersed in places with rolls or bunches of tangled and matted hair, which from its length, evidently belonged to females. In places the bones of small children were lying side by side with those of grown persons, as if parent and child had met death at the same instant and with the same stroke. Small bonets and dresses, and scraps of female apparel were also to be seen in places on the ground there; like the bones of those who wore them, bleached from long exposure, but their shape was, in many instances, entire. In a gulch or hole in the ravine by the side of the road, a large number of leg and arm bones, also of skulls, could be seen sticking above the surface, as if they had been buried there, but the action of the water, and digging of the wolves had again exposed them to sight. The entire scene was one too horrible and sickening for language to describe.

From this spot we proceeded south about one mile to a large spring, where the emigrants were encamped when the attack was first made upon them previous to the massacre. Here, within a few yards of the spring; we could distinctly define the form and size of the corral which they made, from a number of small holes, forming together a circle in the shape of a corral. These holes were dug for the purpose of lowering the wheels of the wagons in them, so as to form a better protection after the attack began. In the center of the corral a pit some twenty feet long, and four or five wide and deep, was dug for the purpose, no doubt, of placing the women and children in order to protect them from the fire of the assailants. To the left of this corral, and about one hundred and fifty or sixty yards distant, on a small mound or knoll, a number of stones were still piled up in a way to form a partial breastwork or protection against the fire which the emigrants no doubt returned for several days against their assailants. Numbers of the stones in this breastwork had bullet marks upon them on the side towards the corral, fully supporting the above construction as to its use. In places around the corral, human bones and imperfect skeletons were lying on the ground, indicating with the corral and the breastwork on the knoll, that it was here, and not at the place spoken of where the great body of the bones were found, that the work of slaugter began. From this spring we proceeded on towards the settlement of the Santa Clara for the purpose of obtaining the children from Mr. Hamblin, who resided there. On the same evening, after we had struck our camp for the night, a man drove up near us with an ox wagon, going also in the direction of Santa Clara. After turning out his oxen, he came to our tent and very soon informed us that he lived at Santa Clara, and that he was returning home from Cedar City with a load of flour, which he had been up to the latter place to obtain. This conversation, after these personal explanations, turned very naturally, after what we had witnessed during the day, upon the Mountain Meadows massacre. And this man, whose name was Carl, or Carlts Shirts, informed us that he lived, at the time the massacre occurred, at the ranch owned by Mr. Hamblin, at the north end of the Mountain Meadows. He was employed by Mr. Hamblin and making adobies at the time. He saw the emigrants when they entered the valley, and talked with several of the men belonging to it. They appeared perfectly civil and gentlemanly. The train, he supposed, contained about forty wagons, and seven or eight hundred head of cattle, including those that were loose, besides a considerable number of horses and mules. The emigrants entered the valley on Friday, and the men with whom he conversed told him they were anxious to stop a few days and rest and recruit their stock before entering the desert, and inquired of him a good place for this purpose. He recommended the vicinity of the spring in the south end of the Meadows, as good water and plenty of grass abounded there. Following this advice, they proceeded there and encamped. The next morning he again saw some of the men, who informed him that they were looking for lost stock. In the evening he saw the men returning, driving some loose cattle. He never saw any of the party afterwards. Early on Monday morning following, he stated that he heard the firing of a great many guns in the south, in the direction of the camp of the emigrants; he also saw on the hills around a great many Indians passing backwards and forwards, as if in a state of commotion or excitement. His impression from hearing the guns and seeing the Indians at the time, was that the latter had attacked the emigrants. On our inquiring why he did not go to Painter Creek to give the alarm if he thought so he stated that he supposed the people knew about it. If not in the words, the foregoing is the exact substance of the statement made by Shirts.

On the day following we reached Santa Clara settlement and found in the possession of Mr. Hamblin thirteen of the children preserved from the massacre, which with one at Painter Creek and two at Cedar City, was all that had then been heard of. These children were well with the exception of sore eyes, which they had, and which prevailed at the time as an epidemic in the place or vicinity where they were. After remaining a few days in Santa Clara in distributing some goods to the Indians, we set out with these children on our return. We did not take the same route by which we came down, but proceeding from Santa Clara direct to Harmony, leaving the Mountain Meadows some 15 or 20 miles to our left. On arriving at Harmony Dr. Forney called on John D. Lee, who was at the time, as he may be at present, a bishop in the Mormon church. The Doctor had information which led him to believe Lee had a portion of the property belonging to these murdered emigrants in his possession, and his object in calling on him was to demand a surrender of the property. On the demand being made, bishop Lee denied having the possession of any of the property, or any knowledge concerning it, further than that, he heard that the Indians took it.

I was not present when this demand was made, but was informed of it as recited by Dr. Forney on his return from Lee's house. Dr. Forney also informed me that, in a conversation with Lee concerning the massacre, he stated that he was not at the massacre but reached there just after it ended. He also stated that Isaac Haight, who presided at Cedar City, and is another prominent dignitary in the Mormon church, holding an office styled "president," which is higher than that of a bishop, also arrived at the spot soon after him. In the same conversation as related to me, Lee applied some foul and indecent epithets to the emigrants—said that they were slandering the Mormons, while passing along, and in general terms justified the killing. The day after this conversation with Lee, we started for Cedar City; Bishop Lee also set out with us for the professed purpose of going to see Prest. Haight and bishop Higby at Cedar City, and talking over with those men, in the presence of Dr. Forney, the circumstances in relation to the massacre, and the suspicions which had been expressed, that they were concerned in it either as actual participants in the deed itself, or in inciting the Indians to do the crime, and then sharing with them the spoils of the slain. Bishop Lee proceeded in company with us about half way from Harmony to Cedar City, when, from some unknown cause, he rode ahead and we did not see him afterwards.

On our arrival at Cedar City he was not there, or if he was, he kept secreted and out of sight. Dr. Forney met there President Haight and Bishop Higby, and made of the ecclesiastics the same demand that he did of Bishop Lee, and received about the same replies from them that Lee gave. They did not, however, attempt to justify the massacre, on the ground of their slandering the Mormons. On leaving Cedar City, on our way back, before arriving at Corn Creek, the Indian chief, Kanosh, who had been with us from the time that we left the Indian farm on Corn Creek, going south, informed Dr. Forney, that some Indians had told him on the way, that there were two more children saved from the massacre than Mr. Hamblin had collected. This information, though not deemed very reliable, the Doctor considered of sufficient importance to make an additional effort, in order to ascertain whether it was correct or not. On arriving at Corn Creek, we found there three companies of U.S. troops from Camp Floyd, under the command of Captain Campbell, who was on his way south to meet Maj. Prince, paymaster in the army, who was returning to Camp Floyd from California, with a large sum of money. On meeting these troops from Camp Floyd, Dr. Forney furnished me with instructions, and directed me to proceed south again with the troops, and see if I could ascertain anything about the two children spoken of by Kanosh. Judge Cradlebaugh, of the U.S. District Court for Utah, was also traveling with Capt. Campbell's command into the vicinity of Mountain Meadows, to see if he could obtain any evidence against persons who had been charged with participating in the massacre, that would justify him in arresting and holding them for trial. He was proceeding as a court inquiry or investigation simply; and informed me that he had authority from Gen. Johnston to retain a portion of the troops under Capt. Campbell, if he deemed it necessary, either to protect the court or to enforce its writs. Judge Cradlebaugh, on setting out was accompanied by deputy marshall, J. H. Stone, but the latter was compelled to stop near Nephi on account of sickness. Judge Cradlebaugh now requested us to take the place of Mr. Stone, as I had been previously sworn in and cited as deputy U.S. Marshall at the U.S. District Court, held at Provo in the preceding month. As the duties of this post could in no way interfere with my search for the two children said to have been left, and might enable me better to find them, I acceded to Judge Cradlebaugh's request to act as marshal.

In the vicinity of Parowan and below Cedar City, where the command of Capt. Campbell encamped, the soldiers, while hunting for wood, discovered human bones scattered in the bushes, and at one place they brought an entire skeleton into camp—the bones of which were still united and held together by sinews, showing that the person, whoever it was, could not have been a great while dead. We had not knowledge at the time, and never received any, as to whose remains these were, or whether they were persons that had died from exposure or starvation or whether they were the victims of treachery and murder. From the distance at which they were found from the place of the Mountain Meadows massacre, it is not presumable that they formed a portion of the party slain there.

271

On arriving at Cedar City, President Haight and Bishop Higby were not seen but at the camping ground a few miles beyond Judge Cradlebaugh issued writs for their arrest; and also for the arrest of Bishop Lee of Harmony, and placed them in my hands for execution. These writs were issued, as I understood, on the authority of affidavits, charging these men with being concerned in the Mountain Meadows massacre, which were made before Judge Cradlebaugh before he set out to investigate the matter.

These writs were given to me when we were about four or five miles below Cedar City and about twelve or fourteen from Harmoney; but as nothing had been seen of Haight or Higby in passing through Cedar City, I thought it best to proceed first to Harmony and try to arrest Haight or Higby in passing through Cedar City, if circumstances gave promise of any success in doing so. It is proper for me to say here, that not only Haight and Higby, but a large portion of the male inhabitant of the different Mormon towns and settlements secreted themselves on the approach of the troops. The cause of this I do not know, unless from a consciousness of guilt of some kind, as the troops were certainly on no hostile expedition against the inhabitants, but were simply on their way to act as an escort to a paymaster, of the army. And Judge Cradlebaugh did not seek to interfere with the right or liberty of any man unaccused of crime. I summoned to attend me, and if necessary act as a civil power, in the arrest of Lee, eight Quartermaster's men who were traveling with Capt. Campbell's command; on their way to California. Accompanied by these men, I started for Harmony on the morning that I received the writs. On the way thither we passed through or near a small settlement containing five or six houses. I stopped here to make inquiries about the two children. The residents of the place, men, women and children mostly came out of their houses when I had stopped, but none of them professed to know anything about any children besides those that Mr. Hamblin had collected. I told them that if the children were in the country at all, every house would be searched if they were not given up. At this, one of the men present, but who did not live in the place, but had arrived there just before me, stated that his wife had one of the children besides those that Mr. Hamblin had collected and that he lived at Pocketville, another small settlement forty or fifty miles distant, named from its location in the mountains. He stated that the child was very young, and that his wife was very much attached to it, and that it would give me much trouble if I took it away, and seemed by all his remarks to be anxious to retain it. I told him that I had no power to give the child away, and that I would send and get it in a few days. Mr. Hamblin went over and brought this child away in a few days after I discovered where it was. This child was a bright eyed and rosy cheeked boy, about two years old, and must have been an infant when the massacre occurred.

On being brought to Salt Lake City, and joining the other children, one of the older boys of the group, whose name was John Calvin Sorel, ran up to it, and kissing it remarked that it was his little brother; and that he did not know where he was. From this circumstance the child received the name of Sorel, after that of the older boy, but whether it was their original name or not I do not know; it is, at all events, expressive of their sad history. The second child said to have been left, I never heard of, although I inquired diligently after it. On arriving at Harmony with the men accompanying me, I went to the house of Bishop Lee and inquired for him, but was informed by one of his wives (I was told that there were thirteen in number) that Mr. Lee had been absent two or three days in the mountains; that he was there looking for copper with the Indians. Others besides his family of whom I inquired, also informed me that he had gone away. As he had thus played the same dodge that President Haight and Bishop Higby gave us at Cedar City I deemed it unwise to wait for his return or to return myself to Cedar City under any expectations of finding Haight or Higby there. I therefore returned again to the camp of Capt. Campbell, and proceeded on with it to the Mountain Meadow, and encamped a second time by the spring in the south end of the meadows, where the emigrants were encamped before being butchered.

From the Mountain Meadows, Capt. Campbell, with his command, proceeded to the Santa Clara, some four or five miles from the Mormon settlement on that stream, and there awaited the arrival of Maj. Prince. We waited here a week before Maj. Prince arrived. During our stay here some Indians in the vicinity came frequently to our camp—the same Indians that had been charged with massacreing the emigrants at the Mountain Meadows. These Indians admitted that a portion of them were present after the attack began at the corral, but denied they joined in it. One of these Indians stated in the presence of others of the same band, that after the attack was made upon the emigrants at the corral, a white man came to them and exhibited a letter, and stated that it was from Brigham Young, and that it directed them to go up and help whip the emigrants. A portion of the band went therefore, but did not assist in the fight and gave us reason for not doing so, that the emigrants had long guns and were good shots, and they were afraid to venture near. A chief of the band stated that a brother of his was killed by a shot from the corral at a distance of two hundred yards, as he was running across the meadow. These Indians also stated that the Mormons who killed the emigrants were painted so as to resemble Indians. They denied that they received any of the stock or property belonging to the emigrants, except a few of the old clothes. These Indians called Bishop Lee "Narguts", which in their language means a crying man. This name was given to Lee they stated, because he once cried when he lost some stock or had it stolen. They stated that "Narguts" was there but would not venture near, being, like themselves, afraid. President Haight and Bishop Higby were also present aiding in the attack.

Maj. Carlton, of the first Dragoons, came as the escort of Maj. Prince from California. On reaching Santa Clara where we were encamped, the two commands went together to the Mountain Meadows—Maj. Carlton to recruit his stock, before setting out on his return to California, and Capt. Campbell on his way to Camp Floyd. Leaving these commands both here, Judge Cradlebaugh and I both proceeded to Cedar City, where the Judge intended to remain some time and make a thorough investigation if he could, concerning the massacre and persons engaged in it.

Owing to some disadvantages in the location of Cedar City, a large portion of the inhabitants that once dwelt there had moved away, and there was, in consequence, a good many vacant houses in the place. Judge Cradlebaugh obtained the use of one of these to stay in while he remained, and for the purpose of a court room. As soon as it became known that Judge C. intended holding a court, and investigating the circumstances of the massacre, and that he would have troops to insure protection, and to serve writs if necessary, several persons visited him at his room, at late hours of the night and informed him of different facts connected with the massacre. All those that called thus, stated that it would be at the risk of their lives if it became known that they had communicated anything to him; and they requested Judge Cradlebaugh, if he met them in public in the day time, not to recognize them as persons that he had before seen.

One of the men who called thus on Judge Cradlebaugh, confessed that he participated in the massacre, and gave the following account of it; Previous to the massacre, there was a council held at Cedar City, which President Haight and Bishop Higby and Lee attended. At this council they designated or appointed a large number of men residing in Cedar City, and in other settlements around, to perform the work of dispatching these emigrants. The men appointed for this purpose, were instructed to report, well armed at a given time, to a spring or small stream, lying a short distance to the left of the road leading onto the meadows, and not very far from Hamblin's ranch, but concealed from it by intervening hills. This was the place of rendezvous; and here the men, when they arrived, painted and otherwise disguised themselves so as to resemble Indians. From thence they proceeded early in Monday morning, by a path or a trail which leads from this spring directly into the meadows and enters the road some distance beyond Hamblin's ranch. By taking this route they could not be seen by anyone at the ranch. On arriving at the corral of the emigrants a number of the men standing in the outside by the campfires, which, from appearances, they had just been building. These were first fired upon, and at the first discharge several of them fell dead or wounded; the remainder immediately ran to the inside of the corral, and began fortifying themselves as well as they could, by shoving their wagons close together and digging holes into which to lower them, so as to keep the shots from going under and striking them. The attack continued in a desultory and irregular manner for four or five days. The corral was closely watched, and if any of the emigrants showed themselves, they were immediately fired at from without. If they attempted to go to the spring, which was only a few yards distant, they were sure to fall by the rifles of their assailants. In consequence of the almost certain death that resulted from any attempt to procure water, the emigrants, before the seige discontinued suffered intensly from thirst. The assailants, believing at length that the emigrants could not be subdued by the

THE MOUNTAIN MEADOWS MASSACRE

means adopted, resorted to treachery and stratagem to accomplish what they had been unable to do by force. They returned to the spring where they had painted and disguised themselves previous to commencing the attack, and there removed that disguise; and again assumed their ordinary dress. After this, Bishop Lee, with a party of men returned to the camp of the emigrants, bearing a white flag as a signal of truce. From the position of the corral, the emigrants were able to see them some time before they reached it. As soon as they discerned it, they dressed a little girl in white, and placed her at the entrance of the corral, to indicate their friendly feeling to the persons bearing the flag. Lee and his party, on arriving, were invited into the corral, where they staid about an hour, talking with them about the attack that had been made upon them. Lee told the emigrants that the Indians had gone off over the hills, and that if they would lay down their arms and give up their property, he and his party would conduct them back to Cedar City; but if they went out with their arms, the Indians would look upon it as an unfriendly act, and would again attack them. The emigrants, trusting to Lee's honor and to the sincerity of his statement, consented to the terms which he proposed, and left their property and all their arms at the corral; and under the escort of Lee and his party, started towards the north in the direction of Cedar City. After they had proceeded about a mile on their way, on a signal given by Bishop Higby, who was not of the party that went to the corral with Lee, the slaughter began.

The men were mostly killed or shot down at the first fire, and the women and children, who immediately fled in different directions, were quickly pursued and dispatched.

Such was the substance, if not the exact words, of a statement made by a man to Judge Cradlebaugh, in my presence, who at the same time confessed that he participated in the horrible events which he related. He also gave Judge C. the name of 25 or 30 other men living in the region, who assisted in the massacre. He offered also to make the same statement in court and under oath, if protection was guaranteed to him. He gave as the reason for divulging these facts, that they had tormented his mind and conscience since they occurred, and he expressed a willingness to stand a trial for his crime.

We had been in Cedar City but two days when Capt. Campbell with his command arrived, and informed Judge Cradlebaugh that he had received an express from Gen Johnston directing him to bring back with him all the troops in his command, as reports were then current that the Mormons were assembling in armed bodies in the mountains, for what purpose was not known. In consequence of this order, Judge Cradlebaugh was left without the means of either protecting witnesses who might be called on to testify in court, or of arresting any parties who might flee or resist his writs. Without assistance of this kind, he deemed it useless to attempt to hold a court, and we accordingly both left on the following day with Capt. Campbell, on his return to Camp Floyd. On our way there we were overtaken by Mr. and Mrs. Hamblin, on their way to Salt Lake City. They had with them the child found at Pocketville. I had employed Mr. Hamblin to take it to the city, knowing that it would be out of my power to devote proper care to it, under the circumstances in which I was placed. Mr. Hamblin traveled in company with us for a day or two, and during this time Mrs. H. informed me that at the time of the massacre, she was living at the ranch at the north end of the Mountain Meadows, and that for several days before these children were brought to her house, or before she had even seen them, she saw several men loitering about in the vicinity of her house without any apparent object of business; this was an unusual circumstance. On the day that the massacre took place, Mrs. Hamblin stated that the children were brought to her house, and there disposed of by Bishop Lee to different white persons who were there at the time. Lee professed to act as agent for the Indians in disposing of these children. He pretended to barter them for guns, blankets, and ponies for the use of the Indians; but Mrs. H. stated that she was of the opinion at the time that the children were not really sold; and that the pretence of doing so by Lee was a mere sham. Lee went through the form of selling or bartering off all the children by two. One of these was an infant whose left arm was nearly shot off above the elbow, the bone being entirely severed; the other was her sister, three or four years older. These two, Mrs. Hamblin stated, Bishop Lee gave to her, and assigned as a reason for doing so, the high esteem which the Indians had for Mr. Hamblin. I have omitted heretofore to state that Mr.

Hamblin the husband of this lady, who has been several times referred to in this narrative, was a "President" in the Mormon church, holding the same office as that of Isaac Haight. From many interviews that I have had with Mr. Hamblin, and from all that I could learn from others, he was absent from home, and in Salt Lake City, when the massacre took place; and I have no evidence or reason to believe that he was in any way concerned or even aware of the massacre, till after it was over.

It will be remembered that I employed Mr. Hamblin to go to Pocketville for the child which I heard of there. After his return with the child, Mr. Hamblin came to the camp of Capt. Campbell, on the Santa Clara, to inform me of the fact.—While there he told me that he had heard more, and learned more about the massacre during his absence after the child, than he ever knew before; that he had been told of a number of men that he knew, that were concerned in it, that he never dreamed or suspected, or would have dreamed or suspected of being concerned in it, but for what he had been told. I inquired of him the names of these men, and he informed me that he was under a promise of secrecy not to divulge them to any one but Gov. Cummings; but that he intended to tell him who they were. Mr. Hamblin was in Salt Lake City not long after, but I was told by Gov. Cumming after he left, that he revealed nothing to him in regard to the massacre or those concerned in it.

These are the principal and most important facts obtained in relation to this noted massacre during the trip to which I have referred. I have omitted many minor facts and circumstances corroborative of those given, on account of the additional length to which they would extend this article, which is already quite lengthy. I have aimed at the narration simply of what I saw and heard, leaving the public to place any construction they deem proper upon the facts and statements given. And this would not have been done by me in this manner if I had seen from any one else a publication embodying these particulars, if this attempt had not been made to sneer away the evidence that exists of Mormon complicity in this horrid massacre, if not of their being the only persons concerned in it.

WM. H. ROGERS.

Appendix XII

APPENDIX XII

UTAH TERRITORY, CEDAR COUNTY.

James Lynch of lawful age being first duly sworn, states on oath: that he was one of the party who accompanied Dr. Jacob Forney, Superintendent of Indian affairs on an expedition to the Mountain Meadows, Santa Clara &c in the months of March & April last, when we received sixteen children, sole survivors of the wholesale massacre perpetrated at the former place in the month of September 1857. The children when we first saw them, were in a most wretched and deplorable condition; *with little or no clothing, covered with filth and dirt.* They presented a sight heart rending and miserable in the extreme. The scene of the fearful murder still bears evidence of the atrocious crime, charged by the Mormons and their friends to have been perpetrated by Indians but really by Mormons disguised as Indians, who in their headlong zeal, bigotry and fanaticism deemed this a favourable opportunity of at once wreaking their vengeance upon the hated people of Arkansas, and of making another of those iniquitous "Blood Offerings" to God so often recommended by Brigham Young and their other leaders. For more than two square miles the ground is strewn with the skulls, bones and other remains of the victims. In places the water has washed many of these remains together, forming little mounds, raising monuments as it were to the cruelty of man to his fellow man. Here and there may be found the remains of an innocent infant beside those of some fond-devoted mother, ruthlessly slain by men worse than demons: their bones lie bleaching in the noon day sun a mute but eloquent appeal to a just but offended God for vengeance. I have witnessed many harrowing sights on the fields of battle, but never did my heart thrill with such horrible emotions, as when standing on that silent plain contemplating the remains of the innocent victims of Mormon Avarice, fanaticism & cruelty. Many of these remains are now in possession of Mr. Rogers, a gentleman who accompanied us on the expedition. Why were not the remains interred if not in a Christian like and proper manner, at least covered from the sight? But no the hatred of the murderers extended to them after death—there they lay, a prey to the famished wolves, that run howling over the desolate plains to the unlooked for feast, food for the croaking ravens that through the tainted air with swift wing wended their way to revel in their banquet of blood.

I enquired of Jacob Hamblin who is a high Church dignitary, why these remains were not buried at some time subsequent to the murder? He said that the bodies were so much decomposed that it was impossible to inter them. No longer let us boast of our citizenship freedom or civilization. There was one hundred and forty poor harmless Emigrants to California, butchered in cold blood, by white men too, and attending circumstances far exceeding anything in cruelty that we have ever heard of or read of being perpetrated by savages. It is now high time that the actors and perpetrators of the dreadful crime should be brought to condign punishment. For years these Mormons have possessed an immunity from punishment or a sort of privilege for committing crimes of this nature, but soon it is to be hoped a new state of things must dawn—a retribution must come, vengeance must be had—civilization humanity and christianity call for it, and the American people must have it. Blood may be shed, difficulties may be encountered, but just as sure as there is a sun at noonday, retribution will yet overtake the guilty wretches—their aiders, abettors, whether open or *hidden under disguise of Government employment.*

John D. Lee, a Mormon President, has knowledge of the whereabouts of much of the property taken from these ill fated emigrants, and if I am not misinformed in possession of a large quantity of it. Why not make him disgorge this illgotten plunder—and disclose the amount escheated to, and sold out by the Mormon Church, as its share of the blood of helpless victims? When he enters into a league with Hell and covenant with death; he should not be allowed to make feasts and entertain government officials at his table as he did Dr. Jacob Forney, Superintendent of Indian Affairs, while the rest of his party refused in his hearing and that of Lee, to share the hospitalities of this *notorious murderer—This scourge of the desert.* This man Lee does not deny, but admits that he was present at the massacre, but pretends that he was there to prevent blood shed, but positive evidence implicate him as the leader of the murderers too deeply for denial. The Children point him out as one of them that did the bloody work. He and other white men had these children, and they never were in the hands of the Indians, but in those that murdered them and Jacob Hamlin [note variant spelling above] and Jacob Forney know it. The children pointed out to us the dresses and jewelry of their mothers and sisters, that now grace the *Angelic* forms of these murderers women and children—verily it would seem that men and women alike combined in this wholesale slaughter. This ill fated train consisted of 18 wagons 820 head of cattle household goods to a large amount, besides money estimated at 80 or 90,000 dollars the greater part of which it is believed now makes rich the harems of John D. Lee. Of this train, a man whose name is unknown, fortunately escaped at the time of the massacre to Vegas one hundred miles distant from the scene of blood on the California Road. Here he was followed by five mormons, who through promises of safety &c prevailed upon him to begin his return to Mountain Meadows & contrary to their promises and his just expectation they inhumanly butchered him—laughing at and disregarding his loud and repeated cries for mercy as witnessed by and told by Ira Hatch one of the five. The object in Killing this man was to leave no witness competent to give testimony in a Court of Justice, but God whose ways are inscrutable has thought proper, through the instrumentality of the "babes and sucklings" recovered by us to bring to light this most horrible tragedy, and made known its barbarous and inhuman prepetrators. Already a step has been taken by Judge Cradlebaugh in the right direction, of which we see the evidence in the flight of Presidents, Bishops, and Elders, to the mountains, to escape the just penalty of the law for their crimes. If the vengeance of the Lord is slow 'tis equally sure. The Mormons, who *know better* have reported that the principles, and in fact all the actors in this fearful massacre, were Indian savages, but subsequent events have thrown sufficient light upon the mystery to fix the foul blot indelibly on the Mormon escutcheon. Many of the leaders are well known. John D. Lee was the Commander in Chief, President Height and Bishop Smith in Cedar City and besides these one hundred actors and accomplices are known to Judge Cradlebaugh and Dr. Forney. Some of these implicated are and have been in the confidence and under employment of the Superintendent of Indian Affairs, Bishop Hamblin for instance who is employed by Dr. Forney among the Indians down south, who knows all the facts but refuses to disclose them, who falsely reported to Dr. Forney that the children we brought away were recovered by him from persons who had bought them from

Indians, and who knew that what he reported was false and was so done to cheat the government out of money to again reward the guilty wretches for their inhuman butcheries. It is pretended that the man is friendly towards the United States Government, yet it is a well known fact that he screened some of these murderers about his house, from justice, among whom are an Indian named George and a white man by the name of Tillis recognized by one of the children—a little girl eight years old, who has been sent off to the States by Dr. Forney, as the man who killed her mother. Hamblin cannot be a Mormon Bishop and a friend of the United States at least where Mormons or Mormonism is concerned. His creed & oaths forbid it & he could not if he would with safety to himself do it. Then why not out with him? Dr. Forney can find another and more trustworthy Agent than he, Why then keep and patronize the abetter of crime. Before I close, my duty to my country calls upon me to state to the public the course of Dr. Forney to engender in the minds of the Mormons feelings of antipathy and opposition to the Judiciary, and the many obligations which he violated, and promises which he disregarded during this trip.

I left Camp Floyd in March last in charge of 39 men, emigrating to Arizona, about the 27th of that month we came up with Dr. Forney at Beaver City who there informed me that he was *en-route* to the scene of the Mountain Meadow massacre and Santa Clara, to procure evidence in relation thereto, and to secure the surviving children. He informed me that all his men had left him being Mormons and who before leaving had informed him, Forney, that if he went down South, that the people down there would make an ewnuch of him, and asked us for aid & assistance. I cheerfully placed the whole party at his command telling him that he had started upon an errand of mercy, and it was strange that he should have employed mormons—the very confederates of these monsters, who had so wantonly murdered unoffending Emigrants, to ferret out the guilty parties.

He was left without a man and we found him guarding his mules & wagons. He requested two of the men of my party (Thomas Dunn & John Lafink) to return to Great Salt Lake City with him, promising to give them employment during the following summer and winter. They consented to abandon their trip to Arizona upon these terms and returned with the Doctor, and I am sorry to say he violated his plighted faith, and his solemn contract on reaching the City, by immediately discharging them without cause and hiring mormons to take their place, as I am informed has been his custom since he came into the Valley. I was with Dr. Forney from the time I joined him until he returned to the City of Salt Lake, having voluntarily abandoned my expedition to Arizona to aid his humane enterprise and during the trip I repeatedly heard him tell the Mormons "That they need not fear Judge Cradlebaugh (whose disclosures & energy had created some alarm) that he (Forney) would have him removed from office, that the Mormons (Murderers and all) were all included in the Presidents proclamation and pardon, and would not be tried or punished for any offence whatever committed prior to his issuing the pardon—That Judge Cradlebaugh was not a fit man for office" in fact abusing and slandering the Judge in unmeasured terms—no language being too low or filthy to apply to him. I could arrive at no other conclusion from his conduct than that the Doctor desired to influence the minds of the Mormons against the judiciary, and that he cared more to create a prejudice against Judge Cradlebaughs course in attempting to bring these murders to light, than he did to elicit the truth relative to the murders, and that he was only following out his instructions from the General Government in going after these children, while he was availing himself of this journey to make a pilgrimage to the south settlements to abuse & traduce Judge Cradlebaugh and arouse a feeling of resistance to his authority among the guilty murderers.

It is to be regretted that the Doctor has manifested so hostile a feeling to his associate Federal Officer and that the course of the Judges, especially that of Judge Cradlebaugh has to be criticized by such a man as Jacob Forney—a more veritable old granny than whom, in my opinion never held an official position in this country, and in this opinion I am borne out by the concurrent opinions of nearly all the Gentile population in Utah who know him, as well as by many of the Mormons people. I now reside in Cedar County U.T.

Signed: JAMES LYNCH

James Lynch being duly sworn states on oath that all the material facts stated by him in the foregoing affidavit, so far as he states the same of his own knowledge are true and so as he states the same as from information derived from others as also the conclusions drawn from the same he believes to be true and further saith not.

Signed: JAMES LYNCH

Sworn and subscribed to

July 27th 1859   *Signed* D. R. ECKELS

Chief Justice of Sup. Court

The undermentioned state on oath that the foregoing affidavit has been carefully read to them that they are the identical persons named in it as having been employed by Dr. Jacob Forney to return with him to Salt Lake City—that they went from Beaver City with said Forney South and back again and that we fully concur in the statements made by James Lynch Esqr in the foregoing affidavit, as to what we saw and heard on the trip, and the conduct of Dr. Forney Superintendent of Indian Affairs and further say not.

(*Signed*) THOMAS DUNN

(*Signed*) JOHN LAFINK

Subscribed and sworn to before me

July 27th 1859   *Signed* D. R. ECKELS

Chief Justice of Sup. Court.

APPENDIX XIII

The deposition of Brigham Young as entered in the court records is as follows:

TERRITORY OF UTAH	)	SS
BEAVER COUNTY	)	
IN THE SECOND JUDICIAL DISTRICT COURT	)	
THE PEOPLE, ETC.	)	INDICTMENT FOR MURDER
VS.	)	SEPTEMBER 16, 1875
JOHN D. LEE, WM. H. DAME,	)	
ISAAC C. HAIGHT, ET AL.	)	

Questions to be propounded to Brigham Young on his examination as a witness in the case of John D. Lee and others, on trial at Beaver City, this 30th day of July, 1875, and the answers of Brigham Young to the interrogatives here to appended, were reduced to writing, and were given after the said Brigham Young had been duly sworn to testify the truth in the above entitled cause, and are as follows:

FIRST—State your age, and the present condition of your health, and whether in its condition you could travel to attend in person, at Beaver, the court now sitting there?

ANSWER—To the first interrogatory, he saith:

I am in my seventy-fifth year. It would be a great risk, both to my health and life, for me to travel to Beaver at this present time. I am, and have been for some time, an invalid.

SECOND—What office, either ecclesiastical, civil, or military, did you hold in the year 1857?

ANSWER—I was Governor of the Territory, and ex-officio Superintendent of Indian Affairs, and President of the Church of Jesus Christ of Latter-Day Saints, during the year 1857.

THIRD—State the condition of affairs between the Territory of Utah and the Federal Government, in the Summer and Fall of 1857.

ANSWER—In May or June, 1857, the United States mails for Utah were stopped by the Government, and all communication by mail was cut off, an army of the United States was enroute for Utah, with the ostensible design of destroying the Latter-Day Saints, according to the reports that reached us from the East.

FOURTH—Were there any United States Judges here during the Summer and Fall of 1857?

ANSWER—To the best of my recollection there was no United States Judge here in the latter part of 1857.

FIFTH—State what you know about trains of emigrants passing through the Territory to the West, and particularly about a company from Arkansas, en route for California, passing through this city in the Summer or Fall of 1857?

ANSWER—As usual, emigrants' trains were passing through our Territory for the west. I heard it rumored that a company from Arkansas, en route to California, had passed through the city.

SIXTH—Was this Arkansas company of emigrants ordered away from Salt Lake City by yourself or any one in authority under you?

ANSWER—No, not that I know of. I never heard of any such thing, and certainly no such order was given by the acting Governor.

SEVENTH—Was any counsel or instructions given by any person to the citizens of Utah not to sell grain or trade with the emigrant trains passing through Utah at that time? If so, what were those instructions and counsel?

ANSWER—Yes, counsel and advice were given to the citizens not to sell grain to the emigrants to feed their stock, but to let them have sufficient for themselves if they were out. The simple reason for this was that for several years our crops had been short, and the prospect was at that time that we might have trouble with the United States army, then enroute for this place, and we wanted to preserve the grain for food. The citizens of the Territory were counseled not to feed grain to their own stock. No person was ever punished or called in question for furnishing supplies to the emigrants, within my knowledge.

EIGHTH—When did you first hear of the attack and destruction of this Arkansas company at Mountain Meadows, in September 1857?

ANSWER—I did not learn anything of the attack or destruction of the Arkansas company until some time after it occurred—then only by floating rumor.

NINTH—Did John D. Lee report to you at any time after this massacre, and if so, what did you reply to him in reference thereto?

ANSWER—Within some two or three months after the massacre he called at my office and had much to say with regard to the Indians, their being stirred up to anger and threatening the settlements of the whites, and then commenced giving an account of the massacre. I told him to stop as from what I had already heard by rumor, I did not wish my feelings harrowed up with a recital of detail.

TENTH—Did Philip Klingensmith call at your office with John D. Lee at the time Lee made his report, and did you at that time order Smith to turn over the stock to Lee, and then order them not to talk about the massacre?

ANSWER—No. He did not call with John D. Lee, and I have no recollection of him ever speaking to me nor I to him concerning the massacre or anything pertaining to the property.

ELEVENTH—Did you ever give any directions concerning the property taken from the emigrants at the Mountain Meadows Massacre, or know anything of its disposition?

ANSWER—No, I never gave any directions concerning the property taken from the emigrants at the Mountain Meadows Massacre, nor did I know anything of that property, or its disposal, and I do not to this day, except from public rumor.

TWELFTH—Why did you not, as Governor, institute proceedings forthwith to investigate that massacre, and bring the guilty authors thereof to justice?

ANSWER—Because another Governor had been appointed by the President of the United States, and was then on the way to take my place, and I did not know how soon he might arrive, and because the United States Judges were not in the Territory. Soon after Governor Cummings arrived, I asked him to take Judge Cradlebaugh, who belonged to the Southern District, with him, and I would accompany them with sufficient aid to investigate the matter and bring the offenders to justice.

THIRTEENTH—Did you, about the 10th of September, 1857, receive a communication from Isaac C. Haight, or any other person of Cedar City, concerning a company of emigrants called the Arkansas company?

ANSWER—I did receive a communication from Isaac C. Haight or John D. Lee, who was a farmer for the Indians.

FOURTEENTH—Have you that communication?

ANSWER—I have not. I have made diligent search for it, but cannot find it.

FIFTEENTH—Did you answer that communication?

ANSWER—I did, to Isaac C. Haight, who was then acting President at Cedar City.

SIXTEENTH—Will you state the substance of your letter to him?

ANSWER—Yes. It was to let this company of emigrants, and all companies of emigrants, pass through the country unmolested, and to allay the angry feelings of the Indians as much as possible.

(*Signed*) BRIGHAM YOUNG

Subscribed and sworn to before me this 30th day of July, A.D., 1875.

WM. CLAYTON, *Notary Public*

The affidavit of George A. Smith, after the legal introduction, reads as follows:

George A. Smith having been first duly sworn, deposes and says that he is aged fifty-eight years. That he is now and has been for several months suffering from a severe and dangerous illness of the head and lungs, and that to attend the court at Beaver, in the present condition of his health, would in all probability end his life.

Deponent further saith, that he had no military command during the year 1857, nor any official position, except that of one of the Twelve Apostles of the Church of Jesus Christ of Latter-Day Saints.

Deponent further saith, that he never in the year 1857, at Parowan or elsewhere, attended a council where Wm. H. Dame, Isaac C. Haight or others were present to discuss any measures for attacking, or in any way injuring an emigrant train from Arkansas or any other place, which is alleged to have been destroyed at Mountain Meadows in September, 1857.

Deponent further saith that he never heard or knew anything of a train of emigrants, which he learned afterwards by rumor was from Arkansas, until he met said train at Corn Creek on his way north to Salt Lake City, on or about the 25th day of August, 1857.

Deponent further saith, that he encamped with Jacob Hamblin, Philo T. Farnsworth, Silas S. Smith and Elijah Hoops, and there for the first time he learned of the existence of said emigrant train, and their intended journey to California.

Deponent further saith, that having been absent from the Territory for a year previous, he returned in the Summer of 1857, and went south to visit his family at Parowan, and to look after some property he had there, and also visit his friends, and for no other purpose, and that on leaving Salt Lake City he had no knowledge whatsoever of the existence of said emigrant train, nor did he acquire any until as before stated.

Deponent further saith, that as an Elder in the Church of Jesus Christ of Latter-Day Saints, he preached several times on his way south, and also on his return, and tried to impress upon the minds of the people the necessity of great care as to their grain crops, as all crops had been short for several years previous to 1857, and many of the people were reduced to actual want and were suffering for the necessaries of life.

Deponent further saith, that he advised the people to furnish all emigrant companies passing through the Territory with what they might actually need for breadstuff, for the support of themselves and families while passing through the Territory, and also advised the people not to feed their grains to their own stock, nor to sell it to the emigrants for that purpose.

Deponent further saith, that he never heard or knew of any attack upon said emigrant train until some time after his return to Salt Lake City, and that while near Fort Bridger he heard for the first time that the Indians had massacred an emigrant company at Mountain Meadows.

Deponent further saith, that he never at any time, either before or after that massacre, was accessory thereto; that he never directly or indirectly aided, abetted, or assisted in its perpetration, or had any knowledge thereof, except by hearsay; that he never knew anything of the distribution of the property taken there, except by hearsay as aforesaid.

Deponent further saith, that all charges and statements as pertaining to him contrary to the above are false and untrue.

(*Signed*) GEO. A. SMITH

Subscribed and sworn to before me this 30th day of July, A.D. 1875.

(*Signed*) WM. CLAYTON

Notary Public.

Afterword
by Jan Shipps

JUANITA BROOKS WAS a fierce proponent of treating the massacre at Mountain Meadows as any other historical incident insofar as studying it with a view only to finding the facts was concerned. Yet because she was clearly aware that this was not simply one more historical incident, she did not conclude her splendid account of this troubling episode with a resounding appeal for openness and full disclosure. Instead, she described the landscape where the emigrants had been slaughtered and John D. Lee shot as a part of the southern Utah terrain that was "so sterile and barren that it would actually seem to bear the curse of God upon it," and brought her history of the event to a close with a complaint about the failure of subsequent generations to properly see to the consecration of the ground where so many bodies were buried.

As unlikely as it may seem to those who believe that the best LDS history is that which keeps unpleasant facts in the Saints' past from coming to light, this is a case in which a historical study that exposed all the facts commenced a healing process. In 1988, almost four decades after the first publication of this brave book, descendants of the Mormon pioneers involved in the massacre and descendants of the victims came together and set in motion activities that would lead to a sanctification of the space where the unthinkable had occurred more than a century before. In a spirit of reconciliation and healing, they planned to memorialize the massacre victims. Collecting contributions from "the family and friends of those involved and those who died," they commissioned a granite monument on which a complete listing of all the known names of the victims and the survivors would be inscribed.

A location on Dan Sill Hill that overlooks the massacre site was selected as an appropriate place for the monument. State Senator Dixie Leavitt, a descendant of Dudley Leavitt (Juanita Brooks's grandfather), convinced the Utah legislature to respond to these initiatives by appropriating funds for the improvement of access roads to Mountain Meadows and the construction of a parking area, as well as paved trails from the parking area to the summit of the hill. President Gordon B. Hinckley, a member of the First Presidency of the Church of Jesus Christ of Latter-day Saints, was approached and asked to speak at the monument's dedication. And plans were made for ceremonies that, finally, would hallow the ground where so many died.

Whether consciously understood as such, the improvement of the site, the new monument, and its dedication can all be understood in a true sense as responses to the call issued at the end of *Mountain Meadows Massacre*. The monument will function henceforth as a collective headstone marking the shared resting place of the dead. The names of the victims, so long lost to history, are memorialized. When J. K. Fancher, a relative of one of the victims, could describe the monument as "a bridge of communication and understanding, compassion and forgiveness," and a member of the First Presidency of the LDS church could deliver a beautiful prayer to consecrate the ground on which it stood, it was obvious that a spirit of reconciliation was at hand. *Mountain Meadows Massacre* has accomplished what its author so clearly wanted.

Bibliography

MANUSCRIPTS AND DOCUMENTARY SOURCES

1. Official Records

Bleak, James G. "Annals of the Southern Utah Mission," Books A and B. (Archives of the L.D.S. church historian, Salt Lake City.)

These handwritten ledgers cover the happenings in southern Utah from the first Mormon exploration to 1877. Appointed as official historian in 1861, the author filled in the period before that time from church and local records. After 1861, happenings in southern Utah, Nevada, and Arizona were carefully recorded as they took place. Book A covers the period to 1869. It was first copied in abridged form by Brigham Young University under the supervision of H. Lorenzo Reid. It has since been copied by a WPA project and by private individuals. Book B, covering the period from 1869 to 1877, has been copied by the Dixie Junior College from a duplicate of the original left with the descendants of James G. Bleak. Books C and D are also in the archives of the L.D.S. church historian, together with other historical records taken from the depository first kept in the St. George Temple and later in the Tabernacle.

"Cedar City Ward Record Book, 1857." (Archives of the L.D.S. church historian, Salt Lake City.) This handwritten ledger contains minutes of meetings and records of general ward activities.

"History of Brigham Young, 1844–1877." (Archives of the L.D.S. church historian, Salt Lake City.)

This compilation includes letters, items of history, and personal incidents, arranged in chronological order. Rewritten from first to third person, it constitutes part of what is called the "Documentary History of the Church."

Bibliography

"Journal History of the Church, 1830–1900." (Archives of the L.D.S. church historian, Salt Lake City.)

This is a day-by-day, loose-leaf record, covering events in the church and containing many transcripts of original documents. It is chronologically arranged.

"Military Records of the Second Brigade, First Division, Nauvoo Legion." (Copy at the Henry E. Huntington Library, San Marino, Calif.)

The handwritten original of this account has been sold to a collector in the East. A second copy is at Brigham Young University, Provo, Utah. It is an illuminating account of the progress of the Mormon War.

"Military Records of the Iron County Battalion, Nauvoo Legion."

These records are carefully kept in the hand of James H. Martineau, adjutant to William H. Dame, colonel commanding. They include full rolls of each company, reports of arms and equipment, correspondence, *etc.*, during this critical period. Originals are in the military records section of the Utah State Historical Society, Archives Division.

"Papers of the Attorney General Prior to 1870." (Records of the Department of Justice, National Archives, Washington, D.C.)

The letters written during the years 1858–59 show the conditions among the Indians along the southern route and the need for troops to protect emigration. These letters are mainly duplicates from the originals in the records of the Adjutant General's Office, War Department, also in the National Archives.

"Parowan Ward Record Book." (Archives of the L.D.S. church historian, Salt Lake City.) This handwritten ledger contains an account of the various ward activities, minutes of meetings, etc.

Richards, Franklin D. "Early Records of Utah (July 21, 1847–December 1851)." (Bancroft Library, University of California, Berkeley.)

———. "Incidents in Utah History (January 1852–January 1855)." (Bancroft Library, University of California, Berkeley.)

———. "Utah Historical Incidents (January 1855–December 1887)." (Bancroft Library, University of California, Berkeley.)

These three companion volumes were prepared for H. H. Bancroft by the author, then official historian for the L.D.S. church. They seem to be an abridgement of the "Documentary History of the Church."

"Transcript of the Trials of John D. Lee." (Henry E. Huntington Library, San Marino, Calif.) The shorthand notes and the complete transcripts of both trials of John D. Lee, as well as letters, affidavits, and other materials introduced as evidence.

"Utah Superintendency, 1855-1860." (Records of the Office of Indian Affairs, National Archives, Washington, D.C.)

This file contains all the correspondence and reports of this department for the years preceding the massacre and immediately following it. They permit insight into the various frictions which developed between Brigham Young and the government officials in this department.

2. Personal Diaries and Records

Adams, William. "History of William Adams." (Copies at the Utah State Historical Society, Salt Lake City, and at the Washington County library, St. George, Utah.) This book was written by Adams in 1894, when he was seventy-two years old.

Arthur, Christopher J. "Journals and Diaries." (Copies of some at the Utah State Historical Society, Salt Lake City, and some at the Washington County library, St. George, Utah.)

This man was a prolific writer, sometimes giving several accounts of the same happening. Part of the time while he was bishop at Cedar City, he kept a diary, the entries of which show both the religious activities of the people and their efforts to establish cooperative enterprises. A son-in-law and ardent admirer of Isaac C. Haight, he speaks often of the leader. Besides the copies mentioned above, the Henry E. Huntington Library has photostats of several.

Ashworth, William. "Life." (Copy at the Brigham Young University Library, Provo, Utah.) This autobiography gives many interesting details, although some dates are inaccurate. Copies were made by the Brigham Young University.

Boreman, Jacob Smith. "Miscellaneous Papers and Writings." (Henry E. Huntington Library, San Marino, Calif.)

Judge Boreman officiated at the trials of John D. Lee, and his papers include letters, an article entitled "Curiosities of Early Utah Legislation," penciled "Reminiscences," and the charge to the jury at the close of the Lee trial.

Brimhall, George Washington. "Autobiography." (Owned and copied from the original by Mrs. Fawn Brodie, a granddaughter of the author.)

This document consists of 73 single-spaced typewritten pages. It gives an excellent picture of the early explorations of southern Utah and Nevada, of the Indians of the region, and the Indian-Mormon councils. This was the original draft of Brimhall's book, *Workers of Utah*, published in Provo, 1889, which is now very rare. A copy of this is in the Library of Congress.

Brown, Lorenzo. "Journals [1823–1900]." The copy made by the Brigham Young University consists of 857 typewritten pages. Photostats of the original are in the Library of Congress. Consisting primarily of daily entries, this record is very valuable to students of Mormon history.

Brown, Thomas D. "Journal of the Southern Indian Mission, April 15, 1854–April 1856." (Archives of the L.D.S. church historian, Salt Lake City.)

The original is handwritten very legibly, in a slightly faded black ink, in a ledger volume approximately eight by thirteen inches in size and consisting of 243 numbered pages. Although the official record of the mission, it is a highly personalized diary of the activities of the missionaries. Appended to it are three letters to Brigham Young and one from him.

Burgess, Melancthon W. "Journal." The original is a small, leather-bound pocket notebook with daily entries written in pencil. It covers the period from April 10 to June 26, 1858, and is a vivid close-up of the activities of the Mormon "army" in Echo Canyon.

Carleton, Major James Henry. "Special Report." (Records of the War Department, National Archives, Washington, D.C.)

Dated "Camp at Mountain Meadows, Utah Territory, May 25, 1859," this report consists of eleven sheets of four pages each, or 44 pages in all, handwritten in ink on blue paper. It is not in Carleton's handwriting but bears his signature.

Conover, Peter Wilson. "Journal, 1840–1875." (Copy in the Utah State Historical Society, Salt Lake City.)

This fascinating document of 64 pages was evidently rewritten from a diary or the events were summarized at intervals. The accounts of the journal to call the Carson saints back to the Valley, the expedients necessary to get their load of ammunition safely to

Great Salt Lake City, and the near-death experiences on the desert are among the most vivid of the contemporary writings.

Dame, William H. "Papers." This remarkable collection contains several letters from George A. Smith to Dame just preceding the massacre, and some following it. There are also letters to and from his wives, a day-by-day record of the exploring company sent out to find a new location for the church, and a record of activities in the Parowan Ward during 1859. Much of it is in the hand of James H. Martineau, clerk. All the papers are on microfilm at the Utah State Historical Society and in typescripts at Brigham Young University.

Farnsworth, Philo T. "Interview." (Bancroft Library, University of California, Berkeley, Calif.) Taken by a representative of H. H. Bancroft, this interview gives information on the emigrant trains which were immediately behind the one that was massacred. The record is now in the Bancroft Collection.

Ginn, John L. "Early Perils of the Far West. The Mountain Meadows Massacre and Other Tragedies Incident to the Mormon Rebellion and Indian Wars of 1857–1858." (Copies in the archives of the L.D.S. church historian, Salt Lake City, and in the Coe Collection, Yale University Library, New Haven.)

Β Β Β Β This is a typewritten manuscript of 161 pages, which was evidently prepared for publication. Corrections and notations are made in a palsied hand. Another copy is owned by Mrs. Emma Shepard of Shepard's Book Store, Salt Lake City.

Haight, Isaac C. "Diaries." Vol. I. (Copies in the Washington County library, St. George, Utah, at the Brigham Young University library, Provo, Utah, and at the Utah State Historical Society, Salt Lake City.)

Β Β Β Β Beginning with a brief summary of the writer's life, the record continues with periodic entries. From February to June, 1853, there are almost daily notations; from that time until 1857, the entries are usually weekly or monthly; after 1857, they are made less frequently, and the volume closes with a brief entry in 1862.

Hamblin, Jacob. "Journal." (Archives of the L.D.S. church historian, Salt Lake City.)

Β Β Β Β This record covers the years 1854–58. It is kept in a notebook from which the back covers are gone and which is worn, somewhat soiled, and slightly faded. The entries are written partly in brown

Bibliography

and partly in blue ink. The notebook has fifty-six pages, with pages 1–6 and pages 39–40 missing. The latter is presumably the leaf which recorded the Mountain Meadows Massacre and the interview between the Indians and President Young, for the entry on the previous page ends with Hamblin on the way to Salt Lake City and the one following begins with his arrival in the south. Although the *Deseret News* has printed excerpts from this record, the whole has never been published.

Higbee, John M. Account of the Mountain Meadows Massacre. (In possession of the Higbee family, Cedar City, Utah.)

With no formal title, this account, written in 1894, fills seventeen pages in an ordinary notebook. The handwriting is clear and distinct; the book is well preserved. It is signed "Snort" after the Preface and "Bull Valley Snort" at the end. See Appendix II. A typewritten copy is at Utah State Historical Society.

Huntington, Oliver B. "Diaries." 18 vols. (Photostats at the Henry E. Huntington Library, San Marino, California; typewritten copy at the Utah State Historical Society, Salt Lake City.) The originals are in eighteen small volumes of varying sizes. The typewritten copy is in three volumes, of which Volume II deals with the periods of this study. Originals and copies at Brigham Young University.

Laub, George. "Diaries." 3 vols. (Photostats at the Henry E. Huntington Library, San Marino, Calif.; typescripts at the Brigham Young University library, Provo, Utah, and at the Utah State Historical Society, Salt Lake City.)

These handwritten diaries give a vivid picture of the evacuation of Nauvoo, the life in exile, and the crossing to Utah in the first volume, which covers the period 1844–57. The coming of the army, the preparations to meet—and later the preparations to flee—and the call to the Cotton Mission are described in the second volume, dated 1858–70. The life and activities in southern Utah are described in the third volume, which begins in 1871. The first and second volumes are especially pertinent to this study.

Lee, John D. "Diaries." 5 vols. (Henry E. Huntington Library, San Marino, Calif.)

These diaries are dated 1848, 1857–58, 1866, 1873, and 1875. The volume quoted in this book begins in December, 1857, and continues with almost daily entries through most of 1858. The "Diaries"

297

were published by the Henry E. Huntington Library in 1955.
————. "Diary 14A." (Archives of the L.D.S. church historian, Salt Lake City.)

On the flyleaf is written, "John D. Lee's Journal bought in St. Louis, May 29, 1844. No. 4." The first entry is dated May 28, and it gives an account of Lee's boarding ship on the Mississippi to go on a mission for the L.D.S. church. It is written in a small, fine hand and is decorated in places with geometric drawings and embellished acrostics. The daily entries tell his experiences as a missionary, his return to Nauvoo upon hearing of the death of Joseph Smith, and his subsequent activities. The last section of the little volume is a day-by-day account of his mission with Howard Egan for the battalion money. The last date is November 18, 1846.

————. "Diary 14B." (Archives of the L.D.S. church historian, Salt Lake City.)

On the flyleaf of this book appear the following captions: "John D. Lee Record. A book Containing an Inventory of all the Camps of the Saints! Also the circumstances connected with the Exodus from Nauvoo, The City of Joseph, West through the Wilderness in search of Home and Place of rest by John D. Lee Young. 1846." This record gives details of the preparations for the exodus of the Mormons, the organization of companies, the purchase of supplies, and the securing of wagons and equipment.

————. "Diary 14C." (Archives of the L.D.S. church historian, Salt Lake City.)

This is the "Journal of the Iron Mission, 1850–1852." It begins with Lee's call to accompany George A. Smith and his group south to establish the town which was later named Parowan, the far southern border of Utah settlement. The happenings en route and the history of the village are entered daily. Published in 1952 in the *Utah Historical Quarterly*.

————. "Missionary Diaries." (Copy at the Henry E. Huntington Library, San Marino, Calif.)

The two small pocket diaries cover Lee's activities as a missionary for his church during the period January, 1841, to January, 1842. The backs of both booklets are gone and some leaves are missing, but they are illuminating in regard to the character of the writer. The Henry E. Huntington Library has a typed copy of the first and a photostat of the second.

Bibliography

————. "Record of the First Council of Seventies." (First Presidency of the Seventies' Quorum, L.D.S. Church Office Building, Salt Lake City.)

The large ledger, bound in red leather, is a record of the Quorums of the Seventies. John D. Lee was clerk and recorder from October, 1844, to January, 1847, and much of the writing is in his hand. Besides the minutes of meetings, items of general history are written in, as well as accounts of work done in the Nauvoo Temple and general problems facing the people in the evacuation of Nauvoo and the preparation to emigrate west.

Lee, Rachel. "Journal." (Henry E. Huntington Library, San Marino, Calif.)

This record, by a wife of John D. Lee, makes note of doings in Harmony, especially of meetings and other community activities. Entries begin on February 17, 1857, and continue with brief weekly notations all that year and through 1858. For the next two years, entries are irregular.

Lewis, David. "Journal." (Photostat at the Henry E. Huntington Library, San Marino, Calif.) The original is a large, leather-bound ledger. The author began to write on January 18, 1854, when he was in his thirty-ninth year. He gave a summary of his early life, with details of the Haun's Mill massacre, of which he was a survivor.

Liston, Commodore Perry. "Journal." (Photostat at the Henry E. Huntington Library, San Marino, Calif.; typewritten copy at the Utah State Historical Society, Salt Lake City.) Though brief, this is a significant record of the period under consideration.

Platte, Benjamin. "Journal." (Photostat at the Henry E. Huntington Library, San Marino, Calif.; typed copy at the Brigham Young University library, Provo, Utah.) This brief, handwritten record was kept by a man who for a number of years was in John D. Lee's employ.

Pulsipher, John. "Diaries." 2 vols. (Photostat at the Henry E. Huntington Library, San Marino, Calif.; typed copies at the Brigham Young University library, Provo, Utah, and at the Utah State Historical Society, Salt Lake City.) Only Volume I, 1835–74, is pertinent here. It gives the story of the Mormon War in a close, intimate way, from the point of view of an ardent believer.

Richards, Samuel W. "Diary, 1846." (Photostat at the Henry E.

Huntington Library, San Marino, Calif.; typed copy at the Brigham Young University library, Provo, Utah.)

Although Samuel W. Richards kept many diaries, only this one seems to apply here. It gives an account of the evacuation of Nauvoo and of conditions during the year of camping out, as well as of the preparations for the final move to the valley of the Great Salt Lake.

Rogerson, Josiah. "Trial of John D. Lee." (Archives of the L.D.S. church historian, Salt Lake City.) This is listed in the subject catalogue of the L.D.S. Church Library as "Trial of John D. Lee. Josiah Rogerson, Reporter. July 1875 to January 1885." Location is given as "1621 (Big Safe)."

Smith, Jesse N. "Diaries." (Archives of the L.D.S. church historian, Salt Lake City.)

This man kept a long and complete account of his doings over many years. At the time of the massacre, he was living at Parowan. A grandson, George A. Smith, of Mesa, Arizona, has a typed copy of the diary, which he has published for the family in serial form in a monthly sheet called *The Kinsman*.

Stout, Hosea. "Diaries." (Photostat at the Henry E. Huntington Library, San Marino, Calif.; typed copies at the Brigham Young University library, Provo, Utah, and the Utah State Historical Society, Salt Lake City.)

At one time legal counsel to Brigham Young, the writer tells much that has been unknown in Mormon history before. He comments upon official church business and policy and records items of general interest. The copy at the Utah State Historical Society has four volumes; the first three contain 396, 497, and 564 pages, respectively.

Woodbury, John Stillman. "Diaries." 6 vols. (Photostat at the Henry E. Huntington Library, San Marino, Calif.; typed copy at the Brigham Young University library, Provo, Utah.)

These handwritten volumes, totaling 744 pages, record the activities of the author through many years. In 1857, he was in the Hawaiian Islands on a mission, but he carefully copied into his record the letters he received from Utah, showing the conditions which prevailed there and the attitudes of the Mormon people.

Woodruff, Wilford. "Diaries." (Archives of the L.D.S. church historian, Salt Lake City.) One of the most careful record-keepers of the Mormon church, the author put down not only his own personal doings, but also general happenings of importance. His diary covering the period of interest here is not paged, but the entries are dated.

3. Records of Contemporary Investigations

Baskin, Robert N. *Reminiscences of Early Utah.* Salt Lake City, 1914. 252 pages.

———. *Reply By R. N. Baskin to Certain Statements by O. F. Whitney in His History of Utah Published in 1916.* Salt Lake City, Lakeside Printing Co., 1916, 29 pages.

Carleton, J. H. *Mountain Meadows Massacre,* 57 Cong., 1 sess., *House Doc. 605.* Washington, D.C.: G. P. O., 1902), 17 pages. This is, in the main, a faithful transcription of the handwritten report in the War Department files.

———. *Report on the Mountain Meadows Massacre, 1859.* Salt Lake City, Handbook Publishing Co., 1882, 95 pages. This is reprinted in part in John M. Conyer, *Handbook on Mormonism.*

———. *Report on the Subject of the Massacre at Mountain Meadows in Utah Territory in September 1857 of One Hundred and Twenty Men, Women, and Children, Who Were from Arkansas. And Report of the Hon. William C. Mitchell, Relative to the Seventeen Surviving Children Who Were Brought Back by the Authorities of the U.S. After Their Parents and Others with Whom They Were Emigrating Had Been Murdered.* Little Rock, Ark., True Democrat Steam Press Printing Co., 1860. The only known copies are in the possession of E. D. Graff, Chicago, and T. W. Streeter, Morristown, N.J.

Conyer, John M. *Handbook on Mormonism.* Salt Lake City, Handbook Publishing Co., 1882, 95 pages.

Cradlebaugh, John. *Utah and the Mormons.* Privately printed, 1863, 67 pages. Pages 1–26 contain a speech delivered in the House of Representatives on February 7, 1863; pages 26–67 contain documents in the form of affidavits and excerpts from letters, results of the author's researches in southern Utah in 1859.

Lee, John Doyle. *J.D. Lee's Bekjendelse, samt Fulbyrdelsen af hans Dom paa de blodige Mountain Meadows Marker.* Translated by

B. A. Froiseth. Salt Lake City, Skandinava Print, 1877, 36 pages. This edition has portraits and crude plates, including one of the massacre.

——. *John D. Lee's Bekjendelse, samt Fulbyrdelsen af hans Dom paa de blodige Mountain Meadows Marker*. Salt Lake City, Trykt i Utah Skandinavs Bogtrykkeri, 1877, 35 pages.

——. *Journals of John D. Lee*. Ed. by Charles Kelly. Salt Lake City, The Western Printing Company, 1938, 261 pages. These *Journals* cover the years 1846–47 and a fragment of 1859. The book was privately printed by Rolla Bishop Watt.

——. *The Life and Confessions of John D. Lee, the Mormon*. Philadelphia, Barclay and Co., 1877, 46 pages; (187?), 64 pages. This is a pamphlet reprint of the abstracts of Lee's confession, which was released to the press immediately after his execution.

——. *Mormonism Unveiled*. St. Louis, 1877, 406 pages. (St. Louis, Ryan, and Rand and Co., 1877, 390 pages; St. Louis, Moffat Publishing Co., 1891, 413 pages; Cleveland, C. C. Wick and Co., 1891, 413 pages. The last two editions listed include an appendix on Brigham Young.)

——. *Mormonism Unveiled. The Life and Confessions of John D. Lee*. Ed. by W. W. Bishop. St. Louis, 1877, 390 pages. (St. Louis, The Sun Publishing Company, 1882, 413 pages; St. Louis, J. H. Mason Co., 1891, 413 pages; St. Louis, Excelsior Publishing Co., 1891, 431 pages. The last edition is textually the same as the Mason one, but it has more plates.)

The Lee Trial: An Exposé of the Mountain Meadows Massacre! Salt Lake City, Salt Lake Tribune Publishing Company, 1875, 64 pages. This pamphlet has a yellow paper cover with an engraving of Lee on the front and one of the massacre on the back. An unsigned Preface occupies pages 3 and 4. The summary of the trial is taken from the reports as originally published in the daily and weekly editions of the *Tribune*. The last pages present "Opinions of the Press Upon the Lee Trial," sampled from all over the country.

Life, Confessions, and Execution of Bishop John D. Lee. Philadelphia, Old Franklin Publishing House, 1877, 48 pages.

Message of the President of the United States, Communicating, in Compliance with a Resolution of the Senate, Information in Relation to the Massacre at Mountain Meadows and Other Massacres in Utah Territory. 36 Cong., 1 sess., *Exec. Doc. 42*. Washington, D.C.,

Bibliography

G. P. O., 1860, 139 pages. This document contains correspondence of officials of the Department of Indian Affairs and the War Department, as well as reports by Jacob Forney, Garland Hurt, Captain R. P. Campbell, and Charles Brewer, assistant surgeon, U. S. Army.

The Mormon Menace. New York, 1905. An abridged version of John D. Lee's confessions, with an introduction by Alfred H. Lewis.

Mountain Meadow Massacre, with the Life, Confession and Execution of John D. Lee, the Mormon. Helpless Women and Children Butchered in Cold Blood by Merciless Mormon Assassins. Philadelphia, 1882, 64 pages. This edition has a portrait and very lurid full-page plates.

Watt, George D. *A Series of Instructions and Remarks by President Brigham Young at a\Special Council, Tabernacle, March 21, 1858.* Salt Lake City, 1858, 19 pages.

Only one copy of this pamphlet is known to be in existence and it is in the Yale University library. The photostat is 19.8 by 12.4 cm. On the first page above the caption, the name "Chislett" is written, very likely that of John Chislett, who presumably preserved the booklet. This seems to be the "printed circular" that was sent out immediately to special people throughout Utah. It shows Brigham Young at the height of his powers and the rhetorical devices by which he convinced his people that they should abandon Great Salt Lake City.

4. Newspaper Reports

Los Angeles *Star.* Issues through October and November, 1857.

Salt Lake City. *Deseret News.* Issues of 1859–60 and 1874–77.

———. *Salt Lake Herald.* Issues from November, 1874, to May 1876.

———. *Salt Lake Tribune.* Issues from November, 1874, to August, 1877.

———. *The Valley Tan.* Issues of 1858–60. This paper published reports of many government officials who investigated conditions in southern Utah during these years.

San Francisco. *Daily Alta California.* Issues of October 12, 17, and 27; November 1 and 12; December 11 and 13, 1857; and January 26, 1858.

———. *Daily Evening Bulletin.* Issues from October 1 to December 31, 1857.

———. *San Francisco Globe.* Issues from October 1 to December 31, 1857.

———. *San Francisco Herald.* Featured articles in the issues of October 27, November 27, and December 11, 1857.

San Jose, California. *The Pioneer.* April 21, 1877 (Vol. 1, No. 16).

OTHER PRINTED SOURCES

1. Historical and Polemical Accounts

Accounts of Brigham Young, Superintendent of Indian Affairs, Utah Territory. 37 Cong., 2 sess., *House Exec. Doc. 29.* Washington, D.C., G. P. O., 1862.

Anderson, Nels. *Desert Saints.* Chicago, The Chicago University Press, 1942.

Bancroft, Hubert H. *History of Utah.* San Francisco, The History Company, 1890.

Birney, Hoffman. *Zealots of Zion.* Philadelphia, Penn Publishing Company, 1931.

Cannon, Frank J., and George L. Knapp. *Brigham Young and His Mormon Empire.* New York, Fleming H. Revell Company, 1913.

Corle, Edwin. *Desert Country.* New York, Duell, Sloan & Pearce, Inc., 1941.

Cowley, Matthias F. *Wilford Woodruff.* Salt Lake City, Deseret News Press, 1909.

Creer, Leland H. *Utah and the Nation, 1846–1869.* Seattle, The University of Washington Press, 1929.

Dunn, J. P. *Massacres of the Mountains. A History of the Indian Wars of the Far West.* New York, Harper & Brothers, 1886.

Dwyer, Robert J. *The Gentile Comes to Utah.* Washington, D.C., The Catholic University of America Press, 1941.

Gates, Susa Young, and Leah D. Widtsoe. *The Life Story of Brigham Young.* New York, The Macmillan Company, 1931.

Gibbs, Josiah F. *Lights and Shadows of Mormonism.* Salt Lake City, Salt Lake Tribune Publishing Company, 1909.

———. *The Mountain Meadows Massacre.* Salt Lake City, Salt Lake Tribune Publishing Company, 1910; 2d ed., 1910.

Gregg, Jacob Ray. *A History of the Oregon Trail, Santa Fe Trail and Other Trails.* Portland, 1955. One chapter on the Massacre.

Hickman, William A. *Brigham's Destroying Angel.* New York,

Bibliography

George A. Crofutt & Company, 1872; reprinted, Salt Lake City, 1904.

James, George Wharton. *Utah, Land of Blossoming Valleys.* Boston, L. C. Page & Company, 1922.

Jenson, Andrew. *Autobiography.* Salt Lake City, Deseret News Press, 1899.

———. *Church Chronology.* Salt Lake City, Deseret News Press, 1899. These *Journals* cover the years 1846–47 and a fragment of 1859. The book was privately printed for Rolla Bishop Watt.

Kelly, Charles, and Hoffman Birney. *Holy Murder.* New York, Minton, Balch & Company, 1934.

Linn, William A. *The Story of the Mormons.* New York, The Macmillan Company, 1902; reprinted, 1923.

Lyford, C. P. *The Mormon Problem.* New York, Phillips & Hunt, 1886.

Martin, Stuart. *The Mystery of Mormonism.* London, Odham's Press, Ltd., 1920; New York, E. P. Dutton & Company, Inc., 1921.

"The Mountain Meadows Massacre," *Hutching's California Magazine*, February, 1860, p. 347.

Neff, Andrew L. *History of Utah, 1847–1869.* Ed. by Leland H. Creer. Salt Lake City, Deseret News Press, 1940.

Nibley, Preston. *Brigham Young, the Man and His Work.* Salt Lake City, Deseret News Press, 1936.

Penrose, Charles W. *The Mountain Meadows Massacre.* Salt Lake City, The Juvenile Instructor Press, 1884.

Richardson, A. D. *Beyond the Mississippi.* Hartford, Conn., The American Publishing Company, 1867.

Roberts, Brigham H. *A Comprehensive History of the Church of Jesus Christ of Latter-Day Saints.* 6 vols. Salt Lake City, Deseret News Press, 1930.

Smith, Joseph Fielding. *Essentials in Church History.* Salt Lake City, Deseret News Press, 1928; revised edition, 1945.

Snowden, James H. *The Truth About Mormonism.* New York, George H. Doran Company, 1936.

Stenhouse, Fanny. *Tell It All.* Hartford, Conn., A. D. Worthington Company, 1874. Other editions were published under the titles: *Exposé of Polygamy in Utah* (1872), *A Lady's Life Among the Mormons* (1872), *An English Woman in Utah* (1880), and *The*

Tyranny of Mormonism (1888). The author was Mrs. Thomas H. B. Stenhouse.

Stenhouse, Thomas H. B. *Rocky Mountain Saints.* New York, D. Appleton & Company, 1873.

Taylor, John. *The Taylor-Colfax Discussion.* Salt Lake City, 1870. A pamphlet collection of John Taylor's answer to a speech made by Schuyler Colfax and the subsequent arguments. Taylor's speeches were printed in the New York *Tribune*; Colfax' in the New York *Independent.*

Triplett, Frank S. *Conquering the Wilderness.* New York, The Thompson Publishing Co., 1886.

Tullidge, Edward W. *History of Salt Lake City.* Salt Lake City, 1866.

Vindex. *Mountain Meadows Massacre.* Salt Lake City, Salt Lake Tribune Publishing Company, 1884. This is a reprint of an article, signed with the pseudonym "Vindex," reviewing Elder Penrose's exculpatory address, delivered October 26, 1884, in the Twelfth Ward Meeting House. The pamphlet (4 pages) has no title page.

Waite, Catherine V. *The Mormon Prophet and His Harem.* Cambridge, Mass., Riverside Press, 1866.

Werner, Morris R. *Brigham Young.* New York, Harcourt, Brace & Co., Inc., 1924.

Whitney, Orson F. *History of Utah.* 4 vols. Salt Lake City, Deseret News Press, 1892.

———. *Popular History of Utah.* Salt Lake City, Deseret News Press, 1916.

2. Biographies and Background

Bailey, Paul. *Jacob Hamblin, Buckskin Apostle.* Los Angeles, Western Lore Press, 1948.

Beattie, George William, and Helen Pruitt. *Heritage of the Valley.* Pasadena, San Pasqual Press, 1939.

Beckwith, Frank. *Indian Joe in Person and Background.* Delta, Utah, the author, 1939. This account is embellished with drawings and photographs, and in one section gives the Indian version of the Mountain Meadows Massacre. The author printed only seven copies.

Brimhall, George W. *The Workers of Utah.* Provo, Utah, 1889.

Brodie, Fawn M. *No Man Knows My History: The Life of Joseph Smith, the Mormon Prophet.* New York, Alfred A. Knopf, Inc., 1945.

Bibliography

Brooks, Juanita. *Dudley Leavitt, Pioneer to Southern Utah*. St. George, Utah, 1942.

——. "Indian Relations on the Mormon Frontier," *Utah Historical Quarterly*, Vol. XII (January–April, 1944), 1–48.

——. *John Doyle Lee: Zealot-Pioneer Builder-Scapegoat*. Glendale, California, 1962. A biography of John D. Lee drawn largely from his own writings.

Collins, Daphney Otis. *Great Western Rides*. Denver, 1961. The last chapter tells the story of James Haslam's ride from Cedar City to Salt Lake City to ask counsel of Brigham Young regarding the treatment of the fated emigrant train. He arrived after the massacre.

Cottam, Walter P. "Man as a Biotic Factor, Illustrated by Recent Floristic and Physiographic Changes at the Mountain Meadows, Washington County, Utah." Reprinted from *Ecology*, Vol. X, No. 4 (October, 1929).

Cottam, Walter P., and George Stewart. "Plant Succession as a Result of Grazing and of Meadow Desiccation by Erosion Since Settlement in 1862." Reprinted from *Journal of Forestry*, Vol. XXXVIII, No. 8 (August, 1930). This article analyzes the plant cycles at Mountain Meadows resulting from overgrazing.

Crosby, Jesse W. "History and Journal of the Life and Travels of Jesse W. Crosby," *Annals of Wyoming*, Vol. XI (July, 1939), 195–217. During the period of the "Utah War," entries were made daily in the journal.

DeVoto, Bernard. "The Centennial of Mormonism," *Forays and Rebuttals*. Boston, Little, Brown & Company, 1936.

——. *The Year of Decision, 1846*. Boston, Little, Brown & Company, 1943.

Fife, Austin E. "Popular Legends of the Mormons," *California Folklore Quarterly*, Vol. I (April, 1942), 105–56.

Flint, Dr. Thomas. "Diary of Thomas Flint from California to Maine and Return, 1851–1855." Reprinted from *Annual Publications of the Historical Society of Southern California*, Vol. XII (1923).

Gove, Captain Jesse A. *The Utah Expedition: Letters of Captain Gove to Mrs. Gove and the New York Herald*. Concord, N.H., New Hampshire Historical Society, 1928.

Hunt, Aurora. *Major General James Henry Carleton (1814–1873), Western Frontier Dragoon*. Glendale, California, 1958. Only pages 171–86 apply here. They are a reprint of his record of the investigation of the massacre made in the spring of 1859, which was printed in *Senate Document 42*, now rare.

Hunter, Milton R. *Brigham Young the Colonizer*. Salt Lake City, Deseret News Press, 1940.

Jenson, Andrew. "History of the Las Vegas Mission," *Nevada State Historical Society Papers*, Vol. V, (1926), 115–284.

Little, James A. *Jacob Hamblin: Personal Narrative*. Salt Lake City, Deseret News Press, 1881; reprint, 1909.

McClintock, James H. *Mormon Settlement in Arizona*. Phoenix, Ariz., 1921.

Metcalf, A. *Ten Years Before the Mast. Shipwrecks and Adventures at Sea! How I Became a Mormon and Why I Became an Infidel!* Elk Horn, Malad Valley, Idaho, 1881. The only known copy is in the Coe Collection in the Yale University library, New Haven.

Morgan, Dale L. *The Humboldt, Highroad of the West*. New York, Farrar & Rinehart, Inc., 1943.

———. "The State of Deseret," *Utah Historical Quarterly*, Vol. VIII (April–October, 1940), 65–239.

Rae, Ralph. *Boone County and Its People*. Arkansas Historical Series, 1955. This includes the story of the Fancher Train.

Remy, Jules, and Julius Brenchley. *A Journey to Great Salt Lake City* [1855]. 2 vols. London, W. Jeffs, 1861.

Spencer, Clarissa Young, and Mabel Harmer. *One Who Was Valiant*. Caldwell, Idaho, Caxton Printers, Ltd., 1940.

Stanley, Reva. *The Archer of Paradise: A Biography of Parley P. Pratt*. Caldwell, Idaho, Caxton Printers, Ltd., 1937.

Tracy, Captain Albert (Haddock). "Journal of Captain Albert Tracy," *Utah Historical Quarterly*, Vol. XIII (1945), 1–119. Tracy was a member of the U.S. Army sent to Utah in 1857.

Twain, Mark. *Roughing It*. Hartford, Conn., American Publishing Company, 1879.

Utah Writers' Project, WPA. *Utah: A Guide to the State*. New York, Hastings House, 1941.

Young, John R. "Reminiscences of John R. Young," *Utah Historical Quarterly*, Vol. III (July, 1930), 83–86.

3. Travelers' Tales

Beadle, John H. *Life in Utah; or the Mysteries and Crimes of Mormonism*. Philadelphia, National Publishing Company, 1870.

————. *The Undeveloped West.* Philadelphia, National Publishing Company, 1873.

————. *Western Wilds and the Men Who Redeem Them.* Chicago, Jones, 1878.

Beaman, E. O. "The Cañons of the Colorado and the Moquis Pueblos: A Wild Boat-Ride Through the Cañons and Rapids—A Visit to the Seven Cities of the Desert. Glimpses of Mormon Life," *Appleton's Journal,* Vol. XI, (April 18–May 30, 1874).

Bishop, F. M. "Journal of F. M. Bishop, 1870–1872" (ed. by Charles Kelly), *Utah Historical Quarterly,* Vol. XV (1947), 159–238.

Bowles, Samuel. *Across the Continent: A Summer's Journey to the Rocky Mountains, the Mormons and the Pacific States with Speaker Colfax.* New York, Hurd & Houghton, 1865.

Burton, Sir Richard. *The City of the Saints.* New York, Harper & Brothers, 1862.

Clark, William. "A Trip Across the Plains in 1857," *Iowa Journal of History and Politics,* Vol. XX (April, 1922), 162–223.

Dellenbaugh, Frederick S. *A Canyon Voyage.* New York, G. P. Putnam's Sons, 1908; reprinted, 1923.

Kenderine, Thaddeus S. *A California Tramp and Later Footprints, or Life on the Plains and in the Golden State 30 Years Ago.* Newton, Pa., 1882.

Swisher, James. *How I Know; or Sixteen Years' Eventful Experiences . . . .* Cincinnati, 1880.

Waters, W. E. *Life Among the Mormons and a March to Their Zion by an Officer of the U.S. Army.* New York, 1868.

FICTION

Alexander, Charles Wesley. *Brigham Young's Daughter.* Philadelphia, 1870.

Bean, Amelia. *The Fancher Train.* New York, Doubleday, 1958.

Brewer, Charles. *Retribution at Last: A Mormon Tragedy of the Rockies. By an Ex-Officer of the U.S. Army.* Cincinnati, 1899. The author visited Mountain Meadows with Captain Campbell in the summer of 1858 and, from his investigation, created this fictional story.

The Crimes of the Latter-Day Saints in Utah, by a Mormon of 1831. A Book of Horrors! San Francisco, A. J. Leary, 1884. This was presented as "history" when printed. The story of the massacre is clearly not based on facts.

Field, Frank Chester (Frank C. Robertson). *The Rocky Road to Jericho*. New York, Hillman-Curl, Inc., 1935.

Fisher, Vardis. *Children of God*. New York, Harper & Brothers, 1939.

Gibbs, Josiah. *Kawich's Gold Mine*. Salt Lake City, Century Publishing Company, 1913.

London, Jack. *The Star Rover*. New York, The Macmillan Company, 1915. The story of the Mountain Meadows Massacre is told from the point of view of a character who was a member of the Fancher train as a small boy.

Thomas, Arthur (Arthur Thomas Hannet). *In the Days of Brigham Young*. New York, Broadway Publishing Company, 1914.

Whipple, Maurine. *The Giant Joshua*. Boston, Houghton Mifflin Company, 1941.

Wilson, Harry Leon. *The Lions of the Lord*. Boston, Lothrop Publishing Company, 1903.

RECENT MAGAZINE ARTICLES

Fife, Austin E. "A Ballad of the Mountain Meadows Massacre," *Western Folklore*, Vol. XII, No. 4 (October, 1953).

Groesbeck, Kathryn D. "The Mountain Meadows Massacre," *True West*, March–April, 1959.

Irwin, Ray W. "The Mountain Meadows Massacre," *Arkansas Historical Quarterly*, Spring, 1950.

Lee, John D. "Journal of the Iron County Mission, John D. Lee, Clerk" (ed. by Gustive O. Larson), *Utah Historical Quarterly*, Vol. XX (1952), 109–34, 253–82, 353–83.

"One Hundred Years After the Mountain Meadows Massacre," *The Saints' Herald*, October 7, 1957.

Widtsoe, John A. "Was Brigham Young Responsible for the Mountain Meadows Massacre?" *Improvement Era*, October, 1951.

Index

311

Index

Index

315

THE MOUNTAIN MEADOWS MASSACRE

Index